scien

THE SALTERS' APPROACH

THE FERRERS SCHOOL

GCSE volume 1   Year 10 units

Bob Campbell ● John Lazonby ● Robin Millar ● Steve Smyth

SALTERS' SCIENCE PROJECT TEAMS

Management team
David Waddington, *University of York (Project Organiser)*
Bob Campbell, *University of York*
David Edwards, *Huntington School*
John Garratt, *University of York*
Peter Kelly, *University of Southampton*
John Lazonby, *University of York*
Robin Millar, *University of York*
Peter Nicolson, *University of York*
John Raffan, *University of Cambridge*
Judith Ramsden, *University of York*

Writing team for the Unit Guides
Susan Adamson, *Poynton County High School, Stockport*
Don Ainley, *University of Hull*
Mary Aitken, *Redland High School, Bristol*
Andrew Boothroyd, *Royds School, Leeds*
Martin Braund, *Boroughbridge High School*
Bob Campbell, *University of York*
Sue Clarke, *The Westgate School, Winchester*
Annabel Curry, *Amersham College of Further Education*
Kevin de Burg, *Avondale College, New South Wales, Australia*
David Edwards, *Huntington School, York*
Beverley Forsyth, *University of York*
Patrick Fullick, *Bournemouth School*
Francesca Garforth, *University of York*
John Garratt, *University of York*
Eluned Harries, *Heinemann Educational Books*
John Holman, *Watford Grammar School*
Andrew Janes, *Boroughbridge High School*
Peter Kelly, *University of Southampton*
Steve Lane, *Watford Grammar School*
John Lazonby, *University of York*
Jim Lewis, *Garforth Comprehensive School, Leeds*
Jean McLean, *Worthing High School*
Miranda Mapletoft, *University of York*
Alan Marsden, *University of York*
Robin Millar, *University of York*
Tom Murray, *Oaklands School, York*
Peter Nicolson, *University of York*
Richard Page-Jones, *North London Science Centre*
John Raffan, *University of Cambridge*
Judith Ramsden, *University of York*
Steve Smyth, *University of York*
Elizabeth Swinbank, *University of York*
Carol Tear, *Garforth Comprehensive School, Leeds*
David Waddington, *University of York*
Carole Walton, *King James's School, Knaresborough*

The following authors also contributed to the development of the Unit Guides
Philip Cheshire, *Rugby School*
Frank Harris, *Malvern College*
Graham Hill, *Dr Challoner's Grammar School, Amersham*
Frank McKim, *Marlborough College*

Mick Price, *Boston Spa Comprehensive School*
Richard Price, *Midland Examining Group*
Alan Pritchard, *University of Southampton*
Katherine Whyman, *Heinemann Educational Books*

Editorial team for the Unit Guides
Mary Aitken
Beverley Forsyth
Jean McLean
Peter Nicolson
Judith Ramsden
Elizabeth Swinbank

Authors and editors for the Student Books
Bob Campbell
Eluned Harries
John Lazonby
Robin Millar
Steve Smyth
Ruth Holmes

INSET support team
Alan Jury
Peter Nicolson

Secretarial team
Nancy Newton
Valmai Firth

For the Midland Examining Group
Howard King, *Secretary to the Oxford and Cambridge Schools Examining Board*
Charles Newbould, *Director of Research, Oxford and Cambridge Schools Examining Board*
Richard Price, *Servicing Officer for Science (to 1990)*
David Barrett, *Servicing Officer for Science (from 1990)*

Writing team for revision of the Unit Guides
John Lazonby, *University of York (Project Co-organiser)*
Peter Nicolson, *University of York (Project Co-organiser)*
Gillian Alderton, *Sheredes School*
Caroline Barnes
Harry Chalton
Roger Essex, *Castledown Comprehensive School*
David Fortun, *Grange School, Bradford*
Jan Hatherall, *Hardenhuish School*
Terry Hayes, *Leigh Environmental Classroom*
Alan Hewitt, *Dinnington Comprehensive School*
Michael Knight, *Highcliffe School*
Malcolm Leigh, *West Hatch High School*
Keith Palfreyman, *Pope Pius X School*
Jonathan Saint, *Heinemann Educational Books*
Ian Saville, *The Robert Smyth School*
Peter Smith, *Withernsea High School*
Stuart Twiss, *Dorset Professional Development Centre*

About this book

Salters' Science 1 is different from conventional textbooks, so read this section carefully to find out how to use it. (It's not just a case of reading each chapter from begining to end!)

This textbook accompanies the first twelve units of the Salters' course at Key Stage 4. These twelve units are:

- Energy Matters
- Keeping Healthy
- Transporting Chemicals
- Construction Materials
- Moving On
- Food for Thought
- Restless Earth
- The Atmosphere
- Electricity in the Home
- Mining and Minerals
- Balancing Acts
- Communicating Information

Each unit has a corresponding chapter in this book. Each chapter is divided into five key sections.

- Introducing
- Looking at
- In brief
- Thinking about
- Things to do

These sections are meant to be used in different ways. Have a quick look at a chapter to see what each section is like and then turn back to this page and read about how to use them.

Introducing

This page sets the scene and tells you why the topic is important and what the chapter covers.

You could read this page before you start to study the topic in class.

Looking at

These are several Looking At pages in each chapter. Each page uses coloured photographs and diagrams to show an important application or use of the science ideas. The page sets you tasks to help you to understand these ideas.

Your teacher will ask you to work through some Looking At pages and to do the tasks on the page.

In brief

This section presents a summary of what you need to know and understand about the topic.

You could use the In Brief when you have finished a unit or when you are revising. Key ideas from this section are explained more fully in the next section.

Thinking about

This explains the key scientific ideas developed in the unit.

When revising, you might find a part of the In Brief that you need to do more work on. You can then move to the Thinking About to find out more about it. Your teacher might ask you to read parts of this section after you have met the ideas in class.

Things to do

This is a collection of things for you to do. There are:

- Activities to try
- Things to find out
- Things to write about
- Points to discuss
- Questions to answer

You could use a selection of these either in class or for homework.

Contents

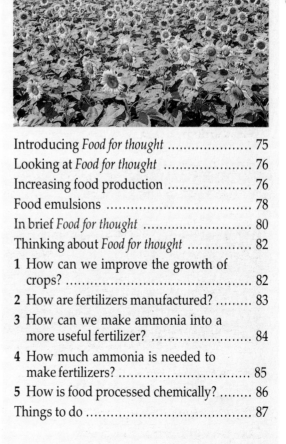

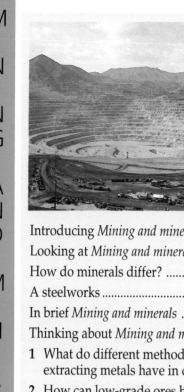

Introducing

ENERGY MATTERS

How often do you stop and think about 'energy matters'? Probably not very often. How important is it for you to care about energy? The picture on this page shows a large number of appliances like toasters, fridges and so on which most definitely affect your life. These appliances use concentrated sources of energy to do jobs for you. You yourself use another source of concentrated energy about three times a day, just to keep you going.

1 Make a list of all the appliances shown which use energy.
2 Try to classify the appliances. For example, you could put them in groups according to what energy source they use, or which you think use a lot of energy and which use hardly any.
3 Which appliances do you think might have required a lot of energy to make them?
4 Which appliances do you think might not use energy very efficiently?

IN THIS CHAPTER YOU WILL FIND OUT

▌ how to measure or calculate the amount of energy used by different appliances or devices

▌ how to calculate the cost of the energy you use

▌ what happens to the energy you use

▌ that energy is also needed to make things

▌ how we can use energy more efficiently.

Looking at

Cutting Heating Costs

Each year we use a vast amount of energy to heat our homes. The cost of this energy in 1989 was about £10 billion in the U.K. How can we reduce this?

Some of the energy used in heating homes is wasted. One way of cutting waste is to use insulation. Of course, insulation itself costs money to install. The diagram shows the different kinds available, how much they cost and how much they save.

1 **Use the information to draw up a chart showing the cost of each type of insulation, and the saving you would expect to make each year.**
2 **Work out how long it would take to recover the cost of each type of insulation from the savings made. This is called the *pay-back time*.**
3 **Make a list of types of insulation in order of cost effectiveness.**
4 **Find out how thick loft insulation should be.**

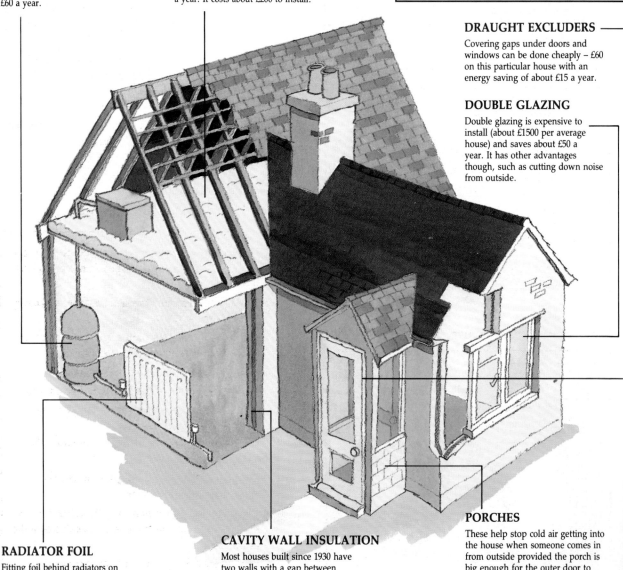

HOT WATER CYLINDER JACKET

It costs £10 to fit an insulating jacket around a hot water tank. The saving is about £60 a year.

LOFT INSULATION

A mineral fibre blanket can be used to cover the floor in the loft. This cuts down energy loss through the roof by 80% and saves about £100 a year. It costs about £200 to install.

DRAUGHT EXCLUDERS

Covering gaps under doors and windows can be done cheaply – £60 on this particular house with an energy saving of about £15 a year.

DOUBLE GLAZING

Double glazing is expensive to install (about £1500 per average house) and saves about £50 a year. It has other advantages though, such as cutting down noise from outside.

RADIATOR FOIL

Fitting foil behind radiators on external walls reflects back energy that would otherwise be lost. It probably only saves £10 a year, but the cost of the foil is just £2.

CAVITY WALL INSULATION

Most houses built since 1930 have two walls with a gap between them. Filling this gap with foam will cost about £500. Less energy will be lost through the walls, saving about £100 a year.

PORCHES

These help stop cold air getting into the house when someone comes in from outside provided the porch is big enough for the outer door to be shut before the inner one is opened. A porch for this house would cost £1000, and save £40 a year in heating costs.

Looking at

Where the Energy Goes

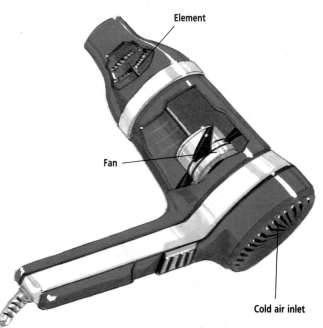

Element

Fan

Cold air inlet

1 Draw an arrow diagram (see page 10) to show the energy changes in a hairdryer when it's working properly.
2 Is the hairdryer using the same amount of energy when its fan stops working?
3 Write a sentence to explain each of the following. In each sentence use one of these words:

conduction, convection, radiation.

- how the handle of the hairdryer becomes hot
- how the energy spreads from the glowing element to Ravinda's hair
- how the air above it also gets hot when the dryer is switched on
- how the energy spreads from the red hot element after the fan stops.
4 Write a sentence to explain why the element glows red hot when the fan stops, but doesn't while the fan is working.
5 What energy changes happen when someone dries their hair with a towel?

Looking at

A Clear Saving

Glass is a very useful material when it comes to making containers and bottles. It is strong and very resistant to corrosion. As it is clear, you can see what is inside. It can also be very beautiful and is a traditional container for drinks.

Why do you think glass is used for these objects?

The Life of a Bottle

Sand, limestone and salt are quarried. The salt is made into soda ash and all these materials are taken to the glass making factory.

All these materials are processed and heated in a furnace. They melt and combine to form glass.

The bottles are filled and taken to the shops.

The glass is shaped, cleaned and sterilised.

1 Make a list of the places where energy is used in making a glass bottle.

 Energy to quarry and transport raw materials.

 Energy to change raw materials into bottles and to transport empty bottles.

 Energy to clean and fill bottles and transport them to the shops.

Save energy by recycling . . .

Recycling glass can save a lot of energy. Broken glass is added to the raw materials in the furnace. This means that less energy has to be used to melt the materials and so make the glass. This saves 1650 MJ (that's 30 gallons of heating oil!) for each tonne of glass used. A tonne of glass is about 4000 milk bottles!

> 2 Look back at the history of a glass bottle. What other major energy costs could be saved by recycling glass, rather than by using raw materials?

. . . and more by re-using

Even more energy savings can be made by re-using bottles. More energy is used to make each refillable bottle because it has to be stronger and more difficult to break. But this extra energy cost is soon saved if the bottle is re-used as the table below shows. The colours on the table and the key show *how* the energy is used.

Recycling glass – where are the bottle banks near you?

How can you persuade people to re-use bottles?

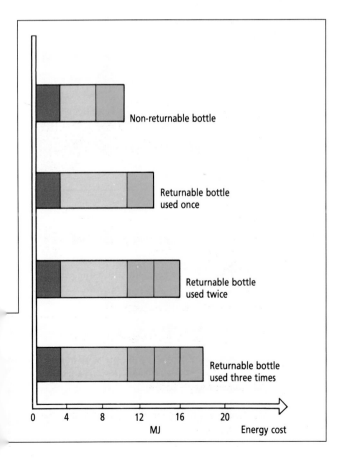

Non-returnable bottle

Returnable bottle used once

Returnable bottle used twice

Returnable bottle used three times

0   4   8   12   16   20
MJ   Energy cost

> 3 What is the *average* energy cost for a refillable bottle that makes:
>   (a) 1 trip, (b) 2 trips, (c) 3 trips?
> 4 Design a poster or a leaflet as part of a campaign to encourage people to re-use bottles rather than recycle broken glass.

Looking at

How Big Should the Bill Be?

These four houses are up for sale. You'll notice that there are a number of similarities and differences between them. In choosing a home, the size of the heating bills will be an important consideration.

1 Decide which of the electricity and gas bills, A to D, probably come from which house. The bills are for the winter quarter.

Start by drawing a table which compares the houses. Include the features of each house which you think could influence the bills.

House No.	Gas c.h.	Insulation

Write a brief explanation for each of your decisions.

1 A well presented 2 year old, 3 bedroomed detached house. Gas central heating, cavity wall insulation, fitted kitchen, burglar alarm, main bedroom with en suite shower room and fitted wardrobes. Garage, gardens.

£85,500

2 A well presented one year old, end of four, 2 bedroomed 'semi'-detached bungalow with excellent features which include Economy 7 electric heaters, feature stone fireplace to lounge. Ent. lobby, lounge/dining room, kitchen, inner lobby, 2 bedrooms and bathroom. Gardens to side and rear. Parking for 2 vehicles.

£52,950

3 A very well presented and surprisingly spacious 2 bedroomed mid terraced house with benefits that include 2 good sized reception rooms, fitted kitchen and first floor modern bathroom. Gas central heating.

£44,500

4
- A sup. individ. des. det. house set in ½ acre
- Solid fuel c.h.
- Porch, hall, lounge, d/room
- Study/bed 4, kitchen, rear hall, utility
- 3 further beds, 1 with en suite, 2 further bathrooms
- Lge dble garage, boiler room, fuel store, ext. w.c.
- Summer house, lge conservatory, sec. system

£190,000

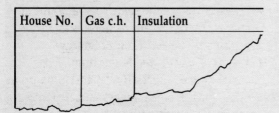

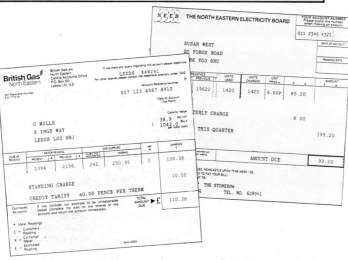

These two bills come from two of the houses. And the summary of bills for each house is given in the table.

Bill	Total from bill	
	Electricity	Gas
A	£220.91	none
B	£93.20	£180.10
C	£62.76	£110.38
D	£150.12	none

2 Suggest a reason why house 4 uses solid fuel for central heating.

3 For which house would it be easiest to reduce the bills? Explain how you would do this.

4 Why do you think there is a standing gas charge and a quarterly electricity charge?

5 Economy 7 is a cheaper alternative electricity tariff (charge rate). It is used to charge people who have night storage heaters. Suggest why the electricity board has two tariffs.

In brief

Energy Matters

1 Our comfortable lifestyle depends on using a lot of energy, at home and at work.

2 Fuels are concentrated stores of energy.

Primary energy sources

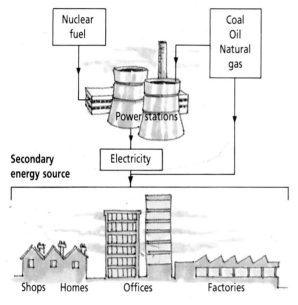

3 Coal, oil and natural gas are fossil fuels. They are the fossilized remains of forests and of small sea creatures which lived millions of years ago. Once we have used them up, they are gone for ever.

4 Different tasks take different amounts of fuel. If we want to measure the amount of energy used, we need a common unit for energy. This is the joule (J).

5 Some electrical appliances use energy more quickly than others. Those which involve heating use a lot of energy.

6 The electricity meter in your home measures how much electrical energy you are using. It 'adds up' the energy used by all your appliances.

7 Every domestic electrical appliance has a power rating in watts (W) written on it. The bigger the power rating, the faster it uses energy. An appliance with a large rating will cost more to run than one with a smaller rating if they are kept switched on for the same time.

8 Appliances do not really 'use' energy – they change it from one form to another, or transfer it from one place to another. This can be illustrated by an energy arrow diagram.

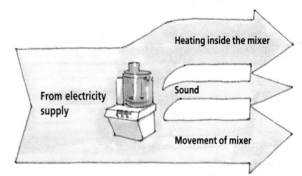

9 There are two important energy *laws*:
● There is always the same total amount of energy after an event as there was at the beginning (**conservation of energy**).
● Energy always spreads out from concentrated sources (fuels) and ends up in many places. Some always ends up causing unwanted heating (**spreading of energy**).

10 Hot objects cool down and their surroundings get slightly warmer. The energy in the hot object has spread further.

ENERGY SPREADS BY ...

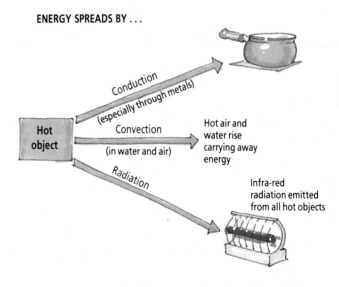

11 We can reduce our fuel bills by insulating our homes better. Insulation makes it harder for energy to spread.

12 Energy is needed to *make* things. Everything has an 'energy cost' as well as a 'raw materials cost'.

Thinking about

Energy Matters

1. *Fuels – making things happen*

To make things happen, we always need an energy source.

To run, these athletes are using the energy stored in the food they have eaten.

To move, the car uses the energy stored in petrol.

When it is switched on, the torch uses the energy stored in the chemicals in its cells.

To raise the lift and its load, energy is supplied by electricity to the lift motor.

This room is heated using the energy stored in natural gas.

Fuels are concentrated energy stores. Coal, oil, natural gas and wood are **primary fuels.** So are the chemicals inside dry cells (batteries). Electricity is a **secondary fuel.** Mains electricity is generated in power stations by burning coal or oil, or by using another primary fuel – uranium.

Fuels are valuable because they provide concentrated energy which we can use to do all sorts of useful jobs.

2. *Measuring energy*

(a) Can we measure how much energy we use to do something? One way is to measure how much fuel the task needs. Here is an example:

To make a pot of tea, you have to boil about 0.5 litres of water. At home, you might do this with an electric kettle, or on a gas ring. If you were on a camping holiday, you might do it using a small portable gas stove.

How much fuel does each heating method use?

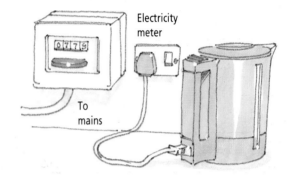

Electricity meter

To mains

The wheel inside the meter turns 37·5 times before the water boils. The meter is marked '375 revs./kWh'.

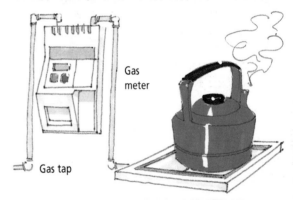

Gas meter

Gas tap

The gas ring uses 18 litres of gas to bring the water to the boil.

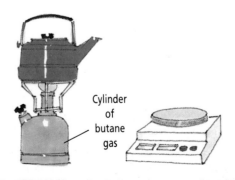

Cylinder of butane gas

The stove weighs 16 grams less after boiling the water than it did before.

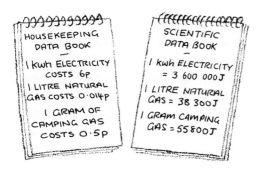

If we know how much we have to pay for each fuel, we can compare the costs of three methods of heating water to make the pot of tea. But for a proper scientific comparison, we need to measure the energy in the same unit each time. The unit used is the joule (J).

Fuel used	Electricity	Natural gas	Camping gas
Amount	0.1 kWh	18 l	16 g
Cost	0.6 p	0.25 p	8 p
Energy	360 000 J	690 000 J	890 000 J

Notice that the numbers of joules are very large. One joule is a very small amount of energy! So it is sometimes more convenient to use the megajoule (MJ). (1 MJ = 1 000 000 J)

Why is the energy used not the same each time? We will come back to that question in *Thinking about 6* on page 12.

(b) Electrical appliances use energy at different rates. Instead of the electric kettle in the diagram, we can connect other appliances to the kilowatt-hour meter and compare how quickly they use electrical energy.

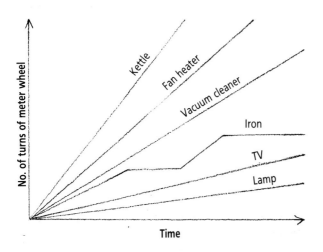

The steeper the graph, the faster the appliance is using energy. Heating is very 'energy greedy'; it uses energy fast! Notice the flat parts of the graph for the iron. An iron has a thermostat. When the iron reaches the temperature it is set for, its heater switches off, even though the iron itself is still switched on. The iron then slowly cools down. At a certain point the thermostat switches the heater back on again. In this way the iron stays at a roughly steady temperature.

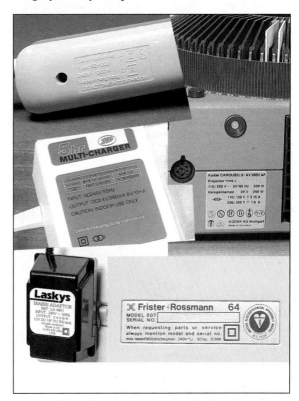

If you want to find out how quickly an appliance uses energy, look at its rating plate. The rating is marked in watts (W) or kilowatts (kW) (1 kW = 1000 W). The bigger the number, the faster the appliance uses energy.

Appliance	Typical rating
Radio	9 W
Lamp	60 W
Television	80 W
Food mixer	300 W
Power drill	315 W
Fan heater	1000 W
Washing machine	1000 W-3000 W
Electric kettle	2000 W
Tumble dryer	2200 W
Immersion heater	2500 W

3. Energy transfers

We often talk about appliances 'using' energy. But what they really do is to transfer energy – from a concentrated fuel to where we want it to go.

An arrow diagram is a good way to picture what is going on from an energy point-of-view. Here are some examples:

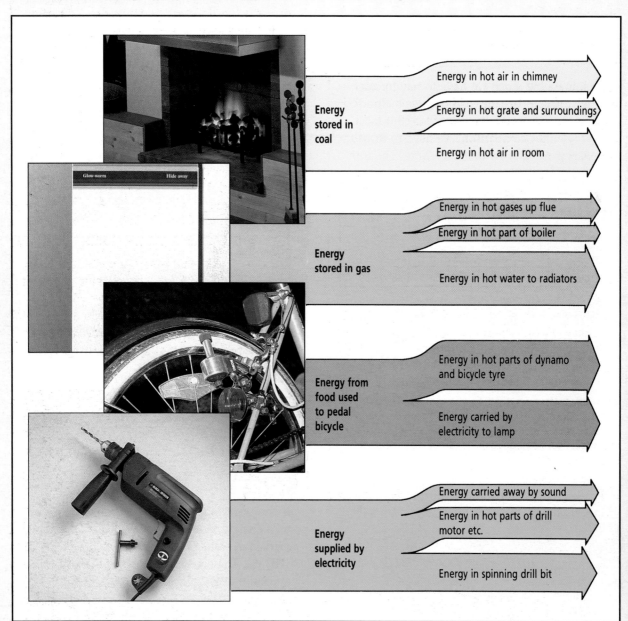

Energy stored in coal
- Energy in hot air in chimney
- Energy in hot grate and surroundings
- Energy in hot air in room

Energy stored in gas
- Energy in hot gases up flue
- Energy in hot part of boiler
- Energy in hot water to radiators

Energy from food used to pedal bicycle
- Energy in hot parts of dynamo and bicycle tyre
- Energy carried by electricity to lamp

Energy supplied by electricity
- Energy carried away by sound
- Energy in hot parts of drill motor etc.
- Energy in spinning drill bit

4. Energy patterns

Energy never disappears. And energy never suddenly appears from nowhere! A fuel is needed to make something happen, but the energy always appears somewhere at the end. Look at the energy arrow diagrams above. There is always energy on the output side as well as the input side. In fact, there is always *the same amount* of energy at the end as there was at the beginning – energy is **conserved**.

But the energy has been changed. It is now much more 'spread out'. Notice how the arrow diagrams always branch, with energy ending up in more and more places. You'll notice that in all the arrow diagrams some heating always happens, even when we don't really want it to.

5. Energy spreading

Not only do most events produce some unwanted heating, but the energy of hot things also goes on spreading! It is hard to keep energy concentrated in one place.

How does the energy in hot bodies spread? There are three main ways:

Conduction:
The only way energy can spread through solids is by conduction. Metals are good conductors, but wood and plastics are poor conductors (good insulators). Water and air are also very poor conductors.

The copper bottom of the saucepan is a good conductor, so energy spreads easily from the hot cooker ring to the pan. The handle is made of plastic – a good insulating material – so that energy does *not* spread along the handle, making it too hot to hold.

Down is the best filling for high performance sleeping bags. Down traps lots of tiny pockets of air, which is a very poor conductor. So the energy cannot spread from your body to the surroundings and you stay warm.

Convection:
When water is heated, it expands a little and gets lighter (less dense). So the hot water rises to the top, carrying its energy with it. Hot air does exactly the same. This method of energy spreading is called convection. Unlike conduction, the hot substance actually moves.

The immersion heater is placed near the bottom of the tank. It heats the water beside it, which then rises to the top of the tank. The pipe going to the hot taps leaves the top of the tank. Then the tank is refilled by cold water which goes in at the bottom.

Radiation:
Energy spreads from the Sun to Earth through 150 million kilometres of empty space. It cannot spread by conduction or convection because there is nothing in between! So there must be a third method of energy transfer – radiation. Radiation travels very rapidly and in straight lines, just like light.

If you stand near a bonfire, you feel the intense heat on your face. You can shield it with your hand. The energy is spreading from the hot fire to your face by radiation travelling rapidly in a straight line.

6. Using energy efficiently

(a) We say that a process is *efficient* if most of the energy goes where we want it to go.

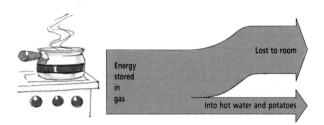

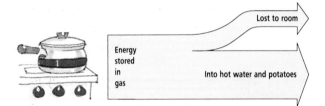

If we put a lid on the saucepan while we boil potatoes, it is more efficient. More of the energy from the fuel goes into the water and less is lost to the surroundings.

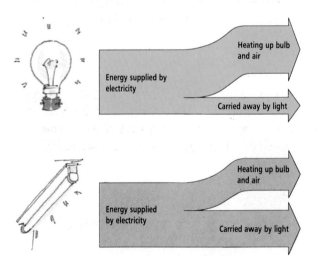

A filament light bulb is not as efficient as a fluorescent tube. Most of the energy which is supplied to the filament lamp just causes unwanted heating.

Efficiency is usually measured as a percentage: how much of the input energy goes where you want it to go?

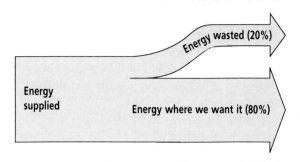

The process shown in the diagram above is 80% efficient.

We can now also explain why the three different methods of boiling water for a pot of tea (*Thinking about 2* on page 8) used different amounts of energy to do the same job. The water has to gain the same amount of energy each time. The electric kettle is the most efficient at transferring energy to water. The gas burners lose more energy to the surroundings.

(b) Insulating your house is a way of using the energy stored in the fuel efficiently.

A house made with good insulating materials will cost less to keep warm than one built with poor insulators.

The **U-value** of a material tells you how much energy will escape every second through each square metre if the temperature inside is 1°C warmer than outside. The bigger the area and the bigger the temperature difference, the more energy escapes every second!

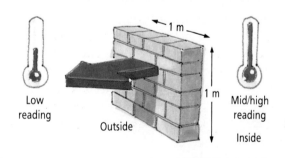

Material	U-value (in W per m² per °C)
Cavity wall	0·75
Insulated cavity wall	0·5
Uninsulated loft	2·0
Loft with 15 cm insulation	0·25
Single glazed windows	5·0
Double glazed windows	3·0

Things to do

Energy Matters

Things to try out

1 An energy-saving bulb (an SL bulb) is really a fluorescent tube coiled up inside a bulb.
It produces the same amount of light as a normal filament bulb – but uses less electrical energy.

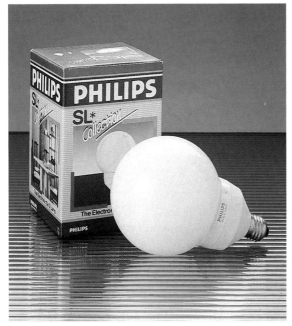

The manufacturers claim that an 18 W SL lamp gives the same amount of light as a normal 75 W filament lamp – the same amount of light for only one quarter of the energy. Design two experiments to test these two claims and try them out.

Hint: One way of comparing the amount of light – the brightness – of two lamps is to use a solar-powered calculator. If you shine a lamp on the calculator's solar cell and then begin to lay sheets of tissue paper over the cell, it eventually stops working and the calculator display goes off. The brighter the light, the more layers of paper it takes before this happens.

2 (a) Watch the wheel turning inside the electricity meter in your house. Count the number of turns in 5 minutes. Work out how many turns this is equal to in an hour.

(b) The number of turns per kilowatt-hour will be written on the meter. Work out how many kilowatt-hours of electrical energy you are using in one hour.

(c) Now go round the house and make a list of all the appliances which are switched on and are using electricity from the meter. Find their rating in kilowatts and add them up. Does this figure agree with your calculation in (b)? If not, why?

3 Design and carry out an investigation to compare different materials for making sleeping bags.

Things to find out

4 Design a questionnaire to find out which fuels people in your class use for heating their homes, and what sorts of insulation they have. You could use the headings on page 2 for the types of insulation.

   Use your questionnaire to conduct a survey in the class. Write a report on your findings, with tables and diagrams to show the main results.

5 Use the Yellow Pages of your local telephone directory to find the number of firms supplying different types of home insulation. Summarize your findings in a table.

   What sort of insulation seems to be the most popular? Is it the most effective form of insulation?

Points to discuss

6 Make a list of the ways you could save energy **(a)** at home; **(b)** at school. Which of these savings could you make with very little effect on your comfort? Which could you make most easily?

Things to write about

7 This letter appeared in a local newspaper:

> **Another 'Save it' energy campaign. What a waste of time. Have the campaigners not heard about the conservation of energy? Energy is always conserved – you cannot waste it. There is no point in using energy more carefully.**

   Write another letter, replying to the comments made in this one.

Questions to answer

8 Draw and label energy arrow diagrams (like the ones on page 10) to show the energy changes in each one of the following:

(a) a gas cooker

(b) a vacuum cleaner

(c) a candle

(d) a cassette-player

(e) a solar-powered calculator

(f) using the brakes on a bicycle

9 Look at the energy arrow diagram on page 10. Assuming it is drawn to scale, estimate the efficiency of each appliance.

10 'Who left the light on all weekend? That's two days that's been wasting electricity!'

'Sorry Dad! Anyway it's not as bad as you leaving the immersion heater on the other night.'

'That was only six hours – not nearly such a waste.'

Use the information on page 9 to settle the argument.

11 (a) The end wall of a house (see diagram) is 2 metres high and 5 metres long and has a U-value of 1.5 W per m² per °C. How much energy is lost per second through this wall when the temperature difference between the inside and the outside is
   (i) 1 °C?
   (ii) 10 °C?

(b) How much energy would be lost if it was an insulated cavity wall with a U-value of 0.5 W per m² per °C?

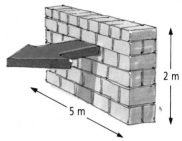

12 Make a table of the features of a vacuum flask and the type of heat loss each one prevents. Why is the stopper made of plastic?

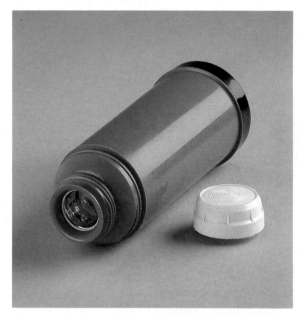

The vacuum flask keeps things hot by making it hard for energy to spread by any of the three methods: conduction, convection and radiation. The flask itself is a double-walled glass bottle, with a vacuum between the walls. And the inside surfaces of the glass bottle are silvered. The stopper is a potential weak link – but it is made of plastic.

Introducing

KEEPING HEALTHY

Your body is a very complex structure. To keep healthy you need to maintain it in good working condition. Keeping healthy also means knowing about what could go wrong, so that you can avoid problems.

1 You would know if your heart, stomach or bones had a problem – you would be able to feel something was wrong. Can you always tell if something is wrong with your body?

2 Does being healthy just mean not having a particular illness? Are you as healthy as a top-class athlete? What can you do to try and stay healthy?

3 If an athlete catches a virus it might make her feel a bit run down, but not too bad. Do you think this would affect her performance? Why?

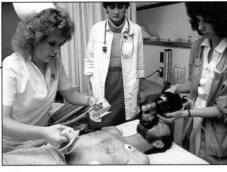

Your heart pumps blood around your body. The blood carries oxygen and food. If your heart goes wrong the cells in your body don't get the oxygen and food they need – you get seriously ill or may even die. This medical team is giving emergency treatment to a patient whose heart has stopped beating (he has had a cardiac arrest).

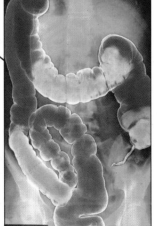

Your digestive system breaks down food so it can be absorbed into your blood. This is an X-ray of the large intestine taken after the patient swallowed a barium meal. The barium shows up on the X-ray.

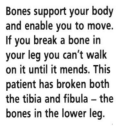

Bones support your body and enable you to move. If you break a bone in your leg you can't walk on it until it mends. This patient has broken both the tibia and fibula – the bones in the lower leg.

IN THIS CHAPTER YOU WILL FIND OUT

▌ what makes people ill

▌ what microbes are, and how the body deals with them

▌ what vaccination and immunity are

▌ how organs that are not working properly can be replaced

▌ how enzymes and drugs work.

Looking at

Influenza

'Flu away?

Have you had 'flu recently? Your symptoms would be a high temperature, a sore throat and a runny nose. Did you have to take any time off school?

During the winter, up to half a class can be away at one time due to a 'flu epidemic. Although most people are back to normal after a couple of days, 'flu can be very dangerous. In 1918 a worldwide 'flu epidemic caused the deaths of 21 640 000 people, one of the world's worst disasters.

In November 1989 there was a 'flu epidemic at Goodsalt school, as you can see from this register for class 4A.

> 1 Imagine you are Ms Anderson, the class teacher. Write a memo to the head teacher about the disruption to pupils' education that the 'flu epidemic has caused, and suggesting that something should be done to prevent it happening again.

NAME OF PUPIL		Week commencing Monday					1 Action taken on absence (initials and date)	Result of Enquiry
1	2	M	T	W	Th	F		
Surname	First Name(s)							
ADAMS	IAN	/	/	/	/	/		
BLOGGS	JANE	/	0	0	0	0		
CHOUDLEY	MEENA	/	0	0	0	0		
DAVIDSON	WINSTON			0	0	0	0	
EARBY	ERROL			0	0	0		
HARRISON	LUKE		0	0	0	/		
IYOTA	GEORGINA							
HO	SHUI LAI	/	0	0	0	0		
JOHNSON	LUCINDA	0	0	0	0			
KELLY	MARY		0	0	0	0		
KELLY	SARAH			0	0	0		
MAN	CHUNG FAI			0	0	0		
MATTHEWS	ROWENA		0	0	0	0		
NORMAN	NIGEL			0	0	0		
OWENS	WAYNE							
PATEL	NISHA	/	0	0	0	0		
PATEL	SUJATA			0	0	0		
PETERS	TOM			0	0	0	0	
RICHARDS	MARK			0	0	0		

Preventing 'flu

> 2 Now imagine that you are the deputy head who has been asked to reply to Ms Anderson's memo. The information you have gathered is on the rest of this page and the next one. Read it and answer the questions, then write your reply. (*In Brief* 6 and 7, pages 22–3, and *Thinking about* 2 and 3, pages 24–5, will also help.)

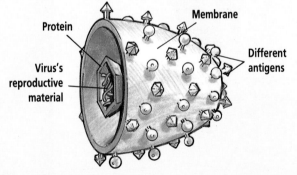

Protein

Membrane

Virus's reproductive material

Different antigens

A model of a virus from the family Orthomyxoviridae ('flu virus). The spikes represent chemicals called *antigens*.

Influenza ('flu): a viral disease. It is very difficult to control because it is caused by not just one virus, but a whole family. To make matters more difficult, the viruses keep changing slightly.

As you can see from the picture, the virus is covered in spiky projections. These represent antigens. The body's immune system detects these and produces antibodies to attack the virus.

'Flu viruses are different from most other viruses because the antigens change slightly from one generation to the next. When the antigens have changed enough, your antibodies are no longer able to attack the virus. So as the 'flu viruses change, you lose your 'flu immunity. You become immune to most illnesses after having them once, but you may be re-infected with 'flu many times during your life.

> 3 Draw a sketch of a 'flu virus. Draw similar sketches showing 'flu viruses 5 and 10 years later. Use colours to show how the antigens have changed.

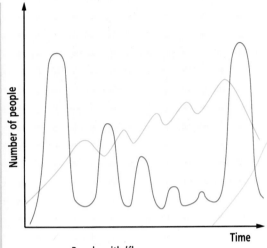

People with 'flu

Average number of people with 'flu antibodies

Average number of people with immunity to new strain of virus

'Flu immunity – the facts

The graph shows how outbreaks of 'flu are linked to changes in the virus. The red line shows the number of people suffering from 'flu. Gradually, after an epidemic, more and more people gain immunity to the disease. The number of people with 'flu immunity is shown by the blue line. Then a new strain of virus emerges, causing another epidemic. Immunity to this is shown in green. This immunity will build up following the previous pattern.

4 Predict the shape of the graph over the next ten years. Make a drawing of your predicted graph.

BEAT THE 'FLU – HAVE A JAB!

You can be vaccinated against 'flu – about 80% of people vaccinated do not catch it. The reason the vaccination is not always successful is that there are so many different kinds of 'flu viruses. Every February a group of doctors meets in Geneva to try to predict what 'flu viruses will be about in the following winter. Vaccines are then made up to protect against the predicted viruses – but if the forecast is wrong and a different type emerges, the vaccine will not work.

The mixture for the year 1990 protects against the following types of virus: A/Shanghai, A/Singapore, B/Yamagata. The first letter of the name is the type of 'flu virus; the second part is the place where that particular strain was first identified.

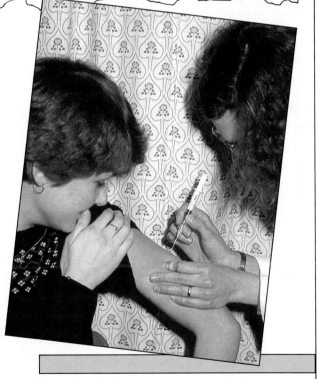

5 Imagine that a new type C virus has just been reported in your town. How will it be named?
    What would happen if this virus began to infect people vaccinated with the 1990 mixture?

Looking at

Pellagra

What is pellagra?

Pellagra is a disease which dries and cracks the skin. It can be very painful. In severe cases the victim may die. In the 1900s there were so many cases of pellagra in the southern states of the USA that the government sent one of their top medical investigators, Dr Joseph Goldberger, to see if the disease could be controlled.

Dr Goldberger was already famous for helping to control two other dangerous diseases, typhus and yellow fever. Both of these were infectious diseases caused by microbes. Dr Goldberger had caught both diseases during his investigations – in fact he nearly died of yellow fever.

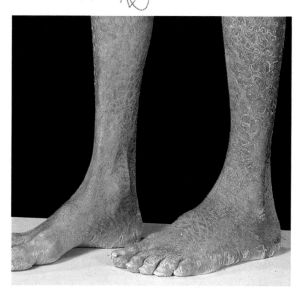

Pellagra is a very unpleasant disease. It was common in some parts of the USA about 100 years ago.

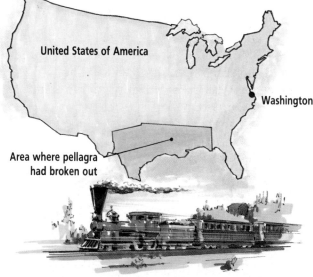

United States of America

Washington

Area where pellagra had broken out

---

1 Imagine you are Dr Goldberger, on your way to the places where the disease has broken out. Make a list of the different types of diseases (*In Brief 1* on page 22 may help). Which type do you think pellagra might belong to?

2 What evidence would you need to show that pellagra belonged to this type of disease?

Was it caused by microbes?

Most doctors at the time thought that pellagra was caused by a microbe. They pointed out that many cases of pellagra were found in orphanages and mental hospitals, where large numbers of people were crowded together. These are ideal conditions for microbes to spread from person to person.

However, Dr Goldberger observed that only orphans and patients caught the disease. Doctors, nurses and other staff did not catch pellagra. This was unusual, and different from typhus and yellow fever, where all sorts of people caught the disease.

---

3 Write a page from Dr Goldberger's diary, setting down the reasons why you think pellagra is a different type of disease from typhus or yellow fever.

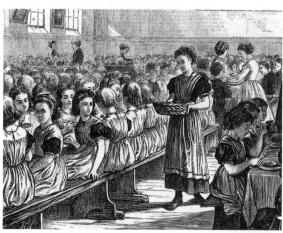

Crowded orphanages gave good conditions for microbes to spread.

Was it caused by poor diet?

Dr Goldberger wondered if the disease was caused by the poor diet that orphans and people in mental hospitals had. He arranged for many people suffering from pellagra to have fresh milk. Many of them quickly recovered. Was there something in milk that cured pellagra?

> **4 Write another extract from Dr Goldberger's diary, with the heading 'At last, a breakthrough'.**

To get more evidence for his theory, Dr Goldberger arranged to conduct an experiment on a group of prisoners. They agreed to take part because they would be released from prison when the experiment was over. The diagram opposite shows what he did.

Convincing evidence

Even after this experiment many doctors still thought that pellagra was infectious. To convince them, Goldberger performed an amazing experiment, using himself, his wife and a group of friends as part of the test.

If pellagra was infectious, then people who were in close contact with the disease should catch it. So, for nearly a year, Dr Goldberger and his group lived with pellagra sufferers. Not only were they in daily contact, they were also injected with blood samples from the diseased group. They also ate food to which they added faeces and urine from the diseased people!

And the result of this unusual experiment? Some of the group had stomach aches (is it any wonder!), but none of them caught pellagra.

> **5 Finish your extracts from Dr Goldberger's diary with an account of his experiments.**

Why was milk important?

Milk contains nicotinic acid (also called niacin), a member of the vitamin B group. It is lack of nicotinic acid which causes pellagra. Meat and flour also contain nicotinic acid. New milling methods introduced around 1890 were so efficient they ground all the nicotinic acid out of flour – so more people were at risk of getting pellagra. Nicotinic acid is now added back into flour.

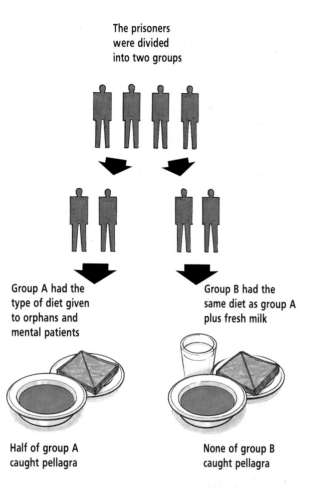

The prisoners were divided into two groups

Group A had the type of diet given to orphans and mental patients

Group B had the same diet as group A plus fresh milk

Half of group A caught pellagra

None of group B caught pellagra

Joseph Goldberger

Looking at

Transplanting kidneys

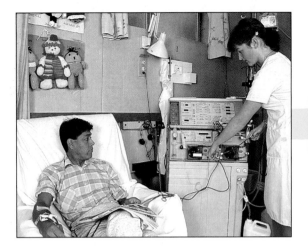

Abdul Khan is suffering from kidney disease. Both his kidneys have failed, so he has to have dialysis.

His sister, Ayesha, leads an active, healthy life.

Ayesha has decided to let Abdul have one of her two kidneys.

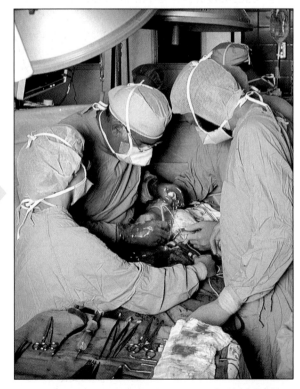

The kidney is removed from Ayesha's body and transplanted into Abdul's body.

Why did Ayesha have to give up one of her kidneys?

After all, sometimes people die and allow their kidneys to be used by other people (that's what kidney donor cards are for).

Transplants are not always successful. Sometimes the body **rejects** the new kidney. The immune system detects that the kidney is different from all the other tissues and starts to make antibodies. The antibodies surround and kill the new kidney, just as if it was a bacterium or a virus.

How can we stop the body rejecting a transplant?

One way is by using drugs. Some drugs stop the immune system working, so no antibodies are produced. The problem is that people have no defence if they catch a disease. The disease may kill them.

Another way of overcoming rejection is to use kidneys from people who are close relatives. The new kidney is similar to the other tissues already in the body, so there is a good chance that the immune system will not detect any difference. In this case antibodies will not be produced so the kidney will not be rejected. The graph shows how using kidneys from relatives improves the chances of success in transplant operations.

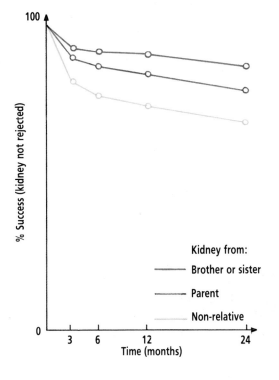

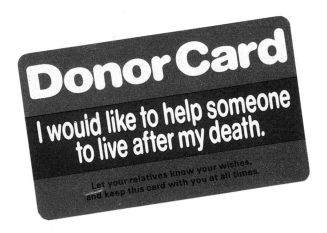

A year later . . .

1 **What do you think antibodies react to in a donated kidney? Why are transplants of kidneys from close relatives likely to be more successful?**

2 **Abdul and Ayesha's parents were against the transplant to start with. They wanted Abdul to wait until a suitable kidney became available. Write a play to show how Abdul, Ayesha and their parents felt, and what changed their parents' minds.**

In brief

Keeping healthy

1 Many complex chemical reactions go on inside your body. If any of these reactions goes wrong, you become ill. This may lead to unusual chemicals in your urine, so examining urine can help in the diagnosis of illness. Reactions can go wrong for various reasons:

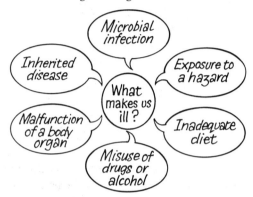

2 **Microbes** are tiny organisms that you need a microscope to see. **Bacteria** and **viruses** are microbes. There are many different types of microbes around us all the time, and your body makes a good environment for them to grow in!

 Pathogenic microbes cause illness when they grow in the body. They can be passed on to other people and so infect them as well.

How microbes enter the body

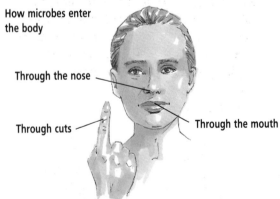

Through the nose

Through cuts

Through the mouth

3 A microbial disease can be controlled by destroying the microbe or by eliminating the conditions it needs to grow. Microbes can be killed by:
- high temperatures
- acid or alkaline conditions
- removal of nutrients
- chemicals that poison them. These are called **germicides**.

4 **Disinfectants** contain concentrated germicides. They are only used on non-living material. **Antiseptics** are weak germicides that can be used on your skin. **Antibiotics** are germicides that are safe enough to be eaten or injected into the body.

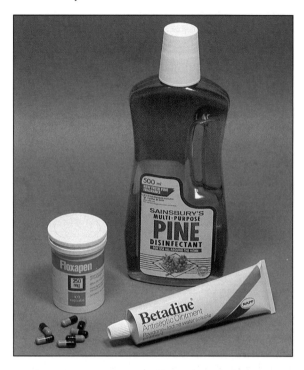

5 Your skin is a barrier to microbe invasion. When your skin gets cut, a blood clot forms to seal the wound and stop microbes entering.

6 When microbes do get into your body they are dealt with by the immune system. White blood cells produce antibodies which destroy the microbes. The next time you are infected with the same microbe, you already have antibodies to destroy it – you are **immune** to it.

White blood cells

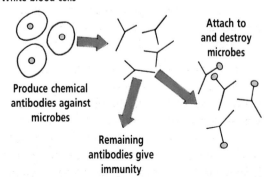

Produce chemical antibodies against microbes

Attach to and destroy microbes

Remaining antibodies give immunity

You become immune to a particular disease if you are vaccinated with a weakened form of the microbe. This stimulates the body to produce antibodies without making you ill. Immunization programmes have eliminated some major diseases.

7   You can also become immune by injection of antibodies.

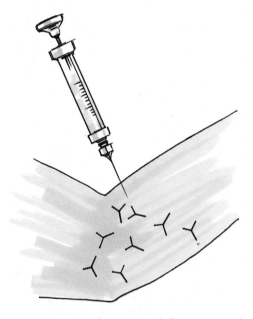

8   AIDS (acquired immune deficiency syndrome) results from infection by the human immuno-deficiency virus (HIV). HIV attacks white blood cells and blocks the immune system by preventing antibody production. AIDS sufferers are unable to offer any natural resistance to microbial infection.

9   When body organs become diseased or do not function properly, they can often be replaced by healthy transplants. Kidneys, livers, lungs, hearts and corneas (from the eye) have all been transplanted. Although transplanted organs are carefully selected, they are often rejected by the body because of the immune response.

10 Your kidneys are high-pressure filter systems which control the amounts of water and dissolved substances in the blood. Although you are born with two kidneys, you can have a full and active life with only one. Kidney failure can be treated by regular dialysis (filtering) on a kidney machine, or by transplanting a healthy kidney from a donor.

11 Coronary heart disease happens when the blood vessels which supply the heart with oxygen get blocked. It can be treated by bypass surgery. An artery from the leg is transplanted to provide an alternative route to the heart.

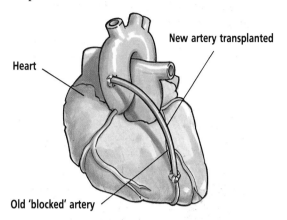

Valves in the heart keep the blood flowing in the right direction. Damaged heart valves may be replaced by artificial ones. Irregular heartbeats can be corrected with an electronic pacemaker.

12 **Enzymes** (biological catalysts) control the complex reactions that go on inside your body. To stay healthy, your body must keep the right conditions for enzymes to work in.

13 The chemical reactions which enzymes catalyse take place at an active site on the enzyme molecule. A substance which has a molecular structure that fits the active site can alter the action of an enzyme. Some drugs work by blocking the active sites of enzymes.

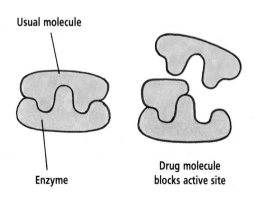

A drug that blocks the active site of an enzyme in a disease-carrying microbe will kill the microbe.

Thinking about

Keeping healthy

1. What happens inside your body?

Your body is made of lots of different chemicals. Like any other animal, you stay alive by taking in more chemicals. You take in water, oxygen and food (food is a mixture of chemicals). These react with other chemicals inside your body. Most of the reactions convert food chemicals into chemcials which are needed by your body and waste chemicals which are excreted from your body.

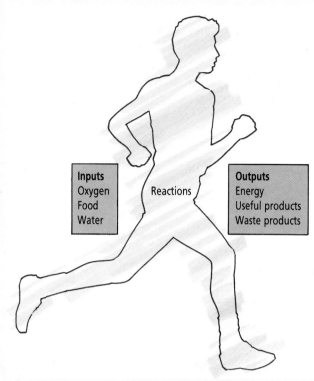

Inputs
Oxygen
Food
Water

Reactions

Outputs
Energy
Useful products
Waste products

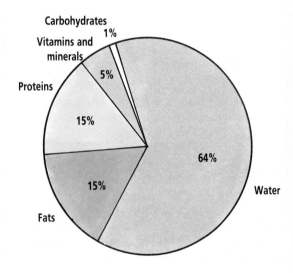

The chemicals which make up your body (percentage masses).

Carbohydrates
1%
Vitamins and minerals
5%
Proteins
15%
Fats
15%
Water
64%

There are many different reactions taking place in your body. When these reactions are working properly, you are healthy. When they go wrong, you become ill.

These reactions are different from reactions you have seen in the laboratory. They are controlled so that they happen steadily, not all at once. The chemicals in the body that do this controlling are called **enzymes**. Enzymes catalyse reactions – they make them happen more easily. Some reactions would happen so slowly without enzymes that they wouldn't appear to react at all.

2. What are enzymes?

Enzymes are molecules that have a special shape. Each enzyme controls just one type of reaction.

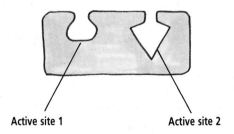

Active site 1   Active site 2

Enzymes have active sites – only one sort of molecule fits into each enzyme's active site.

Computer graphics image of the enzyme chymotrypsin. The active site is coloured.

How do enzymes work?

Enzymes are very sensitive to changes in conditions such as temperature and pH. These factors may change the shape of the molecule, so the enzyme no longer works properly. Microbes can also disrupt enzymes, by producing chemicals which fit into their active sites. When an enzyme is blocked your body chemistry is changed and you feel ill.

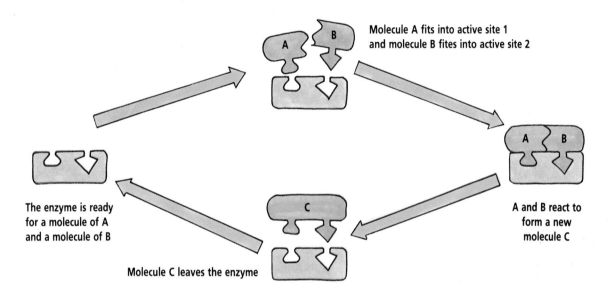

Molecule A fits into active site 1 and molecule B fites into active site 2

A and B react to form a new molecule C

Molecule C leaves the enzyme

The enzyme is ready for a molecule of A and a molecule of B

The enzyme holds A and B together so that C is produced easily. Without the enzyme the reaction would only happen very slowly.

3. How do drugs work?

Microbes are living organisms which have their own enzymes. Antibiotics can block the active site of an enzyme used by the microbe. The microbe's cell chemistry is changed so much that it dies, so the infection clears up. Because we don't have the same enzymes as microbes, the antibiotic doesn't harm our enzymes.

molecule may work even better. Chemists can design different drugs for a disease once they know the shape of one effective drug.

Enzymes are very complex molecules — this chemist is using a computer to design new drugs to block an enzyme.

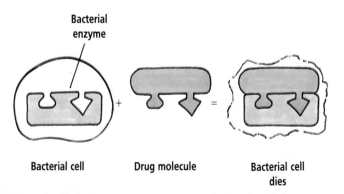

Bacterial enzyme

Bacterial cell   Drug molecule   Bacterial cell dies

If a drug with molecules of a particular shape is effective against an illness, then a similar shaped molecule may also work. In fact, a similar shaped

However, developing a new drug is a long and costly process. A drug must be shown to be pure, safe and effective before it can be used. Even once it is allowed to be used, the drug must be monitored in case it causes any unexpected side effects. A new drug can take 20 years to develop, and the process may cost over £100 million.

4. *What are antibodies?*

Antibodies in your blood help you fight infection
and so help keep you healthy. If you become
infected with microbes, your body reacts by
producing antibodies to them.

How do you produce antibodies?

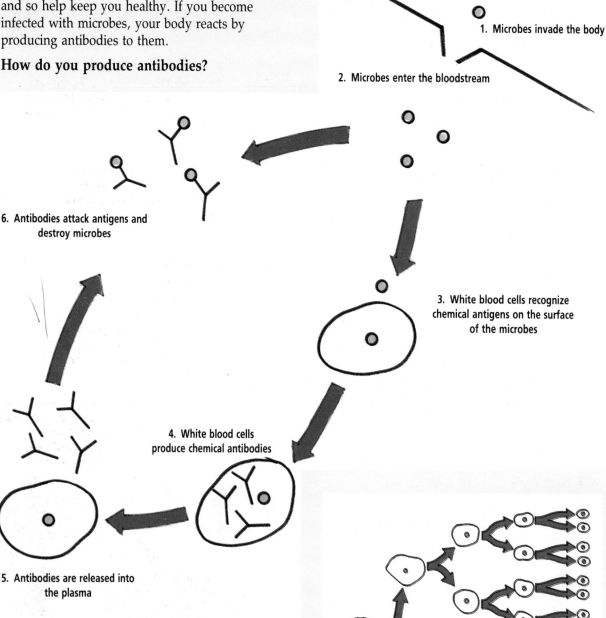

1. Microbes invade the body

2. Microbes enter the bloodstream

3. White blood cells recognize
chemical antigens on the surface
of the microbes

4. White blood cells
produce chemical antibodies

5. Antibodies are released into
the plasma

6. Antibodies attack antigens and
destroy microbes

Antibodies are produced by white blood cells.
When one white blood cell produces an antibody it
enlarges and divides many times to form a large
number of identical cells. Each cell is called a
clone. All the clone cells can produce the same
antibody, so there are lots of antibodies to fight the
infection.

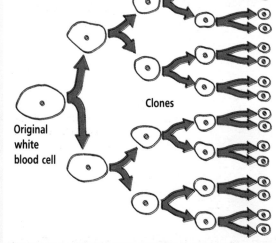

Original
white
blood cell

Clones

Clones are identical cells which are all formed from one original
cell.

Once the infection has been controlled the antibodies are no longer needed and gradually break down. However a few of the white blood cell clones remain in the body. These act as 'memory' cells.

This is why you normally get a disease only once — the memory cells in your body give you lasting protection against the illness. This protection is called **immunity.**

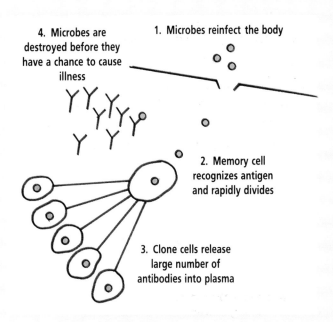

4. Microbes are destroyed before they have a chance to cause illness

1. Microbes reinfect the body

2. Memory cell recognizes antigen and rapidly divides

3. Clone cells release large number of antibodies into plasma

5. *What is immunization?*

Immunization is a process that makes your body 'remember' a disease so it can produce antibodies to it quickly. It can be done in two ways:

Active immunity

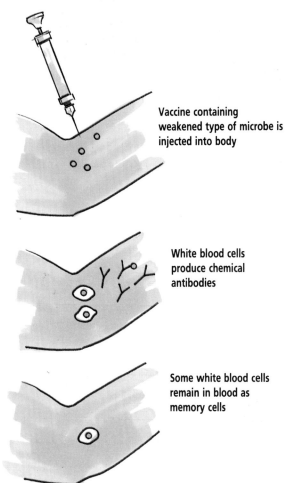

Vaccine containing weakened type of microbe is injected into body

White blood cells produce chemical antibodies

Some white blood cells remain in blood as memory cells

This is called active immunity because your body produces the antibodies for itself. Sometimes the vaccine consists of purified antigen, but you produce antibodies in the same way.

Passive immunity

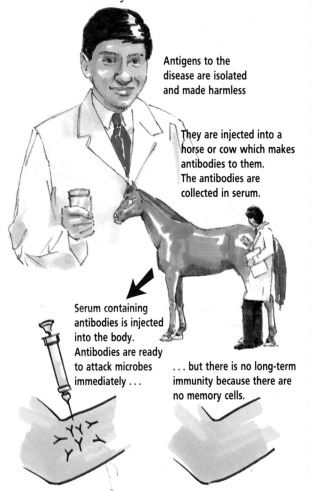

Antigens to the disease are isolated and made harmless

They are injected into a horse or cow which makes antibodies to them. The antibodies are collected in serum.

Serum containing antibodies is injected into the body. Antibodies are ready to attack microbes immediately . . .

. . . but there is no long-term immunity because there are no memory cells.

This is called passive immunity because the antibodies are injected into your body — it doesn't make them for itself.

6. How do kidneys work?

You have two kidneys which work around the clock to get rid of waste products from your blood. They filter about 1 litre of blood each minute.

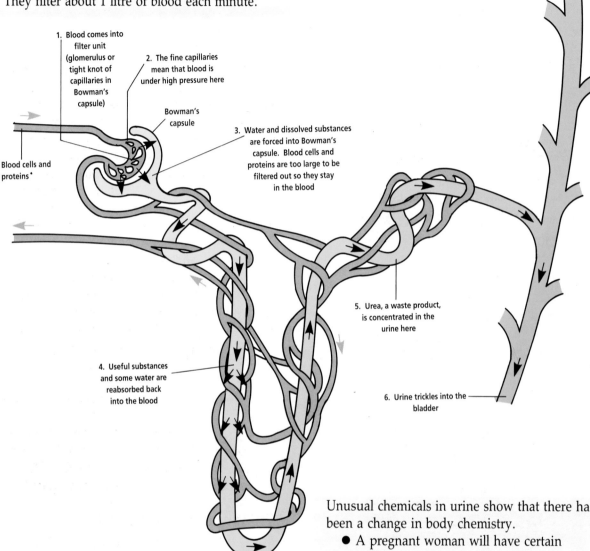

1. Blood comes into filter unit (glomerulus or tight knot of capillaries in Bowman's capsule)

2. The fine capillaries mean that blood is under high pressure here

Bowman's capsule

3. Water and dissolved substances are forced into Bowman's capsule. Blood cells and proteins are too large to be filtered out so they stay in the blood

Blood cells and proteins

4. Useful substances and some water are reabsorbed back into the blood

5. Urea, a waste product, is concentrated in the urine here

6. Urine trickles into the bladder

Healthy kidneys keep:
- the composition of your blood constant
- the water balance of your body constant.

If you drink a lot of water then your kidneys will not reabsorb all the water that passes through them back into the blood. You will produce a lot of dilute urine. If you lose water by sweating, your kidneys will reabsorb most of the water passing through them and so will produce a small amount of concentrated urine.

Unusual chemicals in urine show that there has been a change in body chemistry.
- A pregnant woman will have certain hormones in her urine.
- People suffering from diabetes may have glucose in their urine. People with diabetes lack the hormone insulin, which controls the level of glucose in the body. If the level rises too far glucose is excreted in the urine.
- People with a kidney disorder may have protein in their urine. Protein molecules are too large to be filtered through normal kidneys, but if the kidney is not functioning properly then proteins and other large molecules may be excreted in the urine.

Urine analysis is an important tool used in diagnosing illness.

Things to do

Keeping Healthy

Things to try out

1 Design a questionnaire to find out what common diseases people in your class have had, and what vaccinations they have had. Try out the questionnaire and present your results.

2

Why haven't you dried those plates?

Oh, dad, it's better to leave them to drain. They don't get as many microbes on them as if you used a tea towel.

Use your knowledge of growing bacteria to design an experiment to test the truth of this statement.

Things to find out

3 Since the late 1940s cases of tuberculosis (TB) have been successfully treated by antibiotics. However, at that time, the disease was so common that there were national campaigns to prevent the disease spreading. Using other books, or by interviewing people who can remember, find out what happened during these campaigns.

Points to discuss

4 In 1985-6 there was a whooping cough epidemic and about 35 000 children caught the disease, which can sometimes lead to serious complications like pneumonia. A vaccine which prevents children catching whooping cough is available. A research study has shown that the vaccine can cause brain damage in one case out of every 100 000 vaccinations. Do you think young children should be given the vaccine? What other information would you need to help you decide?

5 Imagine that you have a sore throat, but otherwise you are healthy. Your doctor tells you that if you took antibiotics it would clear up the sore throat quickly. However, she will not give them to you because she believes they should only be taken when absolutely necessary. Do you think the doctor has done the right thing?

6 A drug has been developed that may be effective in fighting AIDS. However, it will take four to five years to show whether it is safe and whether it has any unexpected harmful effects. In that time many people may die of AIDS. Do you think AIDS sufferers should be given this untested drug?

Things to write about

7 Look at *Thinking About 5* on page 27. What is the difference between active and passive immunity? What are the advantages and disadvantages of the two types?

In the country of Tressla there has been an outbreak of the infectious disease typhoid. Both vaccine containing antibodies and serum containing antigens are available for typhoid. If you were a doctor, what advice would you give to the following people?

(a) a tourist going on holiday to Tressla next week

(b) a business person going to Tressla next month, who may make several more trips if the visit is successful.

Questions to answer

8

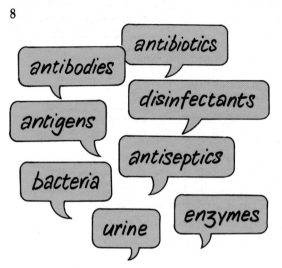

Copy and complete the following sentences. You can use these words more than once.

(a) _____ are a type of drug.

(b) _____ catalyse reactions in the body.

(c) _____ are living things.

(d) _____ are germicides that can be used on the skin.

(e) _____ can cause infections.

(f) _____ are germicides that should not be used on the skin.

(g) _____ are made by cells in the body to help the fight against infection by microbes.

(h) _____ is the name for the waste liquid that comes from the kidney.

(i) _____ are any substance foreign to the body.

9 The proportions of people dying from particular causes have changed a lot over the last 130 years. Table 1 gives the approximate percentages of deaths from four particular causes in 1850, 1910 and 1970.

Table 1

	Infectious diseases	Tuberculosis	Heart disease	Cancer	Other causes
1850	28	17	3	2	50
1910	15	11	9	8	57
1970	1	1	32	32	34

During this time the life expectancy (the averge number of years a person could expect to live) has also changed. Table 2 gives life expectancies, 1850 to 1970.

Table 2

Year of birth	Life expectancy (years)
1850	40
1900	46
1930	58
1970	70

(a) Display the data in each table as pie charts or graphs. Decide which way to present each set of information.

(b) Write a paragraph describing how the proportions of people dying from particular diseases have changed.

(c) Use the charts you have drawn to help you suggest an explanation for
● the increase in the proportion of people dying from heart disease
● the increase in the proportion of people dying from cancer.

10 A kidney machine uses dialysis to remove unwanted substances from a patient's blood. The blood is passed through a cellophane tube which is surrounded by moving fluid which contains dissolved salts. Use *Thinking About 6* on page 28 to help you to answer these questions.

(a) Explain which part of the kidney the cellophane tube corresponds to.

(b) Suggest why the fluid around the tube is moving.

(c) The tube allows water, salts, urea and ammonia to pass through it. Suggest why the fluid which surrounds the tube has salts dissolved in it before it is put into the machine.

(d) Suggest why the presence of protein in a patient's urine indicates a possible kidney disorder.

Introducing

TRANSPORTING CHEMICALS

What does the word 'chemical' suggest to you? Chemicals are not just bottles in the lab — everything is made up of chemicals! Sometimes we need to move chemicals from one place to another. The picture shows how four chemicals get from place to place.

1. List some advantages and disadvantages for each of these four methods of transporting chemicals.

Natural gas gets to the shore through a pipeline.

Petrol is transported from the refinery to the petrol station by road tanker.

This brewery still uses a horse and cart to take its beer to pubs.

Chemicals are moved from the factory where they are made to another factory by train. The second factory uses them to make products such as detergents.

IN THIS CHAPTER YOU WILL FIND OUT

▮ why chemicals are transported around the country and how chemicals are different from each other

▮ different ways of transporting chemicals and how to deal with chemical spillages

▮ the shorthand system to show the emergency services the hazards of the chemicals inside tankers

▮ the shorthand system of representing chemical substances which is used throughout the world

▮ how certain chemicals called elements can be classified.

Looking at

Why are Chemicals Transported?

Most things you eat or use have been manufactured — often from chemicals. The **chemical industry** takes raw materials — oil, gas, coal, minerals, air, water — and makes them into a wide range of chemicals. These chemicals are used to make anything from bread to compact discs.

1 How do you think the layer of rock salt which is under the ground in Cheshire got there in the first place? Write a paragraph showing your ideas.

Rock salt is an important raw material. This earth-moving vehicle is carrying rock salt in a salt mine.

The lorry takes the rock salt to the chemical works. Here it is converted into chlorine and sodium hydroxide.

2 Explain the advantages of siting the factory near the salt mine.

The rock salt is dissolved in water and electricity is passed through the solution. This converts it to sodium hydroxide and chlorine. The photograph shows a row of cells where this happens.

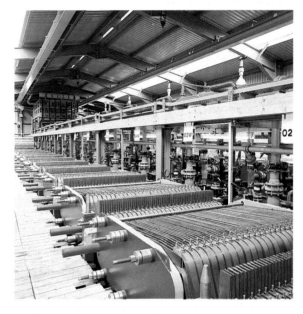

Chlorine and sodium hydroxide are very important chemicals — they are used to make many products which you use every day. But the factories which make these products are often a long way from Cheshire so the chlorine and sodium hydroxide have to be transported to them.

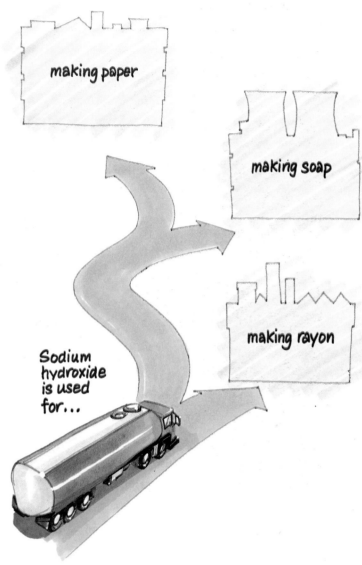

making paper

making soap

making rayon

Sodium hydroxide is used for...

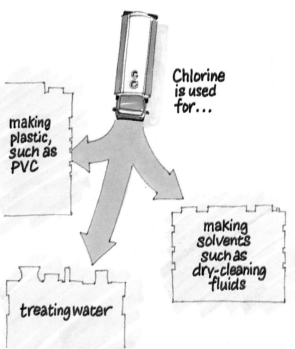

Chlorine is used for...

making plastic, such as PVC

making solvents such as dry-cleaning fluids

treating water

3 Chlorine is a poisonous gas which changes easily into a liquid when you compress it. It is not flammable.

Sodium hydroxide is a solid which absorbs water from the atmosphere. It is very soluble in water and its solution is very corrosive.

Bearing in mind these properties suggest the best way to transport each of these chemicals.

4 Suggest why the paper factory which uses sodium hydroxide might not be near the factory which makes sodium hydroxide, and the factory which uses chlorine to make PVC might not be near the factory which makes chlorine.

Looking at

How Can We Classify the Elements?

1789

It was the year of the French Revolution. A French nobleman called Antoine Lavoisier published a book in which he classified the *elements*. He did this by grouping elements with similar properties together. He might have made further progress with this but the revolutionaries chopped off his head with the guillotine in 1794!

1863

The story continued when John Newlands, a British chemist, arranged all the known elements in the order of the increasing masses of their *atoms*. He noticed that when they were arranged like this there was a pattern in their properties. At a meeting of the Chemical Society in London he announced that:

> *... the eighth element starting from a given one is a kind of repetition of the first, like the eighth note of an octave in music.*

This pattern or generalization only worked for the first 16 elements. This fact, plus the way he linked the pattern to musical notes, led some of the other chemists at the meeting to ridicule his idea.

The repetition of similar properties at regular intervals is called **periodic variation.** Although other people did not accept Newlands' generalization it was the beginnings of the **periodic table of the elements** which scientists now accept and understand.

Lavoisier and one of his groups. As well as the elements oxygen and nitrogen (azote) it contained light and heat.

H Li Be B C N O F Na Mg

The pattern became known as Newland's Octaves.

John Newlands

1 Give a reason *why* scientists wanted to classify the elements.

2 If John Newlands was right, which element would you expect to have properties similar to (a) lithium   (b) beryllium?

1869

Six years later, Dimitri Mendeleev, a Russian, published another periodic table. The basic idea of his table was the same as Newlands in that he

- arranged the elements in order of the masses of their atoms
- and put elements with similar properties under each other in the same vertical column

but where an element did not seem to fit he left a space. He predicted that another element would be discovered with properties which would fit these spaces.

Mendeleev was using his generalization or pattern to **predict** the properties of unknown elements.

For example, he realized that arsenic (As) fitted better under phosphorus (P) than under silicon (Si), so he left a gap (?) under silicon. He predicted this undiscovered element would form an oxide which would be white and have a high melting point and in which one atom of the element would combine with two atoms of oxygen.

1884

Fifteen years later the missing element was discovered. It is called germanium. Germanium forms a white compound with oxygen which has a formula of GeO_2 and a melting point of 1389 °C. Mendeleev was right so chemists began to believe that the periodic table was useful and had some underlying **explanation.**

Mendeleev did not suggest an explanation for the periodic variation of properties. This happened much later, in this century, when **theories** about the structures of atoms were developed.

Dimitri Mendeleev was Professor of Chemistry at St. Petersburg University (now called Leningrad).

	Group 1	Group 2	Group 3	Group 4	Group 5	Group 6	Group 7	Group 8
Period 1	H							
Period 2	Li	Be	B	C	N	O	F	
Period 3	Na	Mg	Al	Si	P	S	Cl	
Period 4	K / Cu	Ca / Zn	? / ?	Ti / ?	V / As	Cr / Se	Mn / Br	Fe Co Ni
Period 5	Rb / Ag	Sr / Cd	Y / In	Zr / Sn	Nb / Te	Mo / I	?	Ru Rh Pd

3 A magazine which is published at regular intervals, such as once a month or once a year, is called a periodical. Why do you think the table of elements is called a *periodic* table of elements?

4 Write a short newspaper article reporting on the Chemical Society meeting at which Newlands announced his 'Law of Octaves'.

5 Lavoisier, Newlands and Mendeleev all published their ideas. Why do you think scientists publish the results of their experiments, and the theories or generalizations based on their results?

6 Mendeleev's periodic table is a generalization or pattern. You can make predictions from it but it is not a theory. Use the ideas discussed on this page to suggest why this is so.

Looking at

Cargoes

Here is a famous poem about transporting chemicals (and other things).

Quinquireme of Ninevah from distant Ophir
Rowing home to haven in sunny Palestine
With a cargo of ivory,
And apes and peacocks,
Sandalwood, cedarwood, and sweet white wine.

Stately Spanish galleon coming from the Isthmus,
Dipping through the Tropics by the palm-green shores,
With a cargo of diamonds,
Emeralds, amethysts,
Topazes, and cinnamon, and gold moidores.

Dirty British coaster with a salt-caked smoke stack
Butting through the Channel in the mad March days,
With a cargo of Tyne coal,
Road-rail, pig-lead,
Firewood, iron-ware, and cheap tin trays.

(John Masefield)

1 Which of the cargoes mentioned in the poem do you think are pure chemicals?
2 The poem was written over 50 years ago. Write a fourth verse about the sort of cargoes carried nowadays.

In brief

Transporting Chemicals

1   The chemical industry is a large and important part of the manufacturing industry. Sometimes it converts raw materials into products which we buy, such as oil into petrol. But often it first converts the raw materials into chemicals (intermediates) which are then used to make products.

2   The factories used to make products are built at different places.
    The choice of site is influenced by:

- source of raw materials
- road, rail and sea links
- available workforce
- environmental factors
- energy supply
- water supply.

3   The intermediate or bulk chemicals can be transported to other factories by:

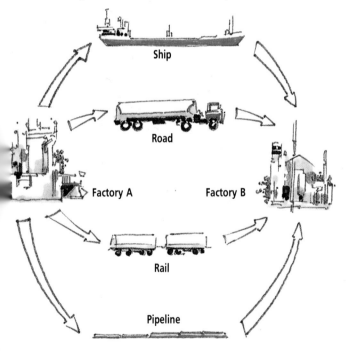

The method used depends on geographical, economic, social and environmental factors.

4   Different chemicals often have different properties. For example, some burn, some are corrosive and some are gases. When they are transported around the country their containers must be carefully labelled. The

Hazchem code system of labelling tells the police and fire services dealing with an emergency what sort of chemicals are involved.

5   An **element** is a substance which cannot be broken down into anything simpler. The smallest particle of an element is called an **atom.** Atoms of one element are different from atoms of all other elements. Each element is represented by a **symbol**, which is shorthand for the element.
    Compounds contain the atoms of more than one element joined together (not just mixed up). Each pure compound is represented by a formula which is shorthand for the compound.
    For example,

$$CaCO_3$$

represents calcium carbonate. This tells you that it contains

calcium, carbon and oxygen

and that these elements are present in the ratio

1 : 1 : 3

The smallest particles of some compounds and elements are called **molecules**. For example, H_2O represents a molecule of water and H_2 a molecule of hydrogen.

6   Chemical reactions between elements or compounds can be represented by word equations. They list the starting substances (reactants) and the products. For example, the burning of natural gas (methane) can be represented by:

methane + oxygen → carbon dioxide + water

Alternatively, an equation which is made up of symbols and formulas can be used:

$$CH_4 + 2O_2 \rightarrow CO_2 + 2H_2O$$

This is called a **balanced** equation because it has the same number of atoms of each element on each side.

7   The **periodic table** is a way of arranging and displaying the elements which helps you remember the similarities and differences between them. It collects similar elements together in vertical columns called **groups**. The horizontal rows are called **periods**.

Thinking about

Transporting Chemicals

1. How should chemicals be transported?

If you ran a factory making chemicals you would sell them to other factories which turn them into useful products. How would you decide on the best way of getting the chemicals to the other factories? You might choose road tankers, trains, ships or pipelines. For small amounts which need to get there quickly you might even use a plane.

Which method do you think is cheapest? You want to make a profit, but the cheapest way might not be the best. If your factory is near a town or village the people won't want your lorries thundering by. There might not be a railway near — you could have one built, but this would be expensive and so you'd have to charge more for your chemicals.

You have to think about lots of questions — here are some for getting chemical X from factory A to factory B.

To predict the cost of a method of transport you need to consider both capital costs and running costs.

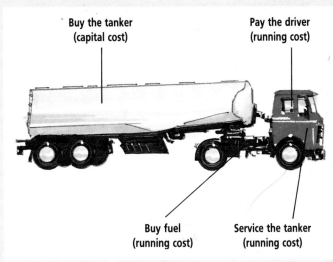

Buy the tanker (capital cost)

Pay the driver (running cost)

Buy fuel (running cost)

Service the tanker (running cost)

A pipeline to transport liquids or gases would be very expensive to build (capital cost) but cheap to maintain (running cost). It would be worth it if you had to transport a chemical from your factory to another for a number of years.

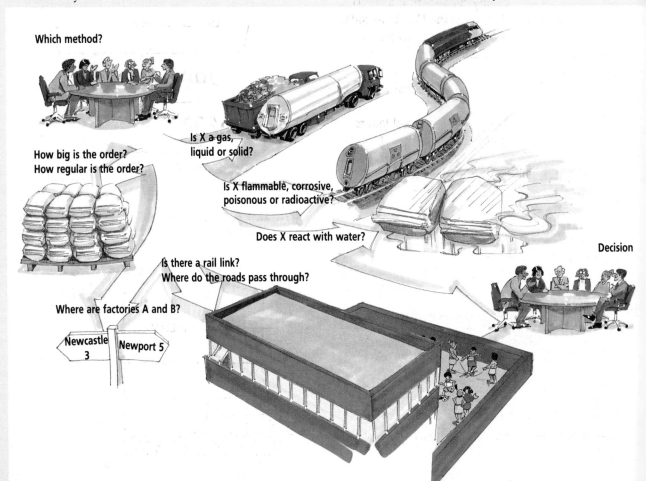

Which method?

How big is the order?
How regular is the order?

Is X a gas, liquid or solid?

Is X flammable, corrosive, poisonous or radioactive?

Does X react with water?

Is there a rail link?
Where do the roads pass through?

Where are factories A and B?

Newcastle 3   Newport 5

Decision

2. Why do we need to know how chemicals differ?

There are millions of known chemicals which are different in many ways. As a first step it is important to know about a few ways they can differ rather than remembering the properties of a particular chemical.

Chlorine is a pale green, poisonous gas which does not burn

Hydrogen is also a gas, but it is colourless, it is not poisonous and it forms an explosive mixture with air

Alcohol is a colourless, flammable liquid which mixes with water

Petrol is also a colourless, flammable liquid but it does not mix with water

Sodium carbonate is a white solid which dissolves in water to form a harmless solution

Sodium hydroxide is also a white solid which dissolves in water but it forms a very corrosive solution

If a lorry or train carrying a chemical has an accident, the police and fire services need to know about the properties of the chemical. So there is an agreed system for labelling containers and vehicles carrying chemicals. It is called the **Hazchem code**.

The emergency workers can look up the name of the chemical from the chemical code number. But the number and letters in the top box are more important – they tell them how to deal with a spillage.

The key shows what the number and letters mean. The 2 means that fog fire equipment can be used. The letter P means that the substance can react violently, the fire fighters should wear full protective clothing and the chemical can be diluted with water and washed down a drain.

In an emergency the Hazchem code gives vital information quickly.

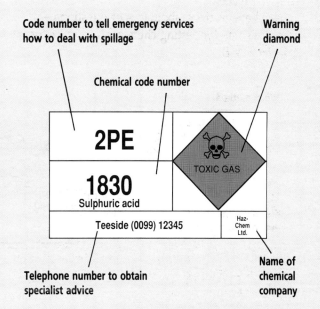

Code number to tell emergency services how to deal with spillage

Warning diamond

Chemical code number

2PE

1830
Sulphuric acid

TOXIC GAS

Teeside (0099) 12345

Haz-Chem Ltd.

Telephone number to obtain specialist advice

Name of chemical company

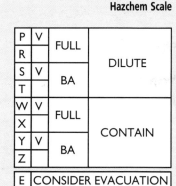

Hazchem Scale

1 JETS
2 FOG
3 FOAM
4 DRY AGENT

P	V	FULL	DILUTE
R			
S	V	BA	
T			
W	V	FULL	CONTAIN
X			
Y	V	BA	
Z			
E	CONSIDER EVACUATION		

3. What are elements, compounds, symbols and formulas?

People in the emergency services who do not usually know a lot about chemistry can understand the Hazchem code (see page 39).

Scientists all over the world also have a shorthand system. It is used to represent *all* pure chemical substances and gives a lot of information.

Every material object, living and non-living, in the whole universe is made of one or more **elements**.

There are about 100 elements. The arrangement of them shown below is called the **periodic table**. Each element is represented by a **symbol**.

Each element consists of tiny particles called **atoms**. The atoms of one element, for example copper, differ from the atoms of all other elements.

The atoms of different elements can combine to form substances which are called **compounds**. The smallest parts of compounds are called **molecules**.

Compounds are represented by **formulas**. The formula is made up of the symbols of the elements which are in the compound and small numbers which show in what ratio the atoms of the elements are present.

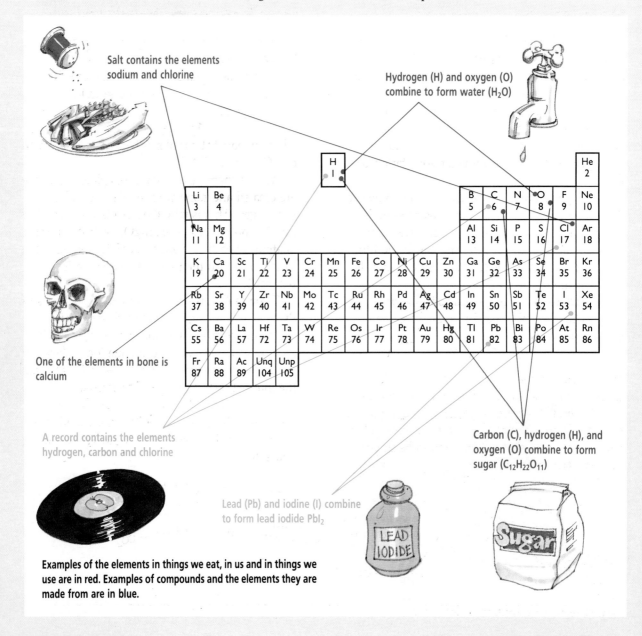

Salt contains the elements sodium and chlorine

Hydrogen (H) and oxygen (O) combine to form water (H_2O)

One of the elements in bone is calcium

A record contains the elements hydrogen, carbon and chlorine

Carbon (C), hydrogen (H), and oxygen (O) combine to form sugar ($C_{12}H_{22}O_{11}$)

Lead (Pb) and iodine (I) combine to form lead iodide PbI_2

LEAD IODIDE

Sugar

Examples of the elements in things we eat, in us and in things we use are in red. Examples of compounds and the elements they are made from are in blue.

4. How are symbols and formulas used to describe chemical reactions?

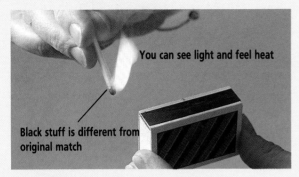

You can see light and feel heat

Black stuff is different from original match

When a match burns new substances are formed.

There is no alcohol to start with

You can see bubbles and smell alcohol

When people make wine new substances are formed.

Both of the changes shown in the photographs are called **chemical changes** because the starting chemicals, the **reactants**, have changed to different chemicals, the **products**.

You cannot always be sure that a chemical change has taken place by just observing what happens. Sometimes you have to test what is left to show it is different from what you started off with.

When you work out what is happening you can describe the change by writing a **word equation**.

For example, if a piece of charcoal (carbon) is burnt in oxygen you can test the gas formed to show it is carbon dioxide. The word equation for this change is:

carbon + oxygen → carbon dioxide

Sometimes symbols and formulas are used instead of words:

$$C + O_2 \rightarrow CO_2$$

This equation tells you that carbon is an element. C represents one atom of the element. Oxygen is also an element. O represents an atom of it but the formula O_2 shows that these atoms go around in pairs. Carbon dioxide is a compound because it contains two elements combined together and the

formula CO_2 shows that they are combined in the ratio of one carbon atom to two oxygen atoms.

Overall the equation tells you that one C combines with one O_2 to form one CO_2.

The equation:

$$2Mg + O_2 \rightarrow 2MgO$$

tells you that: 2 atoms of magnesium combine with one O_2 to form 2MgO.

When a chemical reaction takes place, no atoms are created and none are lost. They are just rearranged. That is why the 2 is placed in front of the Mg and in front of the MgO. The total number of atoms of each element on the left is equal to the total number on the right. The equation is **balanced**.

If you look in science books you will see lots of these equations. They are a quick way of describing chemical reactions and they provide more information than word equations. They are used by scientists throughout the world – they are the international language of scientists.

At this stage it is more important that you understand the information that the equation is telling you rather than be able to write equations yourself.

Metana terbakar dalam udara dengan nyala panas yang tidak bercahaya, untuk membentuk karbon dioksida dan air:

$$CH_4 + 2O_2 \rightarrow CO_2 + 2H_2O$$

El metano arde en el aire, con una flama caliente, no luminosa, formando dioxide de carbono y agua:

$$CH_4 + 2O_2 \rightarrow CO_2 + 2H_2O$$

Methane burns in air, with a hot, non-luminous flame, to form carbon dioxide and water:

$$CH_4 + 2O_2 \rightarrow CO_2 + 2H_2O$$

The same equation is understood in any language.

5. How can you use the periodic table?

An obvious way to arrange the elements is in order of the masses of their atoms, putting the element with the least massive atom first.

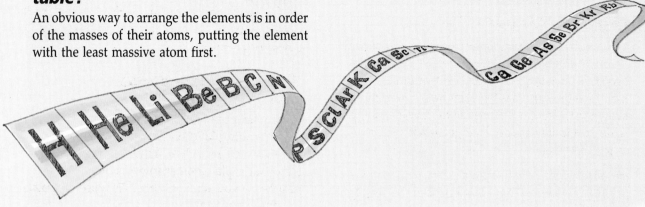

If you do this you might notice that similar elements appear at fairly regular intervals. For example, lithium, sodium and potassium are all soft metals which react with water to form alkaline solutions. The classification can be improved — instead of having the elements in one long row a new row is started every time you come to one of these similar elements.

This arrangement is more compact than the long list. If you look closely at it you will see other examples of where elements in the same vertical column have similar properties.

A more complete table is shown below. The numbers under the symbols show the order of the elements in the table. This number is called the **atomic number** of each element.

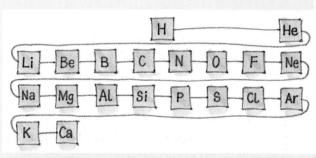

Remember that the table is continuous, but a new row is started at periodic intervals so that similar elements are under one another. The horizontal rows are called **periods**. The vertical columns which contain similar elements are called **groups**.

																group 0
																He 2
group I	group II											group III	group IV	group V	group VI	group VII	
Li 3	Be 4											B 5	C 6	N 7	O 8	F 9	Ne 10
Na 11	Mg 12											Al 13	Si 14	P 15	S 16	Cl 17	Ar 18
K 19	Ca 20	Sc 21	Ti 22	V 23	Cr 24	Mn 25	Fe 26	Co 27	Ni 28	Cu 29	Zn 30	Ga 31	Ge 32	As 33	Se 34	Br 35	Kr 36
Rb 37	Sr 38	Y 39	Zr 40	Nb 41	Mo 42	Tc 43	Ru 44	Rh 45	Pd 46	Ag 47	Cd 48	In 49	Sn 50	Sb 51	Te 52	I 53	Xe 54
Cs 55	Ba 56	La 57	Hf 72	Ta 73	W 74	Re 75	Os 76	Ir 77	Pt 78	Au 79	Hg 80	Tl 81	Pb 82	Bi 83	Po 84	At 85	Rn 86
Fr 87	Ra 88	Ac 89															

H 1

The left-hand block contains the more reactive metals

The central block contains many of the metals which are used to make things

The non-metals sulphur, nitrogen and chlorine, which are all used to make acids, are in the right-hand block

You can link the properties of elements to where the elements are in the periodic table. This will help you to cope with extra information as you learn more about the elements.

Things to do

Transporting Chemicals

Things to try out

1 Baking powder, salt, talcum powder and sugar are four white, solid chemicals which you probably have at home. Like the chemicals mentioned in this chapter, they have different properties. Use the tests below to devise a key which could be used to distinguish between the four substances.

Test 1
Shake a small quantity with water to see if the substance dissolves.

Test 2
If it dissolves, make a more concentrated solution. Test it with a piece of litmus paper.

Test 3
Add vinegar (which is an acid) to each.

Test 4
Line a baking tray with aluminium foil. Place a small heap of each substance at opposite corners of the tray – make sure you can remember which substance is which. Put the tray in an oven set at 200 °C and heat the substances for 15 minutes. Switch off the oven and leave it to cool. Then, using an oven glove, carefully remove the tray and see if the heat has affected the substances differently.

Things to find out

2 Use the periodic table opposite.

(a) Find the position of the element barium. From its position in the table predict
   (i) whether it is likely to be a metal or a non-metal
   (ii) whether it is likely to react more or less vigorously with water than calcium.
   Explain the reasons for your predictions.

(b) Find the position of the element krypton. From its position in the table predict
   (i) whether it is likely to be a solid, liquid or a gas

(ii) whether it is likely to be a metal or a non-metal.
   If possible, check your predictions by looking up the properties of barium and krypton in an advanced chemistry book.

Things to write about

3 In this chapter the words atom, element, compound and molecule are mentioned.
   Write an explanation of what these words represent and how they are related to each other. Aim your explanation at someone who is in the year below you at school. If it helps, use diagrams in your explanation.

Making decisions

4 A tanker has been involved in a road accident. It looks as though some of the chemical it is carrying is leaking out of the tanker. The sign on the back of the tanker is the same as the one below.

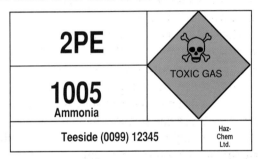

Use the Hazchem code on page 39 to decide what the fire service should do when they arrive at the accident.

5 The Hazchem code for the transportation of chemicals is explained on page 39. There are many chemicals in most homes which are dangerous, for example, cooking oil, bleach, medicines, paintbrush cleaners and weedkillers. Devise a Hazchem code which would be useful in the home. Base it on either the chemicals listed or others which you think are more appropriate.

Points to discuss

6 On your own, try to think of one object used at home which does not use a product of the chemical industry in its manufacture. Then discuss your ideas with each other. If you still think you have thought of an object that does not need the chemical industry, discuss it with your teacher.

7 The formula of vitamin C is $C_6H_8O_6$. What information does this formula tell you about the compound? Vitamin C, whether made artificially from oil or extracted from orange juice, still has the same formula. Think about this and discuss whether or not it is better to buy a drink with added artificial vitamin C.

Questions to answer

8 Look at the ingredients on these labels.

Indigestion tablets
Each tablet contains calcium carbonate, $CaCO_3$, 680 mg and magnesium carbonate, $MgCO_3$, 80 mg.

Cough mixture
Each 5 cm³ contains diphenhydramine hydrochloride, $C_7H_{22}NOCl$, 14 mg.

Make lists of all the different elements in each medicine. Look at the periodic table on page 42 and find out where each element is on the table. Use this to help you to predict whether each element is a metal or non-metal.

Look at *In Brief 5*, page 37. For each ingredient, write out the ratio of the numbers of atoms of each element present in the ingredient.

For questions **9** to **13**:

A	SO_2
B	C_2H_4O
C	$CaCO_3$
D	$C_2H_4O_2$
E	Cl_2

From the formulas A to E, choose the one which

9 contains the element sulphur

10 contains the element calcium

11 contains only one element

12 represents the greatest number of atoms

13 contains the elements carbon, oxygen and hydrogen in the ratio of 2 : 1 : 4.

14 Write the word equations for the reactions represented by each of the following equations.

(a) $2Cu + O_2 \rightarrow 2CuO$
(b) $2K + Cl_2 \rightarrow 2KCl$
(c) $Zn + 2HCl \rightarrow ZnCl_2 + H_2$
(d) $N_2 + 3H_2 \rightarrow 2NH_3$

15 (a) The following two equations are balanced.

$$2Fe + 3Cl_2 \rightarrow 2FeCl_3$$

$$Ca(OH)_2 + 2HCl \rightarrow CaCl_2 + 2H_2O$$

They are called balanced equations because they have the same number of atoms of each element on each side of the equation.

For each equation count the number of atoms of each element on each side and so show they are balanced.

(b) The following two equations are *not* balanced.

$$CO + O_2 \rightarrow CO_2$$

$$NaOH + H_2SO_4 \rightarrow Na_2SO_4 + H_2O$$

For each equation, count the number of atoms of each element on each side. Then by putting appropriate numbers in front of formulas make the equations balance.

For questions **16** to **20**:

A	$CH_4 + 2O_2 \rightarrow CO_2 + 2H_2O$
B	$Mg + Cl_2 \rightarrow MgCl_2$
C	$H_2SO_4 + Fe \rightarrow FeSO_4 + H_2$
D	$H_2 + O_2 \rightarrow H_2O$
E	$Fe + CuCl_2 \rightarrow FeCl_2 + Cu$

From the equations A to E, choose the one which

16 represents a reaction which produces hydrogen

17 contains the greatest number of elements

18 represents a reaction between a metallic element and a non-metallic element to form a compound

19 represents the burning of a fuel to form carbon dioxide and water

20 is *not* a balanced equation.

Introducing
CONSTRUCTION MATERIALS

What materials is your home made of? Are your school, library, town hall and shops all made of the same materials?

When buildings are designed the architect or engineer has to decide which materials to use. The choice will depend on

- the properties of the materials
- the appearance of the materials
- the cost of the materials.

Look at this building site.

1 Make a list of the materials being used and what you think each is being used for.

2 For each material try to think of one alternative material which could be used for the same purpose. Write the names of these alternative materials on your list.

IN THIS CHAPTER YOU WILL FIND OUT

▌ about the properties of construction materials

▌ how these properties are related to the structures of the materials

▌ how you can sometimes modify the properties of materials.

Looking at

A Continuous Process for Making Glass

Glass is a very important construction material — all buildings have windows, and some look as if they are made completely of glass. So we need to produce glass as quickly and cheaply as possible to keep up supplies.

Batch production
Batches of glass can be made like this. ▶

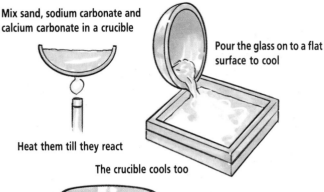

Mix sand, sodium carbonate and calcium carbonate in a crucible

Heat them till they react

Pour the glass on to a flat surface to cool

The crucible cools too

Refill the crucible and start the process again

Only small pieces of glass can be made like this, and on an industrial scale lots of people would be involved in the process.

> 1 Do you think this method uses energy efficiently? Where is energy used inefficiently?

Continuous production
To improve production people have developed a **continuous** process which avoids hold-ups and energy waste. They had to solve a few problems.

Problem 1
How do we get a continuous supply of raw materials into the furnace to be heated?

Solution
Feed them in through hoppers. ▶

Problem 2
How do we get the glass to come out of the furnace continuously?

Solution
A ribbon of molten glass comes out of the furnace. The ribbon is unbroken through the next stages of production, so the cooled glass further along keeps pulling new molten glass out of the furnace.

Problem 3

What can we rest the glass on while it is cooling down? The glass must be kept moving, so it cannot be anything that it will stick to. The glass is very hot, so it cannot be something which will burn.

Solution

Float the glass on molten tin. The tin is very hot — nearly as hot as the glass. This means that the glass cools slowly.

Problem 4

How can we keep very hot solid glass moving?

Solution

Feed the hot ribbon of glass over rollers inside a special oven, where the glass cools down slowly. When the glass reaches the end of the oven it has cooled to 200°C. The glass is now cool enough to be cut up into sheets.

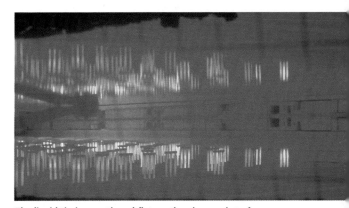

The liquid tin is smooth and flat, so the glass cools to form a smooth, flat surface.

The glass is cut to order – the sizing and cutting are controlled by computer.

2 Draw a diagram of a float glass production line. Make notes on your diagram to show how making glass this way uses energy more efficiently than traditional methods.

Looking at

Pottery in Buildings

What does the word 'pottery' mean to you? Plates and pots? You may be surprised to find that pottery is also used in the construction of your home, and in the buildings around you.

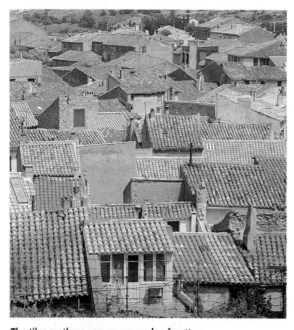

The tiles on these rooves are made of pottery.

How is pottery made?

Like brick, pottery is made from clay. The difference between them is that pottery is normally heated (**fired**) twice, while brick is only fired once. The higher the temperature the pottery is heated to, the less water it will iet through. Pottery surfaces that do not absorb water are extremely useful in bathrooms and kitchens.

Pottery is also easy to decorate. People make it into interesting shapes before firing it, or cover it in special chemicals called **glazes**. Glazes react with the clay during firing to give a shiny and durable coating.

1 Design a model house or other building of your choice. Make a list of places where pottery can be used in it (there are some ideas on this page).
2 Why is pottery chosen for each of the jobs on this page? Add reasons to your list. What other materials could be used instead? Is pottery the only suitable material?

Pottery is used for the wall and floor tiles as well as the pots in this kitchen.

These pottery tiles form cladding on the walls of a house.

The plates are made from pottery as well as the washbasin and toilet.

These are pottery mosaic tiles at the Sheikh Lutfullah Mosque, Iran.

OVERHALL NEEDED!

London's Albert Hall is in danger of falling down. The much-loved London landmark is crumbling away, with water penetrating deeper into the famous stonework each winter. And how has this disaster come about? Now there's the **rub** . . .

In the 1970s the Albert Hall was looking rather dirty. So it was cleaned — by sandblasting. Sandblasting not only rubs off the dirt, it also rubs off the top layer of the building material.

The Albert Hall before sandblasting.

After sandblasting — the Albert Hall is clean but it's also crumbling!

The Albert Hall isn't just any old building. All that elaborate decoration was done in terracotta — a type of pottery. Terracotta has a thin layer of material on the outside which makes it highly resistant to water and very long lasting. But when that layer is rubbed away, the stonework underneath is easily penetrated by water. When this water freezes, it expands. And all those tiny pockets of ice are making the old stones crumble.

If something isn't done soon the ice will be 'bringing the house down'.

3 The owners of the building are extremely worried about what to do. Read through these possibilities and discuss which one you think is the best course of action.
   (a) The building could be left to crumble and collapse.
   (b) The outside could be completely rebuilt in terracotta, which would be very expensive.
   (c) The building could be treated with liquid polymers. These are used to stop water getting into high-rise blocks built of concrete — they soak into the material and form a water-resistant layer. However, using these polymers might be a risk, because no one knows how they will react with terracotta over a long period of time. Once they are applied, the process cannot be reversed.
   (d) The building could be treated with silicone waxes. These act like other waxes and polishes — they form a water-resistant layer. However, unlike liquid polymers, they need to be replaced after about five years, as they are gradually washed away by rain.

4 Write a report for the owners explaining why you reached the conclusion you did, and why you rejected the other three solutions.

5 Imagine that it is one year later and your report has been acted on. Write a follow-up article to the one above, describing what has happened.

Looking at

The Heights of Buildings

One of the laws of Hammurabi, King of Babylonia around 2200 BC, reads:

'If a builder builds a house that is not firmly constructed and it collapses and causes the death of its owner, that builder shall be put to death. If the collapse causes the death of the son of the owner, the son of the builder shall be put to death.'

Even without such penalties, builders want their buildings to last. The sort of building that can be built depends on the strengths of the materials available. As new stronger materials have been developed, so builders have built higher and higher buildings.

These pictures show the tallest structures in the world built of a number of different materials.

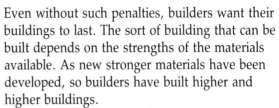

Town Hall, Siena, Italy, 102 m, built of brick in 1348.

Notre Dame Cathedral, Paris, France, 141 m, built of sandstone in 1439.

Timber radio tower, Munich, Germany, 160 m, built in 1932.

Eiffel Tower, Paris, France, 300 m, built of iron in 1889.

Steel radio mast, Plock, Poland, 646 m, built 1974.

The Pyramids, El Gizeh, Egypt, 147 m, built of limestone in 2580 BC.

Washington Memorial, Washington, USA, 169 m, built of stone in 1884.

Canadian National Tower, Toronto, Canada, 555 m, built of concrete in 1975.

1 Make a list of these buildings in the order of when they were built. Start with the one which was built first. What materials have the highest buildings been made of? Have these materials always been available?

2 Use the information on this page to draw a diagram showing how the materials used have influenced the heights of buildings. Draw each building to scale (so if you decide to use a scale of 1 cm = 50 m, the Eiffel Tower drawing would be 6 cm high). Label each drawing with the type of construction material used.

In brief

Construction Materials

1 Bricks:
- are made from fired clay
- are strong and do not absorb much water.
- The atoms in clay are bonded together in layers. During firing the layers become bonded together to form a three-dimensional structure.

2 Metal ties:
- are made from galvanized iron.
- Galvanizing is one way of preventing rusting.
- Both water and oxygen are needed for rusting.

3 Plastics:
- are made by polymerizing certain compounds obtained from crude oil
- are light and weather resistant.
- Some can be reshaped when heated — **thermoplastics**.
- Some cannot be reshaped once formed — **thermosets**.
- During polymerization, large numbers of small molecules (**monomers**) combine to form a very large molecule (**polymer**).

4 Aluminium:
- is resistant to corrosion because of the layer of aluminium oxide on its surface.

5 Glass:
- is made by heating sand, soda ash and limestone together
- has a three-dimensional structure and is hard. But, like a liquid, it does not have a regular structure
- can be made safer by heat-toughening or laminating with plastic.

7 Paint:
- is a mixture of a polymer, a solvent and a pigment
- is used to protect wood from rotting and metal from corroding
- sets when the solvent evaporates and the polymer chains react with oxygen from the atmosphere to bond together.

6 Wood:
- is hard, but can be split along the grain and will absorb water and rot
- has long thin molecules lined up along the grain with weak bonds between them.

Construction Materials

1. Why do different construction materials have different properties?

You choose a particular material because it has the best properties for the job you have in mind. You can use theories about the *structures* of materials to explain their *properties*.

Everything consists of tiny particles which are too small to see. How the particles in a material are arranged and held together is called the **structure** of the material.

Obvious differences between construction materials can be explained by classifying them as one-, two- or three-dimensional structures.

Structures consisting of long, thin particles (one-dimensional structures) explain some properties of wood, wet paint and some plastics.

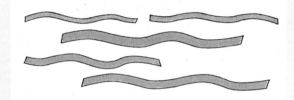

The particles (molecules) are not held strongly together. This means that:

Wet paint — is flexible and runny;

Wood — can be split along its grain.

Graphite (a form of carbon) has particles held together in large flat molecules (a two-dimensional structure). Clay and slate have a similar structure.

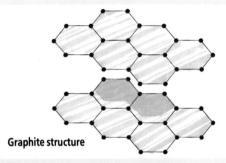

Graphite structure

The flat molecules can slide over each other. This means that:

Clay — is pliable and slippery when wet;

Slate — can be split into sheets.

Diamond (another form of carbon) has particles arranged in a big interlocking structure (a three-dimensional structure). *Hard* materials like brick, stone, concrete, glass, dry paint and some plastics have a similar structure.

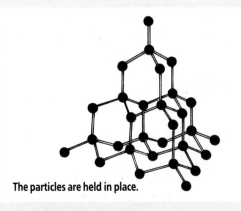

The particles are held in place.

2. How are chemical reactions used to make construction materials?

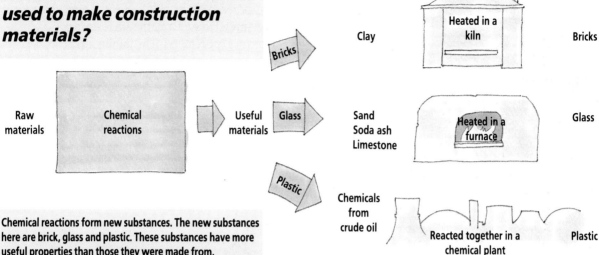

Chemical reactions form new substances. The new substances here are brick, glass and plastic. These substances have more useful properties than those they were made from.

3. What happens during these chemical reactions?

Clay to bricks: Clay contains aluminium, silicon and oxygen atoms bonded together in separate flat layers. When the clay is wet, water molecules get between the layers and allow them to slide over one another.

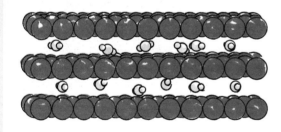

Firing clay (heating it strongly) drives out all the water molecules. Then atoms in one layer form bonds with atoms in another.

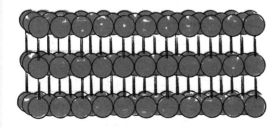

This cross-linking gives brick a three-dimensional structure and makes it hard.

Fired clay cannot be converted back into clay when water is added. So your house is safe in the rain!

Sand, soda ash and limestone to glass: When sand (silicon dioxide) is heated to a very high temperature, it melts and then forms a clear glassy solid when cool.

If sand is heated with soda ash (sodium carbonate), the mixture melts at a lower temperature. This saves energy, but unfortunately the product is soluble in water and so is no use as a glass.

If limestone (calcium carbonate) is also added to the mixture before heating, it still takes less energy to make the glass. The glass formed this time is *not* soluble in water. Normal glass is made by heating these three raw materials together.

Taking it further

When the substances used to make glass are heated together they melt. But there is more to it than that. New substances are formed so chemical reactions have taken place.

Sand is silicon dioxide (SiO_2).
Soda ash is sodium carbonate (Na_2CO_3).
Limestone is calcium carbonate ($CaCO_3$).
The reactions which occur are:

$$\text{silicon dioxide} + \text{sodium carbonate} \rightarrow \text{sodium silicate} + \text{carbon dioxide}$$

$$\text{silicon dioxide} + \text{calcium carbonate} \rightarrow \text{calcium silicate} + \text{carbon dioxide}$$

Ordinary glass is a mixture of sodium and calcium silicates.

Why is glass different? Glass is unusual. It is hard but unlike most solids it does not have a sharp melting point.

Glass can be very tough — it can be reinforced.

Molten glass is runny — it can be poured.

In most solids the particles are in a regular three-dimensional arrangement. In glass, the particles are in a three-dimensional structure but the arrangement is not regular. Glass is really a liquid which has been cooled so quickly that the particles have not had time to organise themselves into a regular pattern. Like a liquid, glass is transparent.

Chemicals from oil to plastic

Plastics are made from lots of small molecules (**monomers**) joined together to form large molecules (**polymers**). The joining up process is called **polymerization**. The monomers are usually made from crude oil.

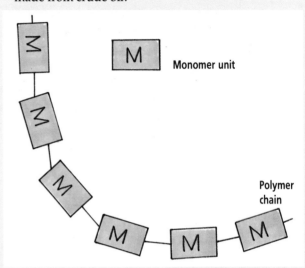

This polymer is made from only one type of monomer.

Adding monomers together like this is called **addition polymerization**. Sometimes monomers combine by a smaller molecule being 'condensed out'. This is called **condensation polymerization**. Many of these polymers are formed from a mixture of two different monomers.

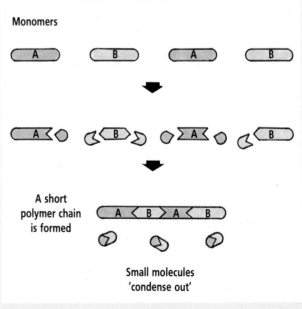

This condensation polymer is made up from two types of monomer.

Sometimes the monomers are gases like ethene or liquids like chloroethene. When they polymerize they become solids. Poly(ethene) (polythene) and poly(chloroethene) are solids. (Chloroethene used to be called vinyl chloride, so the polymer was called poly(vinylchloride) — PVC).

Combining lots of little molecules together to form big molecules has converted the gas or liquid into a solid. Substances made up of little molecules are more likely to be gases or liquids at room temperature. Substances made up of big molecules are more likely to be solids.

Some polymer molecules are long and thin, almost one-dimensional. Then the plastic is flexible. If it is heated it melts and can be reshaped. It is a **thermoplastic**.

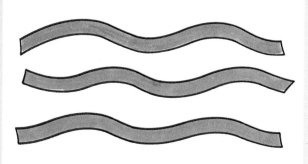

Thermoplastics have no cross-links between their molecules.

Some condensation polymerizations form polymers with three-dimensional structures.

Plastics made from these polymers are more rigid and they do not melt so easily. When they are heated they decompose. These are called **thermosetting plastics** because once set in shape they cannot be reshaped by heating.

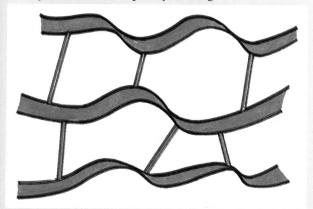

Thermosetting plastics have cross-links between their molecules.

4. What happens when oil paint sets?

There are three main ingredients in paint.

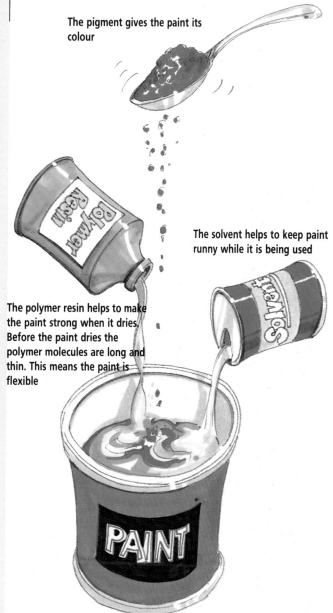

The pigment gives the paint its colour

The solvent helps to keep paint runny while it is being used

The polymer resin helps to make the paint strong when it dries. Before the paint dries the polymer molecules are long and thin. This means the paint is flexible

When paint dries two things happen:
- the solvent evaporates (changes to a gas). That is why wet paint has such a strong smell
- wet paint has a one-dimensional structure like that of thermoplastics. Oxygen from the atmosphere reacts with the paint molecules and forms cross-links between them. This gives a three-dimensional structure like that of thermosetting plastics which is much harder.

5. What happens when metals corrode?

When paint is chipped off a car or bicycle frame the iron underneath gets wet. Wet iron begins to **rust**. Rusting is a special name for the corrosion of iron.

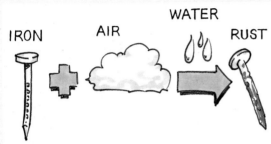

IRON + AIR WATER → RUST

Iron only rusts if the surface of the iron is in contact with the air *and* with moisture.

Although water is necessary for rusting, the reaction can be represented by:

$$iron + oxygen \rightarrow iron\ oxide$$
$$4Fe + 3O_2 \rightarrow 2Fe_2O_3$$

Rust is a form of iron oxide.

Dry rust weighs more than the original iron because it has captured some oxygen from the air. When oxygen is added to another substance the process is called **oxidation.**

Whenever a metal corrodes, oxidation occurs.

When silver goes black or a freshly cut piece of aluminium loses its shine, the same sort of chemical changes are happening. The metal is being attacked (corroded) by the oxygen in the air.

$$aluminium + oxygen \rightarrow aluminium\ oxide$$
$$4Al + 3O_2 \rightarrow 2Al_2O_3$$

But silver and aluminium do not corrode away completely. Silver is not very reactive so it corrodes very slowly.

Aluminium is much more reactive than silver, but as soon as some aluminium oxide is formed on the surface of the metal it protects the rest of the metal. This protective layer makes aluminium very useful. Aluminium door frames do not need painting.

6. How quickly does an acid react with limestone?

Limestone is a very popular building stone. Gases are released into the atmosphere by power stations which burn fossil fuels. Some of these gases can make the rain slightly acidic. This **acid rain** attacks limestone buildings.

Limestone is calcium carbonate. When it reacts with an acid, carbon dioxide gas is given off. For example:

| calcium carbonate $CaCO_3$ | + | hydrochloric acid $2HCl$ |

$$\downarrow$$

| calcium chloride $CaCl_2$ | + | water H_2O | + | carbon dioxide CO_2 |

You can investigate this reaction by measuring the volume of gas given off at regular time intervals. You can plot the results on a graph.

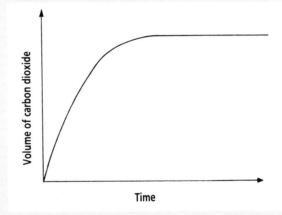

The steeper the curve the quicker the reaction is going (the higher its **rate**). When the curve is flat the reaction has stopped.

If you investigated the reaction in this way you would find that there are three main ways to speed up the reaction:

(a) using small pieces of limestone rather than big lumps. This increases the surface area of the limestone so the acid can attack the stone more quickly

(b) heating the acid. This gives the particles of acid more energy

(c) using more concentrated acid. This means there are more acid particles around to collide with the surface of the limestone.

Things to do

Construction Materials

Things to try out

1 Bricks are slightly porous. So they can absorb water. The amount they absorb can be expressed as 'the percentage increase in their mass when they are placed in water'.

$$\text{water absorption} = \frac{\text{increase in mass}}{\text{mass of dry brick}} \times 100\%$$

Plan how you would compare the amount of water absorbed by different bricks.

Find some different bricks and try out your method.

2 The names of ten building materials are hidden in the wordsearch below. How many can you find?

```
F A Y J E M I O D G E D
I B P O S T E E L N R B
K P E D C O H T U L A I
C A L M I A L E N O T S
H G I A W E B R A E K C
G L A S S D O C F O Y G
N I M U F T E N W A R M
A P O C I J I O L E T U
E N H M B A M C C O G D
L U B G E V A N S H D A
F E O K C I P L V B J L
R C R E D W T H A T C H
```

Things to find out

3 Because bricks are porous they can absorb water from the ground or from driving rain.

(a) How do builders prevent buildings absorbing water from the ground?

(b) Why does driving rain cause greater problems in old buildings which do not have cavity walls?

(c) What problems result when the brickwork of a house is permanently damp?

4 (a) What are the commonest types of rock in your area?

(b) Are there any quarries (open or disused) in your area? If so what do (did) they produce?

(c) What type of stone is used in your local buildings?

5 Colourless glass is made by heating sand, soda ash and limestone together. Coloured glass is made by adding small amounts of other substances. Find out what substances are added to make it **(a)** blue **(b)** green **(c)** red.

Amber Palace, India

Points to discuss

6 All construction materials use natural resources. For example, window frames can be made from wood, steel, aluminium or plastic.

Wood comes from trees, steel and aluminium are extracted from minerals, plastic is made from oil. All these processes which convert raw materials into window frames use energy. Making aluminium and plastic uses most energy, making steel uses less and processing wood uses much less.

Discuss which material should be used for window frames in new houses. Some properties of these materials may make them more suitable. How does this balance against the need to conserve resources?

Questions to answer

7 Read *Thinking about 1* (page 52) and use the ideas to answer the following questions:

(a) Why do you think slate is easier to split than limestone?

(b) Carrier bags and the casings of electric plugs are made from different plastics. Make a list of the ways in which the two plastics are similar and the ways in which they are different. How would you expect the structures of the two plastics to differ?

8

(a) Give the scientific explanation of the difference between addition and condensation polymers.

(b) Look at page 54. If monomer A is:

and monomer B is:

what would be the formula and name of the small molecule produced during the polymerization?

9 This graph shows the rate of reaction between some limestone chips and 1.0 M hydrochloric acid at 25°C.

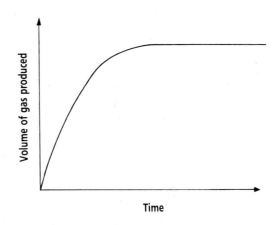

Redraw the graph and sketch in the lines you would expect if:

(a) the same mass of limestone *powder* was used. Label this line A.

(b) the temperature was 15 °C. Label this line B.

(c) half the mass of limestone chips was used. Label this line C.

10 This question is about clay and bricks.

(a) Why is clay slippery and smooth when it is wet?

(b) What happens to the structure of clay when it is changed into brick?

(c) Why are bricks hard and rigid?

(d) How does frost damage bricks?

11 When damp iron rusts it looks as if it is being 'eaten away', but in fact it is combining with oxygen from the air.

(a) Plan an investigation to show that iron gains something from the air when it rusts.

(b) Aluminium is a more reactive metal than iron. Yet when it is used to make window frames it resists corrosion better than iron.

　　(i) Explain why aluminium is more resistant to corrosion than iron.

　　(ii) Describe and explain two ways to prevent the corrosion (rusting) of iron.

Introducing

MOVING ON

How did you and your friends get to school this morning? You probably used various forms of transport between you.

> **1** Make a list of all the different kinds of transport you have used in the past year. Add the advantages and disadvantages of each kind.

Which forms of transport do you think are safest? Although many people feel nervous before flying, it is actually one of the safest forms of transport! Cyclists are involved in far more accidents than aeroplane passengers.

Lots of us use road transport, but there are often accidents on roads. There are many things we can do to make road journeys safer.

> **2** List all the things you can see in these photos which make the various road users safer.

IN THIS CHAPTER YOU WILL FIND OUT

- how forces are involved in changing the motion of objects
- how acceleration is measured and what causes it
- how we can use our knowledge of forces to make travelling safer
- how we can 'spread' forces over longer times and larger areas, so that they do less damage.

Looking at

How to Make Cars Safer

If you have ever been involved in a road accident you will know how frightening it can be. Even if your car is travelling quite slowly, you still feel quite a jolt when it bumps into a solid obstacle. And everything seems to happen so quickly!

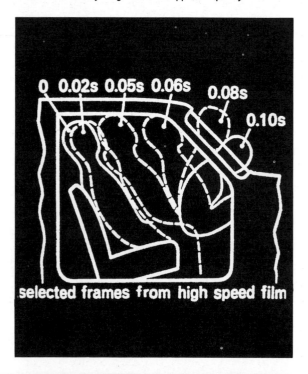

0   0.02s 0.05s 0.06s   0.08s   0.10s

selected frames from high speed film

What really happens in a crash?

At the Motor Industry Research Association (MIRA), cars and car safety devices are tested. In some of these tests, cars with dummy passengers are deliberately crashed into a solid wall. A high-speed camera takes a series of photos during the crash. These help researchers to study the movement of the car and its dummy passengers.

Here are the results of one test. The time starts from the moment the front of the bumper touches the wall.

Time (seconds)	What happened
0.026	bumpers pressed in
0.044	driver hits steering wheel
0.05	force on car is at its maximum; bonnet begins to crumple
0.075	driver's head hits windscreen
0.1	driver probably dead
0.11	bonnet completely crumpled;
	rear passenger hurtles into driver's back
0.15	car completely wrecked
0.2	all movements stop

1 On a sheet of paper, draw a time line. Mark what happened in the test at the appropriate times.

```
|-------------------|-------------------|------------>
0                  0.1                 0.2
                Time (s)
```

2 The average person's reaction time is 0.2 second. The fastest possible reaction time is more than 0.1 second. Could the driver react quickly enough to avoid hitting the windscreen? Could the passenger react quickly enough to avoid being thrown forwards into the driver's back?

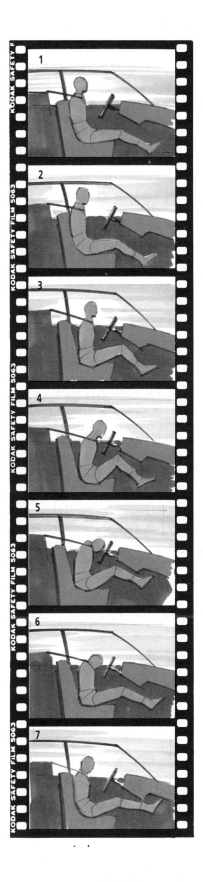

'Belt up': why it makes sense!

The answer to both parts of question 2 is no. This is why seatbelts are such an important safety feature in modern cars. MIRA also test seatbelts. The strip of photos shows how a dummy driver wearing a seatbelt moves during a crash. In photo 1, the crash is just beginning. The time interval between one photo and the next is $\frac{1}{64}$ second (0.0156 s).

> 3 The driver is stationary again in photo 7. How long has the whole crash lasted?
> 4 Does the driver hit the steering wheel? Does the driver's head hit the windscreen?
> 5 Using the photos, estimate how long it takes for the seatbelt to stop the driver's body moving forwards. (*Hint:* Count how many photos it takes for the body to stop moving forward and then use the time interval between photos to work out the total time.)
> 6 Some people think a seatbelt works by holding you completely still. What do the photos show?

How big are the forces?

From the strip of photos, we can also work out how big a force the belt has to exert. The car in these photos was travelling at 80 km/hour (22 m/s) before the crash. This, of course, means that the driver's body was also travelling at 22 m/s before the crash. The driver has a mass of 75 kg. The belt has to slow the driver's body from 22 m/s to zero.

The equation which links these quantities together is:

$$F\,t = mv_{final} - mv_{initial}$$

> 7 Your answer to question 5 is t – the time it takes for the driver's body to stop. v_{final} is zero. Use the equation to work out how big the force F is.

You should find that the force is around 26 000 N. This is almost three times the weight of a small car!

The seatbelt has to be strong enough to exert a force of over 26 000 N. Seatbelts are designed to stretch a little so the body takes a little longer to stop moving. This makes t in the equation larger. This means that F is smaller. If this belt had stopped the driver in just 0.1 s, then F would have had to be over 52 000 N – twice as big.

So there are two reasons why you need to wear a seatbelt:
● You can't react quickly enough to stop yourself, and
● the force you would have to exert with your arms is much bigger than you could possibly manage yourself!

Looking at

Theories about Motion

> 1 Aristotle's theory says that solid objects fall because they 'naturally' return to their proper place — the Earth. Does this theory agree with what we observe? Could the theory be tested by experiment? Is it a scientific theory?

ARISTOTLE'S THEORY OF MOTION, GREECE, AROUND 300 BC.

Everything is made from four elements — fire, earth, air and water — in different mixtures. The way things move is explained by the natural properties of these elements. Things containing a lot of 'fire' go naturally upwards. Things made from 'earth' go naturally downwards — towards the Earth.

Predictions based on Aristotle's theory

According to Aristotle, the heavier an object is, the greater its tendency to move towards the Earth. So heavy objects should fall faster than light ones. In fact, for two objects, one twice as heavy as the other, the heavy one should fall to the ground in half the time the lighter one takes.

> 2 Is this prediction based on everyday experience? Do heavy objects fall faster than light ones? Could this prediction be tested by experiment?

Aristotle's ideas were believed for about 2000 years until . . .

GALILEO'S DEMONSTRATION EXPERIMENT, ITALY, around AD 1600...

I think that all heavy solid objects fall through the air at exactly the same rate, no matter how heavy they are.

See, the one-kilogram mass and the ten-kilogram mass reached the ground at the same time.

But how do things fall?

(THIS IS ONLY A LEGEND)...

Well, I think falling objects get faster by the same amount each second.

You mean they accelerate uniformly?

Yes, so, the distance an object falls will increase as the square of the time. If you drop any heavy object, you'll find that it falls 5m in 1 second. After 2 seconds it will have fallen 20m – four times as far (four is two squared – the square of the time). After 3 seconds, it will have fallen 45m – nine times as far. And so on.

Galileo showed that motion followed the mathematical law he had predicted.

3 How accurate do you think Galileo's methods would have been? Try to think of another way he might have measured time.

4 Did Galileo begin by making observations or by thinking of a theory? What were his experiments for — just to see what happens, or to test a theory?

5 Galileo's results agreed with his predictions. Does this mean that his theories about motion are correct? If he had not found what he expected, would this have proved his theories wrong?

Experimental evidence

Here is a simple way to show that the distance an object falls from rest increases as the **square** of the time.

Take two pieces of thread, just over 1 metre long. Tie five buttons to each thread at the positions shown. Then hold each thread above a table, with the end just touching the table top. Drop one thread, then the other, and listen carefully each time. You should find that the sounds of the buttons landing are equally spaced with thread 1, but not with thread 2.

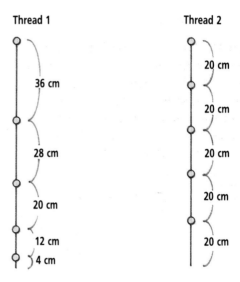

6 How does the result of this simple experiment show that Galileo's prediction was correct?

The importance of Galileo's work

Galileo's work was important for two reasons.

- He challenged Aristotle's theory of motion which had stood unquestioned for almost 2000 years. This started people thinking about motion afresh.
- He linked science and mathematics by looking for a mathematical formula to describe the motion of falling objects.

Galileo was also interested in astronomy. Using a telescope he had invented, he discovered that Jupiter had moons. He also observed mountains on the Moon and sunspots. Strange as it may now seem to us, these discoveries led him into great trouble with the Church authorities. They believed that the Earth was the centre of the universe and that the 'heavens' were perfect. Mountains on the Moon, spots on the Sun and moons revolving round something other than the Earth were difficult for them to accept. Galileo was forced to withdraw his opinions and was kept for many years under house arrest.

Looking at

Cycle Helmets

Everything from cost to the 'wally factor' is deterring cyclists from wearing safety headgear. But helmets can save lives

EVERY year, about 300 cyclists are killed on Britain's roads and 5,000 are seriously injured. Two-thirds of these deaths are caused by head injuries.

Many of these deaths and injuries could be prevented by the use of cycling helmets.

In some accidents, the cyclist's head might hit something sharp like the edge of a kerb. So the design of some helmets is tested by putting them on a metal 'head' and dropping a metal spike on to them. If the spike goes right through, it makes an electrical contact and sets off an alarm.

3 Try to sketch an electric circuit diagram showing how this would work.

This cycle helmet is just a single piece of foam polystyrene, with a chin strap! You have probably come across foam polystyrene as a packaging material.

1 Make a list of the properties of foam polystyrene which make it a suitable material to use for a cycle helmet.

4 Cycle helmets could save lives. But they are expensive and some people think they look silly wearing them — the 'wally factor'. Think up a good caption to make the photo on this page into a poster to encourage people to buy and wear cycle helmets.

A kilogram mass has been dropped on this piece of foam polystyrene from a height of 50 cm. What has the impact done to the foam polystyrene?

2 Use this idea to write a short explanation of how the foam polystyrene helmet protects your head in an accident.

In brief

Moving On

1   If an object is at rest (not moving), all the forces on it must be **balanced**. They add to zero.

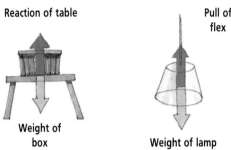

Reaction of table

Weight of box

Pull of flex

Weight of lamp

2   Forces **change** motion. Despite what you might think from everyday experience, a force is *not* needed to keep an object moving at a steady speed. This is called **Newton's first law of motion.**

Driving force

Counter force

Steady speed, so driving force = counter force

3   A force *is* needed:
   ● to start an object moving
   ● to stop an object moving
   ● to make an object move faster
   ● to make an object move slower
   ● to make an object change its direction of motion.
   But a force is *not* needed:
   ● to keep an object moving in a straight line at a steady speed.

4   Left to themselves, objects do not change their motion. This property of all objects is called **inertia.**

5   If a force acts on an object, it makes the object **accelerate.**

Force causes acceleration

6   Acceleration is defined by the equation:

$$\text{acceleration} = \frac{\text{change of velocity}}{\text{time taken}}$$

The units of acceleration are m.p.h. per second, or m/s per second.

   A positive acceleration means that an object is speeding up. A negative acceleration means that it is slowing down.

7   The acceleration of an object depends on the size of the force acting on it and on its mass:

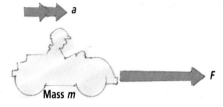

Mass *m*

   ● Acceleration is directly proportional to the force acting.
   ● Acceleration is inversely proportional to the mass of the object.
   This is summarised by the equation:

$$\text{force} = \text{mass} \times \text{acceleration}$$
$$F = ma$$

This is known as **Newton's second law of motion.**

8   The unit of force is the newton (N). One newton is the force needed to give a mass of 1 kg an acceleration of 1 m/s per second.

9   Another useful way to state Newton's second law is:

$$\text{force} \times \text{time} = \text{mass} \times \text{change in velocity}$$
$$Ft = mv_{\text{final}} - mv_{\text{initial}}$$

From this it follows that:
   ● if an object is stopped very quickly, the force involved is large
   ● if an object is stopped in a longer time, the force involved is smaller.

10 When a force acts on a surface, it exerts a **pressure**. The size of the pressure depends on the force and the area on which it acts:

$$\text{pressure} = \frac{\text{force}}{\text{area}}$$

11 The quantity *mv* is called **momentum.** When two objects collide, or spring apart (an explosion), the total momentum is the same afterwards as it was before.

Thinking about

Moving On

1. How do forces keep things still?

If you drop an apple, it falls to the floor. A force pulls it downwards — the force of gravity, its **weight.** But if you put the apple on a table, it does not fall — it sits still. Gravity is still pulling the apple downwards but now another force is balancing this out. The table exerts an upward push on the apple, holding it steady.

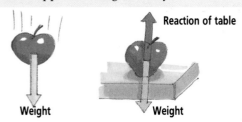

Reaction of table

Weight   Weight

How does the table exert an upwards push? Think what would happen if you put the apple on a piece of foam. The foam would be squeezed down a bit. Foam is springy, so the compressed foam would then exert a push upwards on the apple. The apple sinks in until the upward push is exactly equal to its weight.

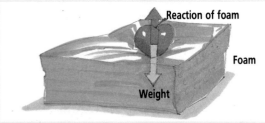

Reaction of foam

Foam

Weight

The same thing happens with the apple on the table. The table top is not so easily squeezed as the foam. It *can* be compressed — though not enough to see with the naked eye. The apple 'sinks in' until the upward force balances its weight.

Anything which is sitting or hanging at rest is being held there by **balanced forces.**

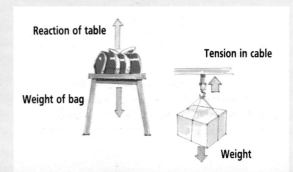

Reaction of table

Tension in cable

Weight of bag

Weight

2. Are forces needed to keep things moving?

If you want to move a box across the floor, you have to give it a push or a pull. When you stop pushing or pulling, it stops. It seems that a continuous force (a push or a pull) is needed to make something move. But there are problems with this simple explanation. Things often carry on moving after a force has stopped acting on them.

When you play tennis, your racket hits the ball and exerts a force on it. But the ball keeps on moving after the racket has hit it — even though the racket is no longer exerting any force on it.

Curling is like bowls on ice! The heavy curling stone is set in motion by a push from the player's hand — but then it keeps on moving as it slides down the ice rink towards its target.

The above photo gives us an important clue. The stone keeps on moving because ice is very smooth. There is very little **friction.** If we could get rid of friction altogether, anything that had been set in motion would carry on moving at a steady speed.

Without friction, no force is needed to keep an object moving at a steady speed in a straight line.

Inertia

Unless a force acts on an object, the object's motion doesn't change. If it is at rest, it stays at rest. If it is moving, it carries on moving at a steady speed in a straight line. We call this observed property of all objects **inertia**. We cannot explain inertia — its just the way all objects behave!

An example: forces in cycling

Here is an example showing how forces are involved in steady motion and changes in motion.

Counter forces ← → **Driving force**

If you are cycling along a road at a steady speed, the forces on you are balanced. The driving force is exactly equal to the counter forces (friction and air resistance). Air resistance is a special case of friction.

Counter forces ← → **Driving force**

If you want to speed up, you have to exert a larger driving force. This is now bigger than the counter forces, so you speed up.

Counter forces ← → **Driving force**

On the other hand, if you want to slow down, you pedal less hard. The counter forces are now bigger than the driving force. The total force is backwards — against the motion. So you slow down.

3. Terminal velocity

Forces are balanced when you are stopped, and forces are balanced when you are riding along at a steady speed. What happens in between? How do you ever get moving in the first place?

When you start to pedal a bicycle you provide a driving force. At this stage the counter forces are small. As you speed up, the counter forces get bigger. You stop speeding up when the counter forces are the same size as the driving force. The speed you are travelling at then is called the **terminal velocity.**

Counter forces ← → **Driving force**

When you start off, the driving force is bigger than the counter forces, so you speed up.

Counter forces ← → **Driving force**

As your speed increases, the counter forces increase. You continue to speed up, but not as quickly as before.

Counter forces ← → **Driving force**

Eventually you reach a speed where the counter forces are exactly equal to the driving force. Now your speed stops increasing. But you don't stop — you keep on travelling at this speed.

4. What is acceleration?

If no force acts on an object (or if the forces are balanced and add to zero), the object's motion stays the same. But if a force does act on an object, its motion changes. A steady force in the direction the object is moving makes it speed up or **accelerate**. A steady force in the opposite direction to its motion makes it slow down — a negative acceleration.

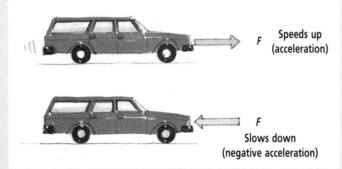

F — Speeds up (acceleration)

F — Slows down (negative acceleration)

Acceleration is defined by this equation:

$$\text{acceleration} = \frac{\text{change of velocity}}{\text{time taken}}$$

Here are some examples of this equation in action.

Example 1: A car can accelerate from 0 to 60 m.p.h. in 8 seconds. What is its acceleration?

$$\text{acceleration} = \frac{60 \text{ m.p.h.}}{8 \text{ s}} = 7.5 \text{ m.p.h. per second}$$

This means that the car's speed increases by 7.5 m.p.h. every second.

Example 2: An ice skater can speed up from rest to 12 m/s in 8 s. What is her acceleration?

$$\text{acceleration} = \frac{12 \text{ m/s}}{8 \text{ s}} = 1.5 \text{ m/s per second}$$

This means that her speed increases by 1.5 m/s every second.

Example 3: A car is travelling at 25 m/s when the driver brakes. The car stops in 5 s. What is the acceleration?

$$\text{acceleration} = \frac{-25 \text{ m/s}}{5 \text{ s}} = -5 \text{ m/s per second}$$

The negative sign means that the car's speed is getting *less* by 5 m/s every second.

5. How are force, mass and acceleration connected?

If a force acts on an object, the object accelerates. But how big is the acceleration? It depends on the size of the force and the mass of the object. We can investigate this in the laboratory.

(a) Force and acceleration

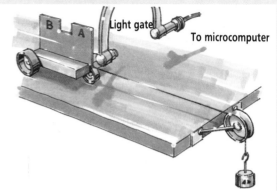

Light gate
B A
To microcomputer

The mass on the end of the thread exerts a force on the trolley. We can increase the force by adding more masses. We measure the acceleration by fixing a double card to the trolley. Part A cuts through a light gate and interrupts the beam. Then part B interrupts it again. The computer measures the times taken for A and B to cut through the beam. If it knows the width of A and B, it can work out the two speeds — one when A goes through, the other when B goes through. It also measures the time interval between these. The computer can then work out the acceleration of the trolley.

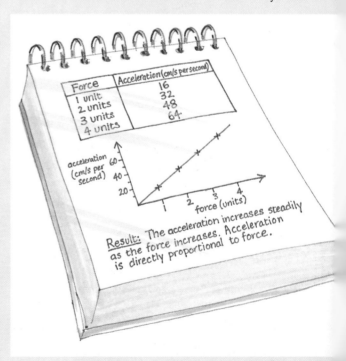

Force	Acceleration (cm/s per second)
1 unit	16
2 units	32
3 units	48
4 units	64

Result: The acceleration increases steadily as the force increases. Acceleration is directly proportional to force.

(b) Mass and acceleration

This time we keep the pulling force constant, but change the mass on the moving object by stacking more trolleys on top.

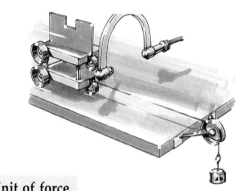

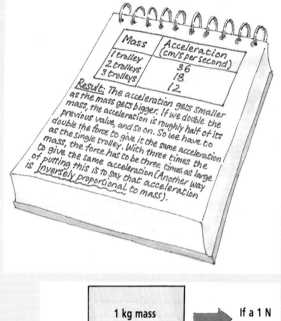

Mass	Acceleration (cm/s per second)
1 trolley	36
2 trolleys	18
3 trolleys	12

Result: The acceleration gets smaller as the mass gets bigger. If we double the mass, the acceleration is roughly half of its previous value, and so on. So we have to double the force to give it the same acceleration as the single trolley. With three times the mass, the force has to be three times as large to give the same acceleration (Another way of putting this is to say that acceleration is inversely proportional to mass).

Unit of force

A force is something which makes a mass accelerate. So we can define the unit of force, the **newton** (N) as follows:

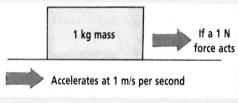

a 1 N force is needed to accelerate 1 kg at 1 m/s per second

So

a 2 N force is needed to accelerate 1 kg at 2 m/s per second
a 3 N force is needed to accelerate 1 kg at 3 m/s per second } **from investigation (a)**

and

a 2 N force is needed to accelerate 2 kg at 1 m/s per second
a 3 N force is needed to accelerate 3 kg at 1 m/s per second } **from investigation (b)**

or

a 4 N force is needed to accelerate 2 kg at 2 m/s per second
a 6 N force is needed to accelerate 2 kg at 3 m/s per second } **from both investigations together**

In all cases,   **force = mass × acceleration**

$$F = m\,a$$

This is called **Newton's second law of motion**.

Taking it further:

There is another very useful way of stating Newton's second law. Imagine a trolley changing its speed from $v_{initial}$ to v_{final} in t seconds.

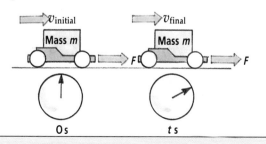

Its acceleration is:

$$a = \frac{(v_{final} - v_{initial})}{t}$$

If we substitute this into the equation for Newton's second law above:

$$F = \frac{m\,(v_{final} - v_{initial})}{t}$$

or

$$Ft = mv_{final} - mv_{initial}$$

We will see in the next section how to use this equation.

6. What happens when you stop suddenly?

Sometimes things change speed very suddenly, for example when a car crashes. A very useful equation for helping us work out what happens then is:

$$Ft = mv_{final} - mv_{initial}$$

F is the force which causes the change of speed and t is the time it takes for the change to happen.

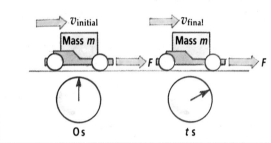

Now imagine a car of mass m travelling along at speed $v_{initial}$ when it is suddenly brought to a stop.

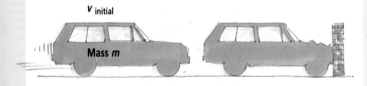

t is the actual duration of the impact — from the moment the car first makes contact with the wall until it stops moving. The equation now becomes simpler, because the final speed v_{final} is zero:

$$Ft = -mv_{initial}$$

The car's $mv_{initial}$ depends on its mass and its speed before the crash. If we know these we can work it out. This equation tells us that F multiplied by t must come to the same number. So if the time taken for the car to stop is small, the force will be large. But if the time is longer, the force will be smaller.

Many modern cars have 'crumple zones'. The front of the car crumples up in a collision, which increases the time the car takes to stop. Other safety features of cars work in the same way. They lengthen the time it takes for a moving object to stop, so that the force is smaller. Seatbelts, crash barriers and safety helmets all make use of this idea. Pages 60–61 and 64 tell you about this in more detail.

7. What happens in a collision?

How hard is it to stop a moving object? The amount of mv it has tells you. If it has a lot of mv, it is hard to stop. If it has only a little mv, it is easier to stop. The quantity mv is given a special name: **momentum.**

Work out the momentum of each of the vehicles in these photos. Which would be the easiest to stop? Which needs the most powerful engine to get it going at this speed?

Mass 10 000 kg
Speed 15 m/s

Mass 1000 kg
Speed 25 m/s

Mass 50 kg
Speed 10 m/s

Momentum plays an important role when two objects collide. The total momentum after the collision is the same as the total momentum before.

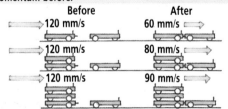

Before			After		
Mass (kg)	Velocity (mm/s)	mv (kg mm/s)	Mass (kg)	Velocity (mm/s)	mv (kg mm/s)
1	120	120	2	60	120
2	120	240	3	80	240
3	120	360	4	90	360

Explosions, where two objects spring apart, are a special type of collision. The total momentum at the beginning is zero — everything is stationary. Afterwards, the two objects have equal and opposite momenta. Direction is important for momentum! Equal and opposite momenta add to zero.

		$(mv)_A$ (Kg mm/s)	$(mv)_B$ (Kg mm/s)
A 200 mm/s	B 200 mm/s	−200	200
230 mm/s	115 mm/s	−230	230
246 mm/s	82 mm/s	−246	246

Taking it further: momentum and energy

All moving things have **kinetic energy** and **momentum**. But momentum is *not* the same as kinetic energy. Think about the explosion experiment. Before the explosion, there was no kinetic energy — everything was standing still. There was also no momentum. After the explosion, the two momenta were equal and opposite. One has a negative sign and they add to zero. But energy does not have direction. Both trolleys have kinetic energy and this does *not* add to zero.

The explosion is an energy transfer. The stored elastic potential energy in the spring is transferred to kinetic energy in the moving trolleys.

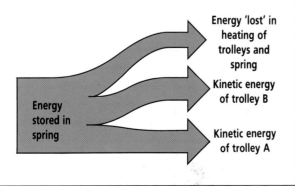

Energy stored in spring →
- Energy 'lost' in heating of trolleys and spring
- Kinetic energy of trolley B
- Kinetic energy of trolley A

8. Pressure

When a force pushes on an object, the force exerts a **pressure** on the surface of the object. The size of this pressure depends on how big the force is and the area it pushes on.

We define pressure using the equation:

$$\text{pressure} = \frac{\text{force}}{\text{area}}$$

The units of pressure are newtons per metre squared (N/m²), or newtons per centimetre squared (N/cm²). 1 N/m² is also called 1 **pascal** (Pa).

Here are two examples, one showing a high pressure and the other a small pressure.

Pressure = 0.15 N/cm²
Force (weight) = 600 N
Area = 4000 cm²

Force = 20 N
Area = $\frac{1}{100}$ cm² (0.01 cm²)
Pressure = 2000 N/cm²

It is the pressure, not the force, which determines how far the pushing object sinks into the other surface. Of course, it also depends on how hard the other surface is. The force exerted by the drawing pin on the wallboard is smaller than the downward force of the skier on the snow. But the pressure of the pin on the board is much bigger than the skier's pressure on the snow. So the pin goes into the board, but the skier does not sink into the snow.

Things to do

Moving On

Things to try out

1 Here are some tricks you can practise and then try out on your friends. They all have a scientific explanation!

(a) Get a medium-sized hardback book and a reel of thread. Tie a length of thread to hold the book. Tie a second length of thread to hang beneath the book.

Now hold the book by the top thread. (You might need to tie a loop in the thread, so that it does not slip out of your fingers. Wearing a glove will also help if the book is heavy.)

Pull gently on the lower thread. Keep pulling . . . which thread breaks first?

Now try this again – but this time pull the lower thread with a sudden jerk. Which thread breaks this time?

(b) Make a pile of pieces from a draughts set. Place this on a smooth tabletop. Take a ruler and quickly sweep it along the table. Can you knock out the bottom draughts piece but leave the others standing?

Try to write a scientific explanation of how these tricks work. The scientific idea of inertia is important in each case.

2 To try this out, you need a bicycle and a small hill on a quiet road near your home. You have to start at the same point each time, somewhere up the hill. So mark a spot on the ground with chalk. Now freewheel down the hill (no pedalling!) and continue freewheeling as far as you can along the level before you stop. Mark the furthest point you reach with chalk.

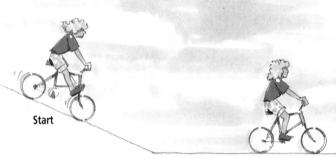

Start

Bicycle stops here

Now go back up the hill to the same starting place. This time let some air out of your tyres until they are only about half pumped up. Try freewheeling down the hill again.

Do you go as far this time? Give a reason for the difference, using science ideas that you have learnt in this unit.

(P.S. Don't forget to pump your tyres up again!)

3 Find a fairly heavy toy car or lorry and an elastic band. Pull the vehicle along with the elastic band and see how long the band gets. You should notice that it is longer when the vehicle is starting than when it is moving steadily.

Try to explain this using the scientific ideas you have learnt in this unit.

Points to discuss

4 In a road accident a car swerves to avoid a child and runs into a wall. The front of the car is completely crumpled in, but the driver is able to open her door and step out uninjured.

A man who saw the accident comments, 'They don't make cars like they used to. Look at that! The front of the car is completely ruined.'

Is the man right in thinking that the car has crushed because it is made of cheaper materials? How would you explain to him why the car is designed to crush easily?

5 Explain each of the following common observations using science ideas in your explanations. Use a diagram if necessary.

(a) If you are standing on a bus when it starts moving, you tend to fall backwards. If you are standing on a moving bus when it suddenly stops, you are thrown forwards.

(b) If you have to brake suddenly on your bicycle, you almost fly off over the handlebars. The back wheel may even lift off the ground.

(c) (Harder) If you are in a car which goes round a corner quickly, you feel as if you are being pushed outwards, towards one side of the car.

6 Some of the worst road accidents happen when a moving car hits a solid fixed object, like the pillar of a motorway bridge. Road engineers have been developing a crushable crash barrier to reduce this danger. The picture shows this barrier being tested.

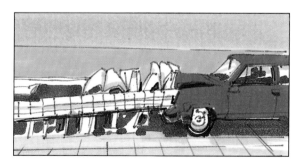

Make a plan drawing of a motorway bridge, showing where you would place a crushable crash barrier.

Explain, using science ideas from this unit, how this sort of barrier works, and how it reduces injury and damage in a crash.

Things to write about

7 Cut out a car advertisement from a newspaper (there are usually lots in the Sunday supplements). Choose one which emphasises the safety aspects of the car.

Make this cutting the centre-piece of a poster. Around the cutting, add some extra information to explain the car's safety features.

8 The pictures show two cars after crash testing. The front end of the car in the top picture was not designed as a crumple zone. The lower car did have a crumple zone design.

Make a list of all the differences you can see between the damage done to the two cars.

Which car would be safest to drive?

Explain how the crumple zone works, using science ideas you have learnt from this unit.

Questions to answer

9

What force is needed to make the discus accelerate at:

(a) 2 m/s² **(b)** 0.5 m/s² **(c)** 10 m/s²?

10 Put the vehicles in the photos below into order, from the largest acceleration to the smallest acceleration.

Boeing 747:
Mass 400 000 kg
Engine force 800 000 N

Ford Fiesta XR2i
Mass 1300 kg
Engine force 6500 N

BMW 1000
Mass 300 kg
Engine force 3000 N

Car ferry
Mass 2 000 000 kg
Engine force 200 000 N

Cyclist
Mass 90 kg
Driving force 135 N

11 A loaded supermarket trolley has a mass of 20 kg. It is rolling along at a speed of 3 m/s, when it bumps into an empty trolley of mass 10 kg.

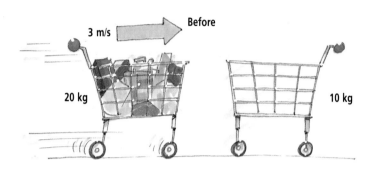

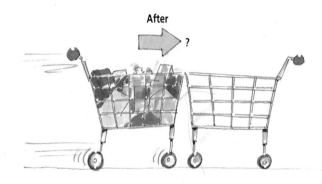

(a) What is the momentum of the first trolley?

(b) If the two trolleys stick together after they crash, what speed will they be moving at?

12 What determines how deep a mark a table makes on a carpet: its weight or the pressure its feet exert?

Which of these tables would make the deepest mark on a carpet?

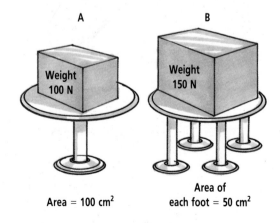

Introducing

FOOD FOR THOUGHT

You probably take it for granted that there will be something for tea tonight. But we see television reports that some people in the world are starving, and many organizations like Band Aid and Oxfam work hard to raise money to help them. There are 5 billion people in the world, and we *do* have enough food to feed them all.

1. Suggest three reasons why some areas of the world have a food shortage while others have plenty of food.
2. In 1900 there were about 2 billion people in the world and there wasn't enough food to go around. Now there is enough for everybody. Make a list of reasons why we can now produce so much more food. The pictures on this page will help you.
3. Scientists have developed ways of producing enough food. How can we make sure the people who need it will get it? Draw a cartoon story explaining who can help and how.

IN THIS CHAPTER YOU WILL FIND OUT

- how we can increase the amount of crops grown on a piece of land (the crop yield)
- how nitrogen-containing fertilizers work and how they are produced
- how foods are processed and preserved.

Looking at

Increasing Food Production

Where does our food come from?

If you think all food comes from supermarkets, think again! To make sure everyone has enough food, we have to look at where the food comes from and how we can produce more of it.

Photosynthesis

Green plants are the original source of all our food. They make their own food by a process called **photosynthesis.** Their leaves are green because they contain a chemical called **chlorophyll.** It can capture light energy and use it to make carbohydrate (sugars). This reaction summarizes photosynthesis.

carbon dioxide + water $\xrightarrow{\text{sunlight}}$ carbohydrate + oxygen

> 1 If you eat nothing but meat (not a healthy diet!) does this mean your food doesn't come from green plants?

Plants use the food they make to grow. We produce crop plants to feed ourselves and farm animals. The more carbohydrate a plant produces the more it grows and the better the crop yield. If we can increase the amount of photosynthesis then we can increase the amount of carbohydrate, improve the crop yield and produce more food. How can we do this? Follow the arrows to find out.

GIVE IT MORE LIGHT

Photosynthesis improves when there is plenty of light. It is not practical to place floodlights over fields but artificial lights can be used in greenhouses.

> 3 These lights are usually controlled to come on in the morning and evening. Why is this?

Another way of increasing photosynthesis is to make sure that most of the light is captured by the plant's chlorophyl. Plants with upright leaves are better at capturing light than plants with horizontal leaves. Plants with leaves that point upwards can be grown close together as the leaves do not overlap. Close-planted crops make better use of the available land and the light.

> 4 Sketch diagrams to show that: (a) plants with upright leaves can collect more light than plants with horizontal leaves (b) plants with upright leaves can be planted closer together than plants with horizontal leaves.

CHOOSE THE BEST PLANT

All living things show variation. Some individual plants in a crop give higher yields than others. By selecting those plants which give the highest yields and breeding them together, new high-yielding varieties can be produced to suit particular conditions. This is one of the main ways in which food crop production has been improved.

> 2 Imagine you were given the task of breeding a variety of corn to be grown in Ethiopia. What conditions would it have to be able to survive? Where might you start looking for varieties?

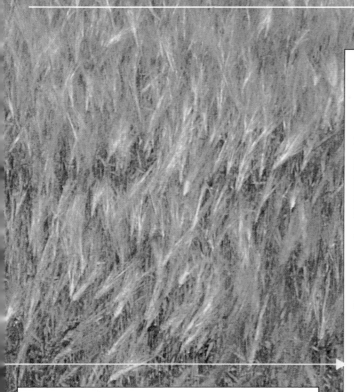

GIVE IT MORE WATER

Crops need plenty of water for photosynthesis. In hot dry climates water can be provided by **irrigation.** About 70% of the world's water supply is used for irrigation.

> 7 List the advantages and disadvantages of each method of irrigation described below.

- **Irrigation canals** bring streams of slow-moving water close to crop fields. They are easy to construct but provide a good place for snails to live. Snails can carry human diseases.
- **Centre-pivot systems** can provide large amounts of water. Too much water can dissolve salts from the ground and leave them in the topsoil when it evaporates. Plants will not grow when the topsoil contains a high concentration of salts.
- **Trickle-feed systems** allow water to drip from pipes placed close to plants. Little water is wasted through evaporation but systems are very expensive to install.

KEEP IT WARM

Increasing the temperature increases the rate of chemical reactions, including photosynthesis. Greenhouses warm up by the heat of the Sun. They are used to grow food plants such as tomatoes. A greenhouse-grown tomato plant will give a greater yield than one grown outdoors. If greenhouses are heated artificially certain food plants can be available for a longer season. Heating can be provided by an electric heater or oil or gas burner inside the greenhouse, or hot water pipes like a central heating system.

> 5 How would you choose to heat (a) a small garden greenhouse (b) a large commercial greenhouse?

GIVE IT MORE CARBON DIOXIDE

Increasing the amount of carbon dioxide around plants can increase the amount of photosynthesis. This is not easy to do in a field but it can be done in a greenhouse.

> 6 Draw a diagram showing how greenhouse crops could be kept warm and have lots of carbon dioxide.

Reaching the limit

Water, carbon dioxide, light and temperature conditions *all* have to be right for the best crop yield. There is no point giving more water if the low temperature is limiting growth! Another factor is the soil. Plants need certain chemicals from it to be healthy.

> 8 What can we do about poor soils?

Looking at

Food Emulsions

Dear Editor,

I approve of the recent campaign in school for healthier eating and so I was horrified when I read the label on the Sunbeam Margarine which I had with my baked potato yesterday. The margarine sold in the school dining room contains an additive called an emulsifier. Why do we have to put up with food with emulsifiers in them? What are they? I thought emulsions were something to do with paint?

Yours

This letter has been published in the school newspaper. You have been asked by the editor to write an article in reply. The article should explain what emulsifiers and emulsions are. It should also give reasons whether or not people ought to be concerned about their use. On this page and the next there is some information that will help in writing the article.

What is an emulsifier?

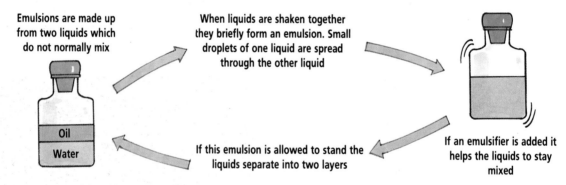

Emulsions are made up from two liquids which do not normally mix

When liquids are shaken together they briefly form an emulsion. Small droplets of one liquid are spread through the other liquid

If an emulsifier is added it helps the liquids to stay mixed

If this emulsion is allowed to stand the liquids separate into two layers

Oil
Water

Emulsifiers are usually long molecules with different groups of atoms at either end.

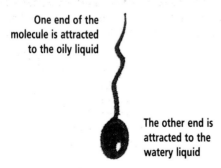

One end of the molecule is attracted to the oily liquid

The other end is attracted to the watery liquid

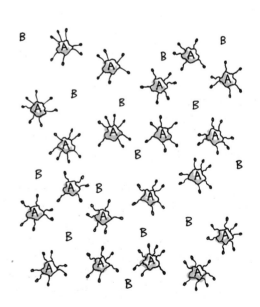

How emulsifiers work

The diagram shows how the emulsifier keeps the two liquids A (oily) and B (watery) mixed.

The oil is broken up into small droplets. Each droplet is surrounded by molecules of the emulsifier.

Salad dressings

Some people like to put a mixture of vinegar and oil on their salad. Vinegar and oil do not mix but if you shake them together they form an emulsion. But this emulsion separates into two layers.

An emulsifier is needed to make it last longer. The emulsifier in 'French dressing' is mustard.

Milk and butter

Milk is a natural emulsion. It contains a watery part and an oily part. The oil is known as butter fat. This oil in water emulsion is held together by the protein molecules contained in milk. These protein emulsifiers keep the fat dispersed as small droplets.

Egg white contains the protein lecithin, which is an emulsifier. Eggs are added to oil and vinegar to make mayonnaise.

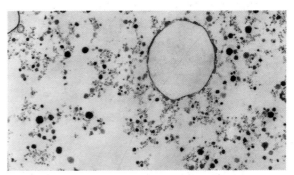

Milk magnified 25 000 times through a microscope — the large fat globule is suspended in a water solution. The dots are protein particles.

If milk is allowed to stand a layer of cream floats to the top.

The layer of cream is some of the fat separating out from the emulsion. If you shake the bottle you can re-make the emulsion.

The cream can be skimmed off to make a mixture with a higher proportion of butter fat. If this mixture is shaken (churned) it eventually changes from an oil in water emulsion to a water in oil emulsion. This water in oil emulsion is butter.

Many foods you eat contain a mixture of fat and water. They are more pleasant if the fat and water do not separate. If you examine food labels you will see which foods contain emulsifiers to stop the fat and water separating.

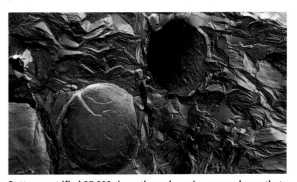

Butter magnified 35 000 times through a microscope shows that droplets of water are dispersed through the fat — a water in oil emulsion.

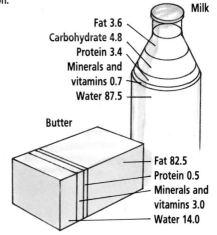

Milk
Fat 3.6
Carbohydrate 4.8
Protein 3.4
Minerals and vitamins 0.7
Water 87.5

Butter
Fat 82.5
Protein 0.5
Minerals and vitamins 3.0
Water 14.0

In brief

Food for Thought

1 People have increased world food production by:

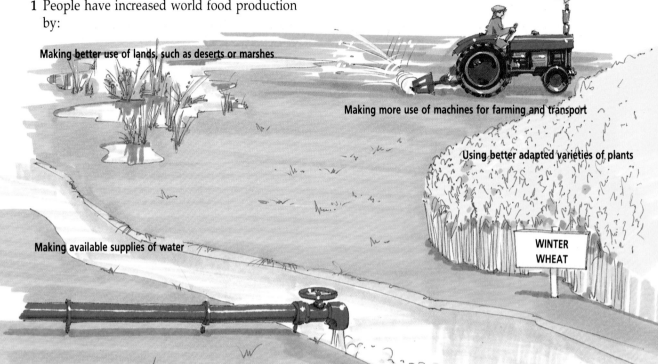

Making better use of lands, such as deserts or marshes

Using chemicals, such as pesticides and fertilizers

Making more use of machines for farming and transport

Using better adapted varieties of plants

Making available supplies of water

WINTER WHEAT

2 Growing and harvesting crops removes nutrients from the soil which are essential for healthy growth.

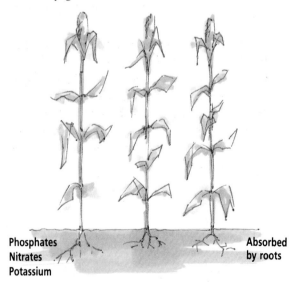

Phosphates
Nitrates
Potassium

Absorbed by roots

Nutrient-deficient soil can be improved by adding chemical fertilizers. Most chemical fertilizers contain compounds of nitrogen, potassium and phosphorus.

3 Compounds of nitrogen are particularly good for encouraging plant growth. Although there is plenty of nitrogen gas in the air, most crop plants cannot use it directly. But the nitrogen can be combined with hydrogen to form ammonia. The industrial process developed by Fritz Haber is used to do this.

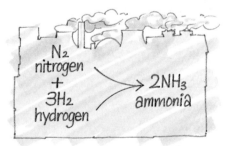

N_2 nitrogen + $3H_2$ hydrogen → $2NH_3$ ammonia

4 Ammonia can be used as a fertilizer, but it is a **base** — it dissolves in water to form an alkaline solution. This means it would change the pH of the soil. It is also smelly and difficult to handle.

   This problem is overcome by reacting ammonia with acids to form **salts.** These are solids and almost neutral. This reaction is called a **neutralisation.**

5 Fertilizer manufacturers need to know how much of each chemical to react together to produce the required quantity of the fertilizer. This can be calculated from the balanced equation for the reaction and the relative molecular masses of the substances involved.

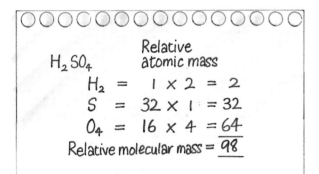

$$2NH_3 + H_2SO_4 \rightarrow (NH_4)_2SO_4$$

RMM 34   98   132

34 tonnes of ammonia and 98 tonnes of sulphuric acid give 132 tonnes of ammonium sulphate.

Relative molecular masses are calculated from the relative atomic masses of the elements in the molecule.

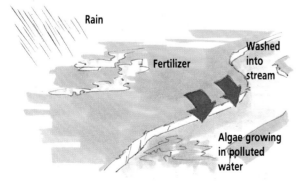

H_2SO_4 Relative atomic mass

$H_2 = 1 \times 2 = 2$

$S = 32 \times 1 = 32$

$O_4 = 16 \times 4 = 64$

Relative molecular mass = 98

6 Because salts used as fertilizers are soluble, they may be washed or **leached** out of soil and reach streams and rivers, causing pollution. For example, an increase in the nitrate concentration of a river can result in unwanted growths of algae and a lower quality of drinking water.

Rain

Fertilizer

Washed into stream

Algae growing in polluted water

7 To keep our stored food fit to eat we need to prevent the growth of microbes and keep out animal pests. Many animal pests are controlled by chemical pesticides, but non-chemical means can also be used. For example, instead of spraying aphids (greenfly), ladybirds can be released on the crop to eat the aphids. Some foods have preservatives added to them to make them keep longer.

Locusts can devastate crops. Chemical sprays are used to kill them.

Food can be stored raised from the ground to keep out mice and rats.

8 Food can be processed to make it more useful or attractive. This can be done by
  ● chemical reactions, such as adding hydrogen to vegetable oil to make margarine
  ● biological reactions, such as using the enzyme pectinase to extract juice from apples
  ● food additives which improve the flavour or appearance of the food.

Recently people have found that some food additives can be harmful. However, foods go 'off' much more quickly without preservatives.

Thinking about

Food for Thought

1. How can we improve the growth of crops?

Plants need certain elements from the soil to be healthy and grow well. Soil which does not contain these essential nutrients is infertile. Fertilizers are chemicals which farmers add to the soil to provide the right nutrients. Sometimes natural fertilizers like manure or compost are used instead of chemical fertilizers. Growing crops and harvesting them removes

- nitrogen (N)
- phosphorus (P)
- potassium (K)

from soil, so these elements have to be replaced.

Nitrogen as nitrates or ammonium salts

Phophorus as phosphates

Potassium as potassium salts

Most manufactured fertilizers contain these three elements.

Chemicals are also used to protect healthy plants from damage. Pesticides are substances which kill pests and herbicides are substances which kill weeds.

Pests spoil or eat up to one-third of the world's food while it is being grown, harvested or stored. These Colorado beetles are eating potato leaves.

In some regions pests can waste up to 40% of crops. Pesticides can help to reduce this loss. However pesticides must be chosen with care. They must break down into non-harmful chemicals. They must not destroy non-harmful animals.

2. How are fertilizers manufactured?

The raw materials for making fertilizers are either dug out of the ground or extracted from the air.

- Phosphorus comes mainly from rock phosphate — a mineral containing calcium phosphate.
- Potassium comes from minerals such as sylvinite which contains potassium chloride.
- Nitrogen, as you might expect, comes from the air.

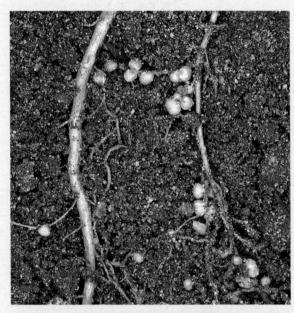

Nitrogen is converted into a usable form by bacteria in nodules on the roots of some plants such as peas and beans.

Lightning converts some nitrogen and oxygen from the air into oxides of nitrogen and then nitrates.

Bacteria and lightning cannot replace all the nitrogen in soil that crops use. So we need to manufacture fertilizers from nitrogen.

People realized they needed to 'fix' nitrogen from the air (convert it to a form plants can use) in the early part of this century. A German chemist, Fritz Haber, invented a method of converting nitrogen and hydrogen into ammonia (NH_3).

Fritz Haber used small-scale equipment to develop the process.

The large-scale manufacture of ammonia in this fertiliser factory is still based on the Haber process.

By 1913 an engineer, Carl Bosch, had scaled up Haber's process so that ammonia could be produced on an industrial scale. The process is still known as the Haber process.

In the modern version of the process a mixture of hydrogen and nitrogen is passed over a **catalyst** at 400°C and 200 atmospheres pressure (this is 200 times greater than normal atmospheric pressure). A catalyst speeds up a chemical reaction without being used up itself. Iron is the catalyst for the Haber process. The reaction is **reversible** – this is shown by the sign $\rightleftharpoons$

$$N_2 + 3H_2 \rightleftharpoons 2NH_3$$

A reversible reaction can be encouraged to go in either direction by changing the conditions.

If the reaction moves to the right the yield of ammonia increases.

The yield would be higher if the pressure was high and the temperature low. But the problem is that at a low temperature it would take a long time for the ammonia to form. A reasonably high temperature together with a catalyst produce the ammonia more quickly.

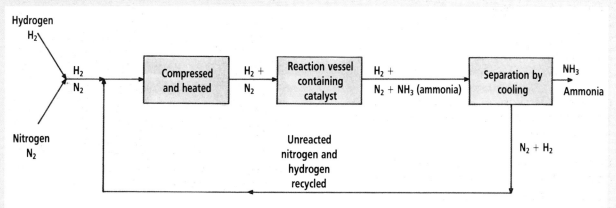

The ammonia is removed by cooling it to a liquid. The unreacted hydrogen and nitrogen are re-circulated so they are not wasted.

3. How can we make ammonia into a more useful fertilizer?

Pure ammonia is a very unpleasant smelly gas. High concentrations of it in the air would be extremely dangerous.

It dissolves easily in water, but even the solution smells very strongly of ammonia. The solution is alkaline so it would change the pH of soil if it was used as a fertilizer.

To make a more useful fertilizer we need to convert ammonia into a solid which does not smell much, is not washed away as quickly as ammonia and does not have much effect on the pH of soil.

The substance formed when any acid reacts with a base is known as a salt. Ammonium sulphate and ammonium nitrate are both salts. They are used as fertilizers. They are solids and so are easier to handle than ammonia. They do not upset the pH of soil. Reactions between acids and bases are called **neutralisations**.

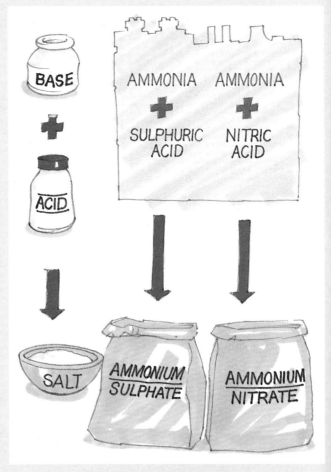

Taking it further

All acids contain hydrogen. **Salts** are formed when these hydrogens are replaced by metals. The name of the salt formed depends on the acid used and the metal which replaces the hydrogen.

It is easy to work out the name of a salt formed from an acid and a base. The table gives the names and formulas of salts formed from sodium hydroxide with three different acids.

Sodium hydroxide is a soluble base and so it is called an **alkali**.

Acid	Formula	Salt	Formula
hydrochloric acid	HCl	sodium chloride	NaCl
nitric acid	HNO_3	sodium nitrate	$NaNO_3$
sulphuric acid	H_2SO_4	sodium sulphate	Na_2SO_4

When these acids react with a solution of ammonia, the ammonium group replaces the hydrogen. The salts formed are
- ammonium chloride, NH_4Cl
- ammonium nitrate, NH_4NO_3
- ammonium sulphate, $(NH_4)_2SO_4$.

Sodium chloride is one of many salts. It is called common salt, or often just 'salt' or 'table salt'.

4. *How much ammonia is needed to make fertilizers?*

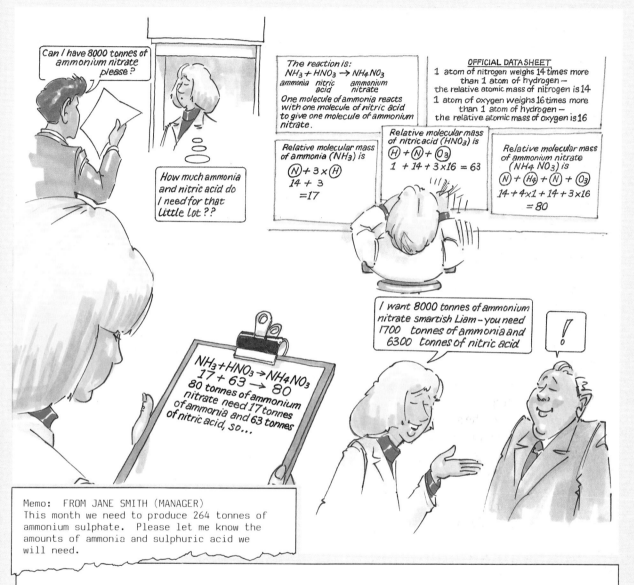

Memo: FROM JANE SMITH (MANAGER)
This month we need to produce 264 tonnes of
ammonium sulphate. Please let me know the
amounts of ammonia and sulphuric acid we
will need.

Memo: FROM LIAM O'GRADY (PRODUCTION)
The balanced equation for the reaction is:

$$2NH_3 \quad + \quad H_2SO_4 \quad \rightarrow \quad (NH_4)_2SO_4$$
ammonia   sulphuric   ammonium
acid   sulphate

The relative atomic masses of these elements are:

H = 1, N = 14, S = 32, O = 16

The relative molecular masses are:

NH_3	= 14 + (3 × 1)	=	17
H_2SO_4	= (2 × 1) + 32 + (4 × 16)	=	98
$(NH_4)_2SO_4$	= 2(14 + 4) + 32 + (4 × 16)	=	132

The equation for the reaction shows that
2 molecules of ammonia react with 1 molecule of
sulphuric acid to form 1 molecule of ammonium
sulphate.
   So (2 x 17) = 34 tonnes of ammonia react with
98 tonnes of sulphuric acid to form 132 tonnes of
ammonium sulphate.
   So for 132 tonnes of ammonium sulphate, you
need 34 tonnes of ammonia and 98 tonnes of
sulphuric acid.
   For 264 tonnes of ammonium sulphate you
need (2 x 34) = 68 tonnes of ammonia and
(2 x 98) = 196 tonnes of sulphuric acid.

5. How is food processed chemically?

Oil is extracted from sunflower seeds. It is good for frying but too runny to spread on bread.

The oil is processed to make a soft solid which can be spread on bread.

Oil molecules are very long and have double bonds in them. Molecules with double bonds are called **unsaturated** — hydrogen can add on across the double bonds. Molecules with lots of double bonds are called **polyunsaturated**.

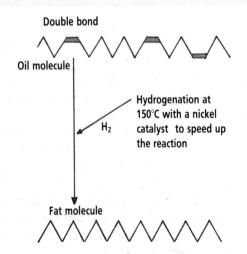

Double bond

Oil molecule

H_2

Hydrogenation at 150°C with a nickel catalyst to speed up the reaction

Fat molecule

Margarine is a blend of oils, fats and milk. Bacteria in the milk act on some of the compounds to give a buttery taste. Vitamins A and D, which are fat soluble, are added.

Fat molecules are also very long but have no double bonds. They are **saturated** — no more hydrogen can add to their bonds. The fat has a higher melting point than the oil, so the liquid has been converted to a solid.

Things to do

Food for Thought

Things to try out

1 Eggshell is mainly calcium carbonate. Most acids react with the calcium carbonate to give soluble calcium salts.

From the acids you have at home, find out which is best at dissolving eggshell. Here are some ideas to try

- lemon juice
- vinegar
- Coca-Cola.

Things to find out

2 Why are vitamins A and D added to margarine?

ENERGY	735 K/CALORIES
	3015 K/JOULES
PROTEIN	0.2 g
CARBOHYDRATE	0.8 g
TOTAL FAT	81.0 g
of which POLYUNSATURATES	41.3 g
SATURATES	14.7 g
ADDED SALT	2.0 g
VITAMINS	% OF THE RECOMMEN
	DAILY AMOUNT
VITAMIN A	125%
VITAMIN D	300%

MARGARINE IS A USEFUL SOURCE OF ENERGY (CALORIES
VITAMIN A (WHICH IS NEEDED FOR GOOD VISION IN DIM
AND HEALTHY SKIN) AND VITAMIN D (WHICH IS NEEDED
STRONG BONES AND TEETH)

3 Find out which substances found at home people use to put on

(a) bee stings

(b) wasp stings.

Why are different substances used?

4 Survey food labels at home and make a list of the E-numbers of food additives present. The first digit of the E-number usually tells you the type of additive. Use the information in the table to identify the type of food additive in each food.

Type of additive	First digit of the E-number
Colourings	1
Preservatives	2
Emulsifiers and stabilizers	3 or 4
Acids, bases and buffers	5 and some 2/3
Sweeteners/flavour enhancers	4 or 6
Antioxidants	3

Points to discuss

5

A valley in Malaysia

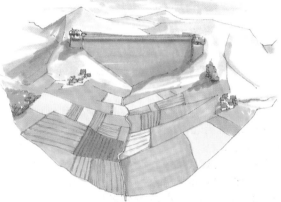

A dam was built to allow increased irrigation

Once the dam was built a new variety of rice was grown that produced a much better yield of food. It could give two crops a year, and rice output tripled in a few years. Farmers with large farms increased their income by 150%, those with small farms by 50%.

However, the new variety of rice needed more fertilizer than the old one. Fertilizer is expensive. This was no problem for the richer farmers, but those with small farms found after ten years that they were worse off than before the dam was built.

The small farmers sold their land to the farmers who already had large farms. These rich farmers invested in machinery to farm their bigger farms and gradually became even richer. The small farmers moved to the forests of Malaysia and became even poorer.

Is this an acceptable outcome? With the benefit of hindsight, how could the pattern have been changed?

Questions to answer

6 What acids will be needed to make the following salts:
- ammonium nitrate
- ammonium phosphate
- ammonium sulphate?

Write word equations to describe the neutralizations that produce these salts.

Use reference books to write balanced equations for these neutralizations.

7 Use the following words to complete the sentences:
- titrations
- neutralization
- indicators
- fungicides
- phosphorus
- leaching

(a) _____ occurs when soluble salts are washed out of the soil.

(b) _____ occurs when equal reacting quantities of an acid and an alkali are mixed together.

(c) _____-containing compounds are important fertilizers.

(d) _____ are chemicals which kill certain types of pests.

(e) _____ can be used to show when an acid has neutralized an alkali.

(f) _____ are done to work out the quantities of acid and alkali required for neutralizaton.

8 Use the relative atomic masses to work out the relative molecular masses of:
- copper sulphate, $CuSO_4$
- sodium chloride, $NaCl$
- ammonium chloride, NH_4Cl
- sulphur dioxide, SO_2
- sodium hydroxide, $NaOH$
- ozone, O_3

9 Using the information on page 85, work out how much ammonia will be needed to

(a) produce 13.2 tonnes of ammonium sulphate

(b) produce 500 tonnes of ammonium sulphate

(c) neutralize 392 tonnes of sulphuric acid.

How much sodium hydroxide would be needed to neutralize 365 tonnes of hydrochloric acid? How much sodium chloride would be produced in this reaction?

10 Iodine reacts with the double bonds in unsaturated fats and oils. The table shows the amount of iodine that will react with 100 grams of a fat or oil.

Fat/oil	Amount of iodine (g)
butter	36
coconut oil	9
lard	56
linseed oil	186
peanut oil	90

(a) Present these figures as a bar chart.

(b) Comment on what the figures tell you about these fats and oils.

11 Ammonium sulphate has the formula $(NH_4)_2SO_4$. Ammonium nitrate has the formula NH_4NO_3. They are both important fertilizers.

(a) Work out the number of nitrogen atoms in each molecule.

(b) Use the relative atomic masses to work out the relative molecular mass of each molecule.

(c) Which of the two fertilizers gives the most nitrogen atoms per tonne?

Relative atomic masses	
Copper	63.5
Sulphur	32
Oxygen	16
Sodium	23
Chlorine	35.5
Nitrogen	14
Hydrogen	1

Introducing

RESTLESS EARTH

The surface of the Earth is constantly changing. Some of the changes are spectacular, such as the formation of the volcanic island Surtsey shown here. Some of the changes are very much slower, taking thousands of years.

A massive steam cloud rises from the volcano as the sea enters the vent.

The volcano grows. Steam rises from the sea as lava flows into it, and steam and gas rise from the crater.

The sea has gradually eroded the cliffs right up to these houses in Sussex.

1 What do you think is happening when a volcano erupts?

2 What do you think is happening when a cliff is eroded?

IN THIS CHAPTER YOU WILL FIND OUT

▌ about different types of rock and how they are formed

▌ about the structure of the Earth

▌ how structures and rocks change, and how long it takes for this to happen

▌ how the geology of an area affects the scenery.

Looking at

A Volcano Erupting

Mount St Helens is a volcano in Washington state, USA. It has erupted at least 20 times in the last 5000 years. In May 1980 the side of the mountain began to bulge. There were many small earthquakes. On 18 May there was a huge explosion, 20 times bigger than the atomic bomb dropped on Hiroshima.

Mount St Helens before the eruption in 1980.

The eruption was photographed from a plane 20 seconds after it began.

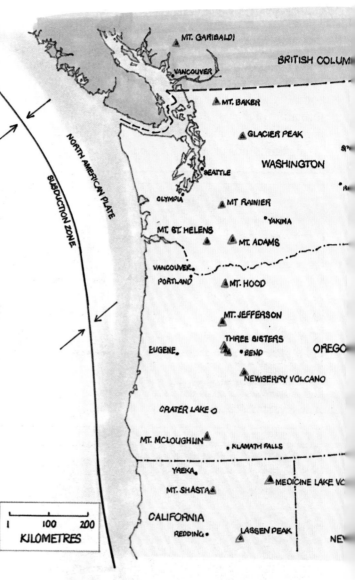

The triangles show active volcanoes caused by the collision of the Pacific plate and the North American plate.

Mt St Helens after the blast.

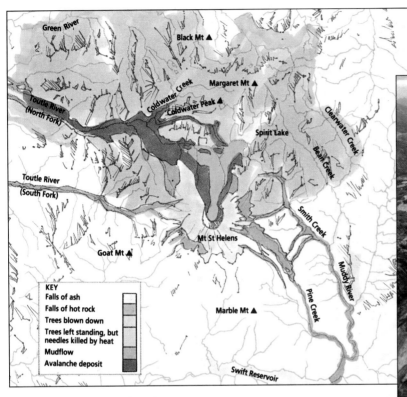

Geological map of the area affected by the blast.

KEY
- Falls of ash
- Falls of hot rock
- Trees blown down
- Trees left standing, but needles killed by heat
- Mudflow
- Avalanche deposit

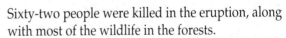

Mud flows blocked 8 miles of valley west of Spirit Lake.

Sixty-two people were killed in the eruption, along with most of the wildlife in the forests.

The forests had been used to provide timber, so this industry was very badly affected. Huge amounts of mud were washed downstream and clogged rivers and harbours.

Smaller eruptions and earthquakes continued in the area until October 1980.

These trees were felled by the blast.

1 Imagine you are a journalist, flying in the aircraft that took the pictures of the eruption. You can 'phone a story through to your paper, but there is no time to send pictures. Write a graphic description of the eruption.

2 A few days later you are asked to do a follow-up article explaining how movements in the Earth's crust are thought to have caused the eruption. You can use diagrams for this article. *Thinking About 4* on page 99 will also help.

Looking at

A Day Out

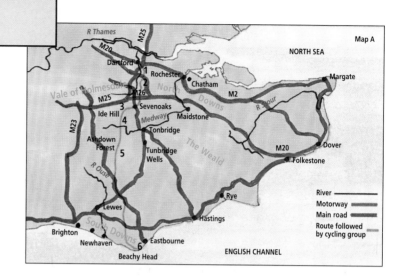

You may not realise it, but wherever you stand, there are various types of rocks under your feet. Different sorts of scenery result from different rocks. Even in towns and cities you can see evidence of the type of rock that the area is built on.

---

1 Where can you see different types of rock in your area?
2 How do these different rock types affect the look of the area?

One area with an interesting geology is the Weald of Kent and Sussex.
The area is shown on map A.
Map B is a geological map of the area.

How did the Weald get that way?
About 135 million years ago the area of the Weald was covered by a lake.

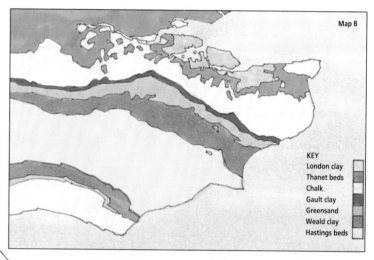

Layers of sediment collected at the bottom of the lake. The first layer was the weald sand, and then this was covered by weald clay.

115 million years ago the lake became part of the sea, and different deposits were laid down. These were greensand, then gault clay, and finally chalk.

Over the next 40 million years these rocks were gradually pressed together to form sedimentary rocks. Originally these rocks formed in flat layers, but huge Earth movements 75 million years ago pushed them into a dome shape.

Over the last 75 million years rain has gradually worn the top of the dome away. The different layers have eroded at different rates, as different rocks have different resistances to water.

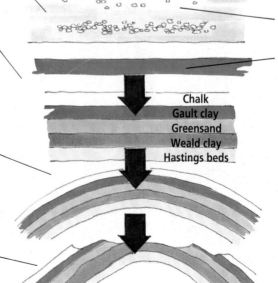

The rocks have been changed by more sedimentation, buckling and weathering over hundreds of millions of years. Today the dome of the Weald looks like this.

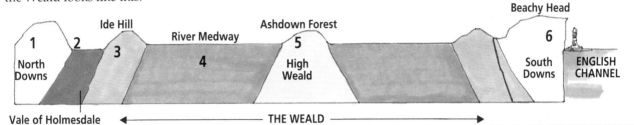

A group of young people decided to cycle from Dartford to Eastbourne. They took these photos and notes on the way. The numbers on the maps and diagram show where they stopped.

3 **Write an account of their journey describing each geological feature they come across. Give an explanation of how each feature formed.**

1 *Stopped for a drink. Sujata showed us the cross cut out of chalk on the hillside.*

2 *Ian had a flat on the bridge over the M26. The motorway runs on the flat ground of the Vale of Holmesdale.*

3 *Top of Ide Hill. Looking at how far we've got to go across the Weald.*

4 *Mapreading stop as we cross the River Medway.*

5 *Guess where!*

6 *Can't go any further!*

Looking at

Preventing Earthquakes

San Francisco is a city with a problem. It is built on two different plates on the Earth's surface, and the dividing line, the San Andreas fault, runs through the city. What is worse, these two plates, the North American and the Pacific, are moving in different directions.

Because they are so big, the two plates don't slip easily past one another. They stick and jam and pressure builds up. When the pressure becomes great enough the plates jerk past each other, and this sudden movement creates earthquakes, as happened in 1989.

San Francisco has been hit by earthquakes before. In 1906 a huge earthquake devastated the city, which had to be completely rebuilt. The 1989 earthquake was not nearly as destructive, but more and bigger earthquakes are forecast.

Can anything be done to stop this? One idea is to pump water down into the rocks to lubricate them. The theory is that this would ease the movement of the plates so they could slide continuously, without building up the strain that causes earthquakes. However, it might cause an enormous amount of movement when the plates are first lubricated.

Another idea is exactly the reverse. All the water is pumped out of the rocks, so that they lock tightly together and can no longer move. The problem here is that this might work well for some time, only to produce an enormous earthquake as the plates finally wrench free.

A third idea uses a combination of these two methods. The diagram shows how.

1 A company has been asked to drill some trial boreholes. Design a leaflet for the company to distribute to local people explaining what they are doing and why.

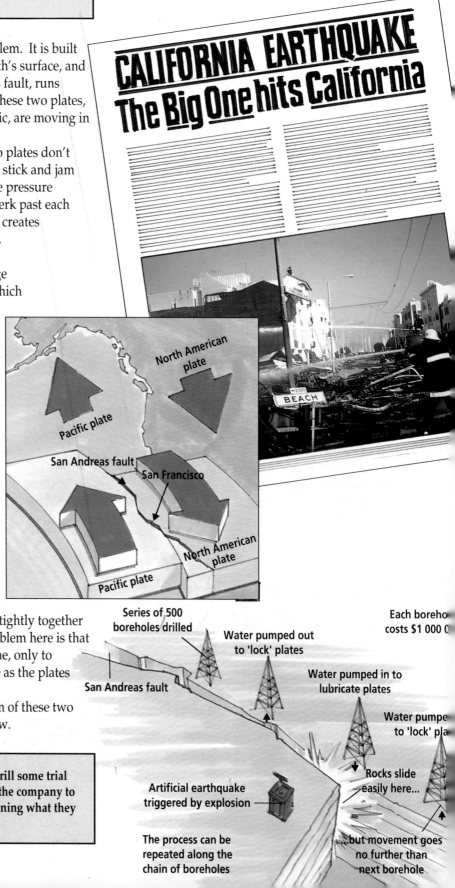

CALIFORNIA EARTHQUAKE
The Big One hits California

North American plate
Pacific plate
San Andreas fault
San Francisco
North American plate
Pacific plate

Series of 500 boreholes drilled
Water pumped out to 'lock' plates
Each boreho costs $1 000 0
San Andreas fault
Water pumped in to lubricate plates
Water pumpe to 'lock' pla
Artificial earthquake triggered by explosion
Rocks slide easily here...
The process can be repeated along the chain of boreholes
...but movement goes no further than next borehole

In Brief

Restless Earth

1 The Earth is made up of three zones: the **core**, the **mantle** and a thin **crust** on which we live. This diagram shows the structure of the Earth and the composition of the different parts.

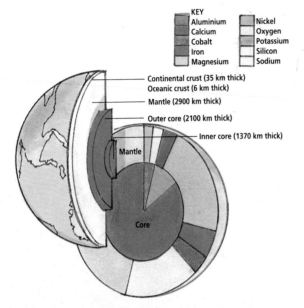

KEY
Aluminium	Nickel
Calcium	Oxygen
Cobalt	Potassium
Iron	Silicon
Magnesium	Sodium

Continental crust (35 km thick)
Oceanic crust (6 km thick)
Mantle (2900 km thick)
Outer core (2100 km thick)
Inner core (1370 km thick)

Mantle

Core

2 People have found out about the structure of the Earth by studying earthquakes. Earthquakes send out shock waves which can be felt at places all over the world. By recording where the waves are felt and where they are not, geologists have built up a picture of the inside of the Earth.

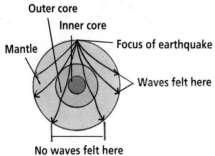

Outer core
Inner core
Mantle
Focus of earthquake
Waves felt here
No waves felt here

3 Earthquakes are caused by the Earth's crust moving. The crust is broken into different plates, which float on the liquid mantle.

There are convection currents in the mantle which move the plates. As the plates move they scrape and bump against other plates. This uneven movement causes violent movements in the surrounding rocks.

4 There are three types of rock in the crust.
Igneous rocks have been formed by volcanic action. They were molten, but have now cooled.
Sedimentary rocks have been laid down over very long periods of time. They are formed from sediments that have slowly built up at the bottom of shallow seas.
Metamorphic rocks form when heat and pressure in the Earth change igneous or sedimentary rocks into a different form.

5 Layers of rock may be bent or folded as a result of movements in the Earth.

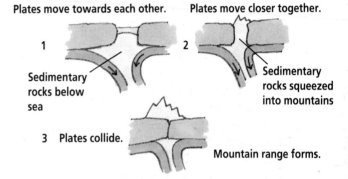

Plates move towards each other.
Plates move closer together.
1
2
Sedimentary rocks below sea
Sedimentary rocks squeezed into mountains
3 Plates collide.
Mountain range forms.

6 Sometimes folding rocks push up to produce mountains. Mountains are gradually worn away by wind and rain. The worn away rock is carried out to sea by rivers.

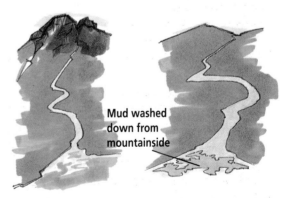

Mud washed down from mountainside

7 Occasionally, when animals or plants die, their remains are preserved as **fossils**. Fossils become part of the rock, as sediment is laid down around them.

Some organisms exist for a time and then become extinct. Knowing how long ago certain organisms lived is very useful to geologists – they can tell the relative ages of different rocks by looking at the fossils inside them.

Thinking about

Restless Earth

1. How can we tell different types of rock apart?

Igneous rocks have been formed from liquid rock. As the liquid cools the chemicals in the rock form crystals. If you can see regularly shaped crystals in a rock, it is likely to be igneous.

When this granite formed from molten rock, some chemicals crystallized out first forming large crystals. Then spaces between these crystals were filled by smaller crystals of other chemicals.

Metamorphic rocks are rocks that have been changed from their original form by heat or pressure. The temperatures and forces involved are very high – you cannot metamorphose rock with a Bunsen burner!

Slate is shale (a sedimentary rock) which has been subjected to very high pressures.

Marble is a metamorphic form of limestone. It is much more shiny and hard than limestone.

Sedimentary rocks are formed from the debris that falls to the bottom of seas and lakes. Most sedimentary rocks show a structure of layers. They are likely to be made up of rounded grains rather than straight-sided crystals.

Some sedimentary rocks contain **fossils**, where the remains of creatures have been preserved in the sediments. When the creature died and was buried in the sediment, the fleshy parts rotted away and were replaced by sediment which eventually changed to rock. Any shell or bones the creatures had are preserved in the rock.

This oolitic limestone contains circular pieces of calcium carbonate cemented together in a matrix.

The shapes of these ammonites have been preserved by rock.

2. How do we know how old rocks are?

We can judge the relative ages of rocks and fossils by looking at other rocks.

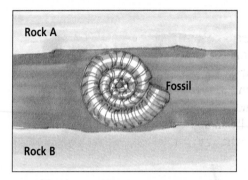

Rock A
Fossil
Rock B

If we know that the rocks at A are 100 million years old and the rocks at B are 200 million years old, then the rock in the middle is between 100 and 200 million years old. Fossils found in this rock will be of the same age. If we assume that the rocks have been laid down at a steady rate, then the fossil in the middle of the rock is about 150 million years old.

The problem with this method is that we cannot judge any of the ages until we know at least one. To provide an absolute age, geologists use radioactivity to date fossils and rocks.

The atoms of some elements break down over a period of time. This is known as **radioactive decay**, because it produces radiation. Scientists have found out how quickly some of these elements decay. For some elements the time for half the atoms to decay (the **half-life**) is a few seconds. For others it is millions of years. By measuring how much of certain elements are left in the rock, we can estimate how old it is.

In 1643, James Usher, Bishop of Armagh, using evidence from the Bible, claimed that the world began in 4004 BC. More recent estimates, based on radioactive dating, give the Earth's age as 4600 million years. People have only existed for the last 40 000 years or so!

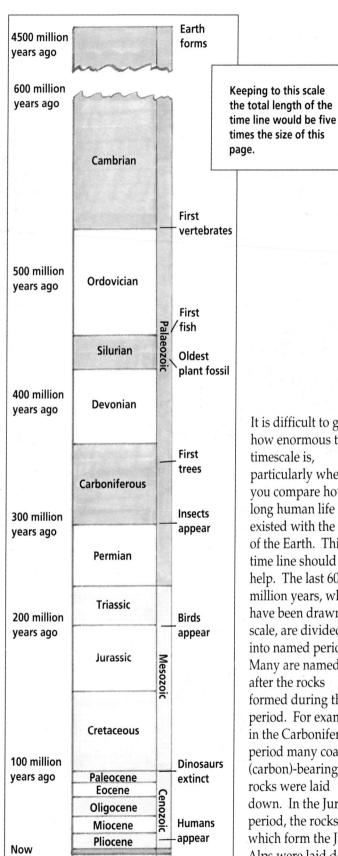

4500 million years ago — Earth forms

Keeping to this scale the total length of the time line would be five times the size of this page.

600 million years ago

Cambrian

First vertebrates

500 million years ago — Ordovician

First fish

Palaeozoic

Silurian — Oldest plant fossil

400 million years ago — Devonian

Carboniferous — First trees

300 million years ago — Insects appear

Permian

Triassic

200 million years ago — Birds appear

Jurassic

Mesozoic

Cretaceous

100 million years ago — Dinosaurs extinct

Paleocene
Eocene
Oligocene
Miocene — Humans appear
Pliocene

Cenozoic

Now

It is difficult to grasp how enormous this timescale is, particularly when you compare how long human life has existed with the age of the Earth. This time line should help. The last 600 million years, which have been drawn to scale, are divided up into named periods. Many are named after the rocks formed during that period. For example, in the Carboniferous period many coal (carbon)-bearing rocks were laid down. In the Jurassic period, the rocks which form the Jura Alps were laid down.

3. How were the mountain ranges formed?

At the beginning of this century people thought that the Earth was slowly cooling. As it cooled the outer crust of the Earth was shrinking and wrinkling like the skin of an old apple. The mountain ranges were thought to be wrinkles on the Earth's crust.

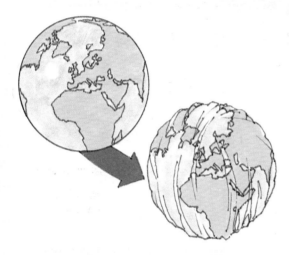

Nowadays the theory of **plate tectonics** is used to explain mountain ranges. This theory suggests that the Earth's crust is made of plates, like a cracked egg-shell. The plates are moving because of convection currents in the liquid mantle below. These convection currents result from heating, caused by reactions going on deep inside the Earth. Where the plates meet, some rocks, over periods of millions of years, have been folded and pushed upwards to form mountain ranges.

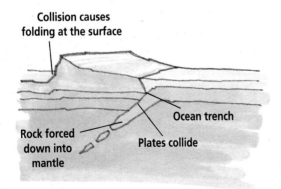

Collision causes folding at the surface
Ocean trench
Rock forced down into mantle
Plates collide

Taking it further:
How the theory came about
The beginning of an alternative theory to the cooling, shrinking Earth idea started with Alfred Wegener, a German meteorologist. He suggested that the eastern coast of the American continent had originally been joined to the west coast of Europe and Africa. He suggested that the continents were drifting apart. This is the **continental drift theory**. He based his idea on the observation that the shapes of the two continents fit well together and that similar rocks and fossils can be found on opposite sides of the Atlantic ocean.

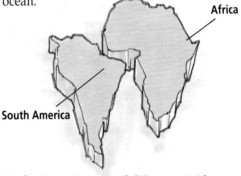

Africa
South America

At the time no one took Wegener's idea seriously. There was no way of testing it and there was no theory as to what could be causing the continents to drift apart. It was not until 1968 that it became possible to explain Wegener's continental drift idea. This happened because the **sea floor spreading theory** was suggested.

This theory suggested that new rock is continually being pushed to the Earth's surface in the middle of the Atlantic ocean. So the ocean bed is spreading out and pushing the continents apart. This was a much stronger theory than Wegener's because it could be tested experimentally. Scientists drilled into the sea bed and examined the samples of rock. They showed that at equal distances from the ridge in the middle of the Atlantic ocean, there are stripes of rock of identical age.

This theory provided the explanation of Wegener's continental drift theory and led to the theory of **plate tectonics**.

4. How does the theory of plate tectonics explain earthquakes and volcanoes?

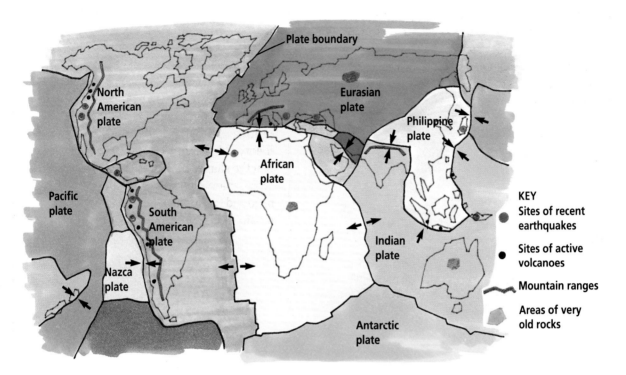

Plate boundary

North American plate

Eurasian plate

Philippine plate

African plate

Pacific plate

South American plate

Indian plate

Nazca plate

Antarctic plate

KEY

● Sites of recent earthquakes

● Sites of active volcanoes

〰 Mountain ranges

▬ Areas of very old rocks

The surface of the Earth is made up of various **tectonic plates** which are moving This map shows the plates. It also shows the sites of major earthquakes and active volcanoes. You can see that many earthquakes and volcanoes happen where the plates meet.

As the plates move they rub against other plates, which makes the movement irregular. One plate may jam against another for fifty years or more.

The pressure builds up so much that the plates do eventually move. The movement may happen with a violent jerk. This movement is known as an earthquake. The effect at the surface may be very slight, or extremely destructive.

The violence of earthquakes is measure on the **Richter scale**. This runs from 0 (no measurable effect) to 9 (extremely violent). The worst earthquake recorded so far was 8.9 on the Richter scale.

Volcanoes also happen around the points where plates meet. Magma (molten rock) is forced upwards under pressure. The greater the pressure build-up, the greater the violence of the volcanic eruption.

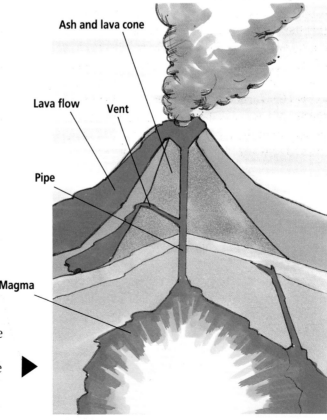

Ash and lava cone

Lava flow   **Vent**

Pipe

Magma

▶

5. How can rocks change?

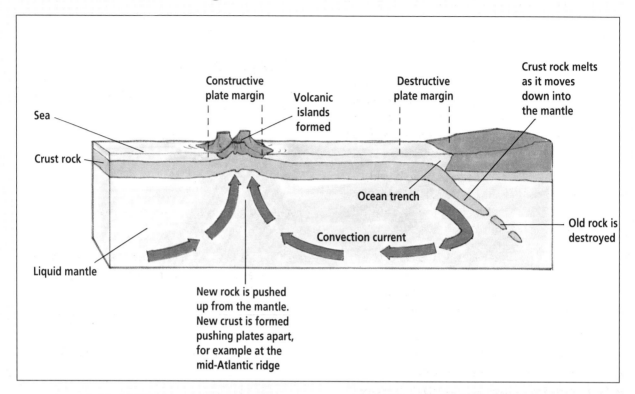

Rocks are continuously made and destroyed. New rocks are produced from the **mantle**, the layer of molten rock below the Earth's crust. The liquid rock of the mantle is continually moving in convection currents because of the heat being generated deep inside the Earth.

This new rock comes to the surface in the mid-ocean ridges. Where the plates meet and push against each other, some old rock is pushed back down into the mantle and becomes liquid again. This process is called the **rock cycle**.

There is another rock cycle which starts with the erosion of rocks by the weather. Little pieces of rock break off and are washed down by rivers into the sea. They are deposited at the bottom of the sea. This is the first stage of the formation of sedimentary rock.

Movements in the Earth may push the sedimentary rock up into mountains. In millions of years' time those mountains are eroded and the whole process begins again.

The timescale of rock cycles is enormous. Every time a volcano erupts or the sea erodes a piece of cliff, you can see a tiny part of a rock cycle in action.

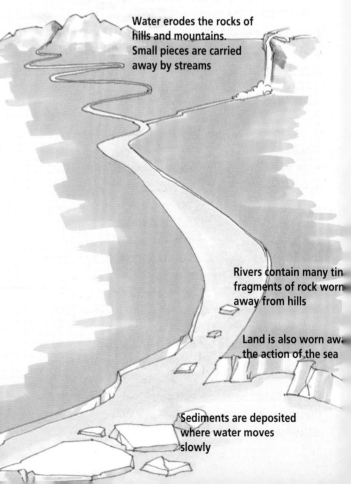

Things to do

Restless Earth

Things to try out

1 Gravestones can be made from igneous, sedimentary or metamorphic rocks. Read *Thinking About 1* on page 96 to help you recognize each type of rock. Then visit your local cemetery and, without touching any of the gravestones, see if you can find examples of each type of rock.

2 Draw a time line for the history of the Weald. Use the information on pages 92–3.

Things to discuss

3 The Richter scale for measuring the violence of earthquakes runs from 0 to 9. Below are some measurements and descriptions of earthquakes. Match each description to the best measurements.

2.0,   3.5,   4.2,   4.4,   4.8,   5.1,
5.8,   6.4,   6.9,   7.2,   7.7,   8.7

- Chimneys fall, branches break from trees.
- Only detected by seismographs (sensitive instruments that measure movements in the Earth).
- Felt by everyone, trees sway.
- Few buildings survive, bridges collapse.
- Few people notice.
- Ground cracks, houses collapse, pipes crack.
- Hanging objects swing.
- Many houses collapse, landslides happen, ground opens wide.
- People panic, walls crack, difficult to stand.
- People wake up. Bells ring because of the vibrations.
- Total destruction.
- Windows rattle, felt by people walking.

4 Look at the 'time line' on page 97. The age of the Earth is about 4600 million years. Humans have probably existed for about 40 000 years. Discuss the implications of this by talking about how you think the Earth changed

(a) from when humans first existed to the Bronze Age, which was about 5000 years ago

(b) from the Bronze Age to the European Industrial Revolution, which started about 200 years ago

(c) from the Industrial Revolution until now.

What do you expect the Earth to be like in another 200 years' time?

Things to find out

5 By looking at geology books, find out what each of the following types of fossils look like

brachiopods
trilobites
ammonites
sea urchins.

Arrange them in order of age and draw pictures of them along a time line.

6 Find the location of each of the volcanoes below. Then mark where they are on an outline map of the world.

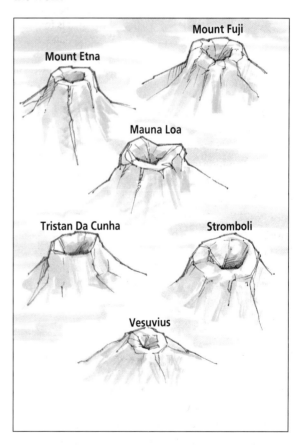

By comparing your map with the one on page 99, decide which of these volcanoes occur where two crust plates are pushing against each other. Which occur where convection currents in the mantle are forcing molten rock to the surface?

Things to write about

7 *South America was once joined to Africa!*

When scientists make major discoveries or put forward what appear to be unusual theories, newspapers sometimes write about what they have said. The journalist tries to write the story in a way which will capture the readers' interest. After the 1914–18 war, Wegener's book on continental drift (see *Thinking About 3*, page 98) was translated into English. Using a headline like the one above, write a newspaper article dated 1919 reporting on Wegener's theory.

Questions to answer

8 Look at the pictures of rocks below. Write down whether you think they are igneous, metamorphic or sedimentary and the reasons for your decision.

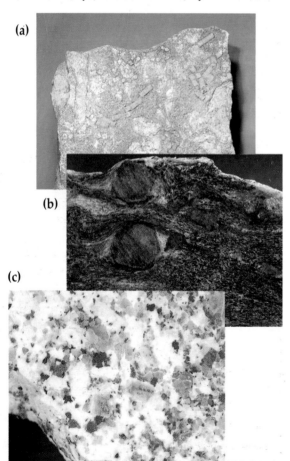

(a)

(b)

(c)

9

Find out where Mount Everest is on a world map. Then explain how it is possible that it is made of limestone.

10

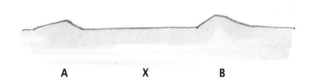

A team of geologists examined rock outcrops at site A and at site B, which is due east of A. They found that at both sites the rock was limestone of similar age. At site A, the rock was dipping at an angle of about 10° to the west. At site B the rock was dipping at an angle of about 10° to the east.

(a) The geologists used fossil evidence to date the rock. Explain what this technique involves.

(b) Draw a sketch showing how you think the layer of limestone was before any weathering took place.

(c) The geologists decided to drill at site X to obtain samples of the underlying rocks. They were hoping to find oil and gas deposits. What types of rock layers should they find and in what order if there is a good chance of finding oil and gas? Explain your answer.

Introducing

THE ATMOSPHERE

Why do you think there is life on the Earth, but not on the Moon? One important reason is that there's no air to breathe on the Moon. It has no **atmosphere**. The Earth's atmosphere is an invisible layer of gases which surrounds the planet.

1 You can see differences between the Earth and the Moon in these pictures. You may already know about other differences. Which differences exist because of the atmosphere? Make a list.

If the atmosphere is invisible, why do you see clouds swirling and mist forming? The atmosphere contains invisible water vapour. Sometimes this vapour condenses into water droplets, which form clouds and mist (like the 'steam' you see when water vapour condenses above a boiling kettle).

The Earth has an atmosphere...

...but the Moon does not.

What lifts the ocean into clouds
and dries our ink upon the page?
What gives the porous pavement, an hour after rain,
its sycamore-bark-splotchy steaminess
as molecules of H_2O leap from the fading film
to find lodging in air's loose lattices?
Evaporation, ...
*   .... as delicate as a mist,*
more mighty than a waterfall.

(John Updike)

2 What is the answer to the question at the beginning of the poem? Is there just one possible answer?
3 Explain in your own words what you think John Updike means by 'molecules of H_2O leaping from the fading film'.

IN THIS CHAPTER YOU WILL FIND OUT

▌ what the atmosphere is and why it is important

▌ how the action of the Sun on the atmosphere causes the weather

▌ about weather patterns and how they change

▌ how gases behave.

Looking at

The Earth's Blanket

What is the greenhouse effect?

1 Look at this cartoon. What do *you* think the
  greenhouse effect is? Write a short explanation.
  These words might help:

  atmosphere   gases   Sun's rays

       heat   reflect   trapped

The Earth's atmosphere is made up of various
gases. Some of these gases, such as carbon dioxide
and methane, are called **greenhouse gases**. There
is more about these on pages 150–51. Radiation
from the Sun heats the Earth. The Earth then
radiates heat too, but its radiation is trapped by the
greenhouse gases in the atmosphere and reflected
back to Earth. The greenhouse gases act as a
blanket. The diagram below shows how this
happens.

Greenhouse gases behave like the glass in a
greenhouse – it lets in radiation from the Sun but
doesn't let radiation from the plants back out
again.

Because of this **greenhouse effect**, the
temperature on the Earth's surface is fairly
constant. At night, when the Earth is facing away
from the Sun, it is still relatively warm. Earth
temperatures are usually between -20°C and 40°C.

**What would it be like without the greenhouse
effect?**
The Moon is about the same distance from the Sun
as the Earth is. But the Moon has no atmosphere,
so there are no greenhouse gases around it.

Radiation from the Moon goes straight off into
space. The temperature on the Moon fluctuates
much more than on Earth – it gets to 150°C facing
the Sun and drops below -150°C facing away from
the Sun. The average Moon temperature is around
-20°C – about 35°C lower than the average Earth
temperature.

2 Predict what would happen if the average
  temperature on the Earth fell to -20°C.
3 Draw a diagram similar to the one on this page
  showing what happens to the Sun's rays which
  reach the Moon.

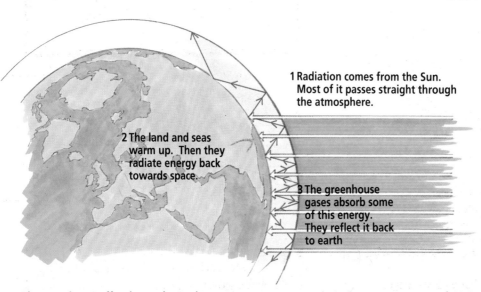

1 Radiation comes from the Sun.
  Most of it passes straight through
  the atmosphere.

2 The land and seas
  warm up. Then they
  radiate energy back
  towards space.

3 The greenhouse
  gases absorb some
  of this energy.
  They reflect it back
  to earth

The greenhouse effect keeps the Earth's average temperature relatively constant at around 15°C at sea level.

What is global warming?

You have probably heard people talking about global warming. They mean that the Earth is getting gradually warmer. Some people blame global warming for the strong winds and floods in the UK in the last few years.

This graph shows the average temperature of the Earth over the last 100 years.

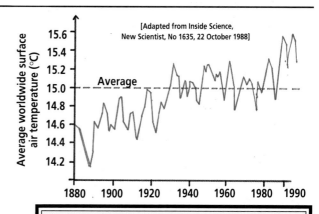

[Adapted from Inside Science, New Scientist, No 1635, 22 October 1988]

Average worldwide surface air temperature (°C)	

4 Do you think the Earth is getting warmer?
   Write reasons for your answer.

Question 4 is something the experts disagree on – the temperature might be slowly rising, or it might be fluctuating randomly.

How are we affecting the atmosphere?

The greenhouse gases keep the Earth at a steady comfortable temperature. Over the last 100 years industry, agriculture and transport have developed very quickly. As the diagram below shows, we have been producing large quantities of greenhouse gases. So there are more greenhouse gases in the atmosphere than there used to be. This is like making the blanket around the Earth thicker – it keeps more heat in.

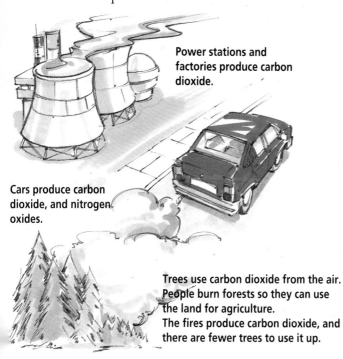

Power stations and factories produce carbon dioxide.

Cars produce carbon dioxide, and nitrogen oxides.

Trees use carbon dioxide from the air. People burn forests so they can use the land for agriculture. The fires produce carbon dioxide, and there are fewer trees to use it up.

We are producing more carbon dioxide and nitrogen oxides – greenhouse gases – than we used to.

The Effects of Global Warming

Scientists predict that production of greenhouse gases could warm the Earth up by about 5°C. The results:

● Sea levels could rise by about 30 cm as ice melts from the Poles and sea water expands – disaster for low-lying areas e.g. Bangladesh and the Nile Delta.
● Local climates could change – floods and droughts might happen more often in some regions.
● Agriculture could suffer – some crops won't adapt to climate changes and pests could survive warmer winters.

What can we do?

● Use energy more efficiently – to cut down carbon dioxide production from fossil fuel power stations.
● Use wood from managed forests – so we know the trees are being replaced by new ones.
● Plant more trees.

---

5 Look back at your answer to question 1. How have your ideas changed?
6 Design and make a leaflet explaining what causes global warming. Show people how they can do the things listed above to help slow it down, or stop it altogether.

Ozone is a gas in the atmosphere which keeps out some harmful ultraviolet radiation. People are concerned about depletion of the ozone layer. This has nothing to do with the greenhouse effect.

Looking at

Forecasting the Weather

Weather has an important effect on everybody. Some people, such as farmers or pilots, need very detailed knowledge of the weather. Others only need to know how it will affect their leisure activities. Newspapers, radio and television supply a range of forecasts to reflect the needs of different people.

1 List six jobs that require detailed knowledge of the weather.
2 Make a list of times when *you* might need to know what the weather will be like.
3 Where have you seen weather charts like the one in the diagram (below left)?

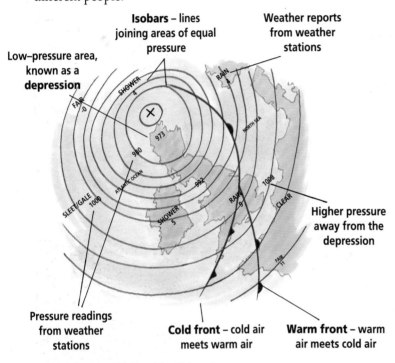

Isobars – lines joining areas of equal pressure

Weather reports from weather stations

Low–pressure area, known as a depression

Higher pressure away from the depression

Pressure readings from weather stations

Cold front – cold air meets warm air

Warm front – warm air meets cold air

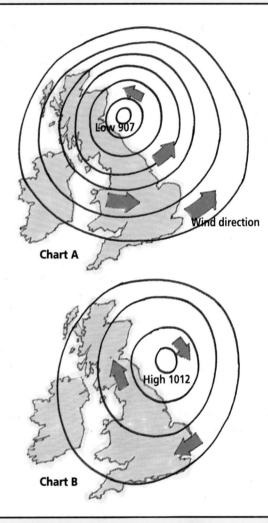

Chart A

Wind direction

Low 907

High 1012

Chart B

Which way will the wind blow?

Weather charts help us predict speed, direction and strength of the wind. Wind is air rushing from one part of the Earth's atmosphere to another. The direction and strength of the wind can be predicted by looking at the areas of high and low pressure and the isobars around them.

You might expect the wind to blow straight from an area of high pressure to an area of low pressure, but this is complicated by the Earth spinning.

North of the equator, wind blows anticlockwise around a depression and clockwise around an area of high pressure. South of the equator the situation is reversed.

Closely packed isobars show large pressure differences in a small area causing the air to move more quickly. The closer the isobars are together, the stronger the wind will be.

4 Look at the weather forecast map (above left). In which direction would you expect the wind to be blowing over
  (a) the Atlantic Ocean
  (b) the North Sea?
5 Look at the charts (above right). From which of the charts would you forecast the wind to be least strong?
6 In the UK, does the wind blow clockwise or anticlockwise around a depression?

What else can we tell from weather charts?

Weather charts also help us to predict rain. Warm air holds more water vapour than cold air. When warm and cold air meet, the warm air is pushed upwards and will be cooled down. As the warm air cools some of the water vapour condenses into tiny drops of liquid water and forms clouds and rain.

Masses of air which are moving from polar regions will be colder than those moving from nearer the equator. Where two air masses meet, a front is formed. If the warm air is following the cold air, we call it a warm front. If the cold air follows the warm air, it is a cold front. When a front passes across the country, you can expect rain.

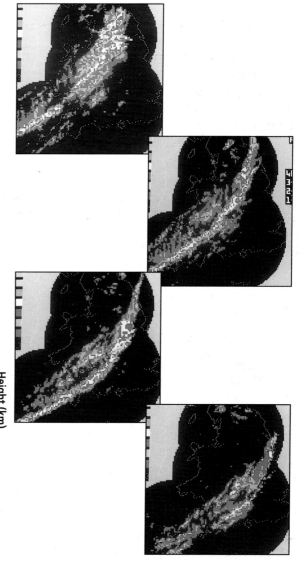

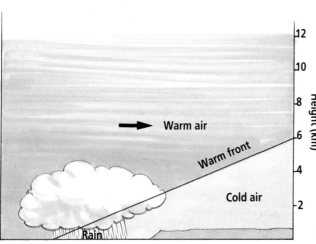

As the warm front moves it is forced upwards above the cold air. This results in clouds and rain.

By using satellites we can photograph movement of weather fronts. These four photographs show the movement of the weather fronts on the day the map on the left was drawn.

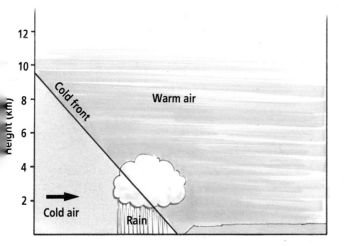

As the cold front moves it forces the warm air upwards. This results in clouds and rain.

Look at the photographs.
7 In which direction is the rain moving?
8 What changes in the sky would someone have seen as the weather fronts moved over them?
9 What temperature changes would the same person have felt?
10 The different colours in the photographs show how the rainfall changes as the fronts move. Write a summary of the changes that could be used as part of a weather report on the radio.

Looking at

Athletes and Altitude

Altitude means height above sea level. At high altitudes, as you go up into the atmosphere, the air 'thins out'. There are fewer gas molecules in a given volume. The **air pressure** becomes less.

1 **This mountaineer is near the top of Mount Everest. Why do you think he is carrying oxygen?**

Dave Peterson on the south-west face, 23 000 feet.

As altitude increases, the amount of oxygen available to breathe becomes less. If you visit a place at a high altitude you may have difficulty breathing at first, until your body gets used to less oxygen in the air.

Living in Mexico City

Mexico City is at an altitude of 2500 metres. People there live perfectly normal lives because they have got used to the low level of oxygen in the atmosphere. **Haemoglobin** is a chemical in blood which carries oxygen. People who live in Mexico City have extra haemoglobin in their blood, so it can carry more oxygen. The increase in haemoglobin makes up for the decrease in oxygen.

Visitors to Mexico City also react in this way. After a week or two they produce more haemoglobin. When they return to a lower altitude, they stop producing so much haemoglobin, and their blood slowly returns to its original composition.

While people have more haemoglobin in their blood they can be more active. Their blood can carry more oxygen, so they can produce more energy by respiration.

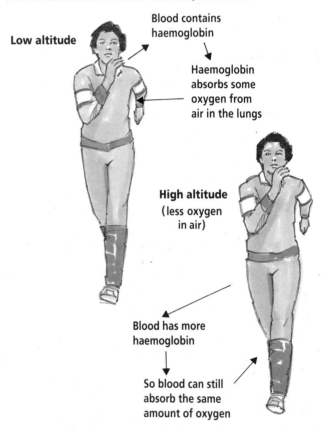

Low altitude

Blood contains haemoglobin

Haemoglobin absorbs some oxygen from air in the lungs

High altitude (less oxygen in air)

Blood has more haemoglobin

So blood can still absorb the same amount of oxygen

Mexico City – 2500 metres above sea level

2 **Why do you think athletes train at high altitudes just before an important event?**

3 **Imagine you are a 5000 metre runner. Write a letter to your sponsor explaining why you want to go to a training camp 1500 metres up in the Rocky Mountains for a fortnight before your next big race.**

In brief

The Atmosphere

1 The **atmosphere** is a thin layer of gases around the Earth. The inner layer is the **troposphere.** The gases in the troposphere get gradually thinner as you go higher. At about 20 km up, almost all the gas is gone. Above this is the **ionosphere** – the outer layer of the atmosphere which contains ions (charged atoms).

2 The pie chart shows the gases which make up the atmosphere.

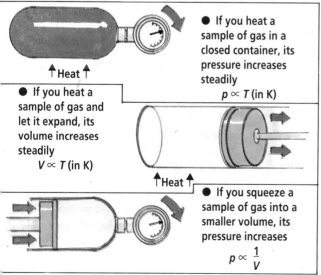

Nitrogen, 79%

Oxygen, 20%

Argon, 1%

Other gases (including carbon dioxide, 0.03%)

3 The atmosphere is so large that the air temperature and pressure vary within it. There are different **air masses** in different places, for example warm, humid air near the equator and colder, drier air near the poles.

4 These air masses are continually moving above the Earth. This movement is caused by the heating effect of the Sun's radiation. Air near the equator is heated strongly and becomes less dense. So it rises and colder air moves in to take its place. This causes **convection currents.**

5 To understand how the atmosphere behaves it helps to know how gases behave in simpler situations. Investigations show that:

- If you heat a sample of gas in a closed container, its pressure increases steadily
  $$p \propto T \text{ (in K)}$$

- If you heat a sample of gas and let it expand, its volume increases steadily
  $$V \propto T \text{ (in K)}$$

↑Heat↑

- If you squeeze a sample of gas into a smaller volume, its pressure increases
  $$p \propto \frac{1}{V}$$

6 The behaviour of gases can be explained using the **kinetic model of gases.** A gas consists of lots of tiny particles moving rapidly in all directions. Heating the gas makes the particles speed up. Pressure is caused by collisions of the particles with the sides of the container.

7 To convert temperatures from degrees Celsius to kelvin, add 273. So 0°C is 273 K and 100°C is 373 K.

8 The air near the equator is less dense than in other places – the pressure is low. The air near the poles is colder and denser – the pressure is high. Air moves from high pressure areas to low pressure areas, causing winds. As the Earth is rotating, the winds tend to swirl around the high and low pressure regions.

9 Sometimes a cold air mass meets a warm air mass, forming a **weather front.** The denser cold air forces the warmer air upwards. The warmer air cools. Water vapour in the rising warmer air begins to condense into tiny water droplets, forming clouds. The droplets join together and fall as rain. Rain is associated with weather fronts.

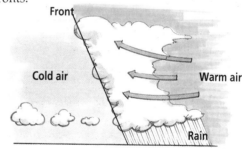

Front

Cold air

Warm air

Rain

10 **Isobars** on a weather map join points where the air pressure is the same. They help us to locate weather fronts and to predict the wind direction.

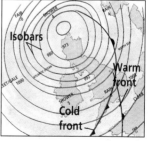

Isobars

Warm front

Cold front

11 Energy is involved when a substance changes from one **state** to another. When ice melts to form water, it absorbs energy to break the strong bonds holding the water molecules together as solid ice. When liquid water cools to form snow crystals, it releases energy.

Thinking about

The Atmosphere

1. What is the atmosphere?

The atmosphere is an envelope of gas that surrounds the Earth. It goes up over 10 000 kilometres above the surface. As you go further up in the atmosphere it becomes thinner and thinner until it is difficult to decide whether it is still there or not. The atmosphere does not have a definite ending point. These diagrams show the layers in the atmosphere.

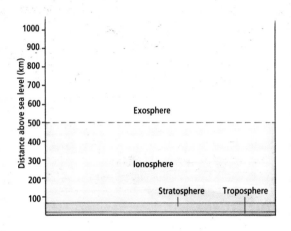

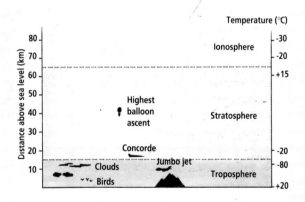

The lower diagram enlarges the bottom layers shown in the top diagram. You can see that

- Weather balloons reach 35 km up
- Concorde flies at around 15 km up } stratosphere
- Clouds and rain form at about 10 km up
- Mount Everest reaches about 9 km up. } troposphere

2. How does the Sun's heat affect the atmosphere?

There are a number of gases in the atmosphere, but only three are present in large amounts. Look at the pie chart in *In Brief 2*. Notice how small the amount of carbon dioxide is.

Without an atmosphere, the parts of the Earth facing the Sun would be very hot, while other parts would be very cold. The atmosphere evens out these temperature differences. This happens because of **convection currents**.

You have probably seen convection currents when you heat water. You can see the water moving in a particular way as it warms up – the diagrams show why. Adding a dye or a coloured crystal to the water makes the convection currents easier to see.

When you heat water it expands. Its density becomes less, because the same amount of water now takes up a larger volume.

The part of the water you heated is now less dense than the cold part, so it rises.

Cold water falls to replace the moving warm water. As the warm water rises, it cools and falls, setting up a current.

Convection currents happen in both liquids and gases, including the atmosphere. They spread heat around more evenly. Without them the regions around the equator would become much hotter and the regions around the poles much colder. This diagram shows the convection currents in the atmosphere.

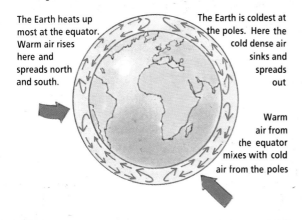

The Earth heats up most at the equator. Warm air rises here and spreads north and south.

The Earth is coldest at the poles. Here the cold dense air sinks and spreads out

Warm air from the equator mixes with cold air from the poles

This movement and mixing of air takes place in the troposphere. This is how the troposphere gets its name – from *tropos*, the Greek word for movement..

3. How does temperature affect the pressure and volume of a gas?

The behaviour of the atmosphere is very complicated. To understand it, it helps to know how gases behave in much simpler situations.

Temperature and volume

What happens when you heat a sample of gas? If you put a half-blown up balloon in a warm place and watch, you will see the balloon getting bigger. The air inside expands as it heats up.

You can investigate this using an air sample trapped inside a glass syringe. When you put the syringe into hot water, the piston slowly moves out. The air inside the syringe expands as it heats up.

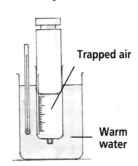

Trapped air

Warm water

As $T\uparrow$, $V\uparrow$ (if the gas can expand freely)

Temperature and pressure

What happens if you heat a gas sample in a container that cannot expand? Imagine blowing cold air into a plastic bag, sealing it, and heating it. The air 'wants' to expand but cannot – the bag will burst. The **pressure** of the air increases as it gets hotter. Pressure builds up inside the bag until it is much higher than the pressure outside – then the bag bursts.

With this apparatus you can measure the pressure of air inside a flask as it heats up. The pressure rises steadily as the air gets hotter.

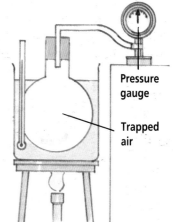

Pressure gauge

Trapped air

As $T\uparrow$, $p\uparrow$ (if the volume is fixed)

Pressure and volume

Now think about keeping the temperature of a gas sample fixed, but changing its volume.

What happens if you (accidentally!) sit on a balloon? Your weight compresses the air in the balloon, trying to squeeze it into a smaller volume. This increases the pressure of the air inside, and the balloon bursts.

Again you can investigate this using a glass syringe. If you add weights to the piston, the air inside the syringe is squeezed into a smaller and smaller volume.

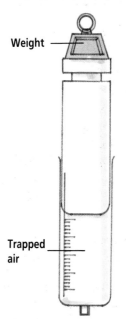

Weight

Trapped air

As $p\uparrow$, $V\downarrow$ (with temperature staying the same)

Taking it further: Finding the link

If you did the investigations in *Thinking About 3* and took some measurements, you would get results similar to these. These results give you a relationship between the pressure, volume and temperature of a gas sample.

TEMPERATURE (°C)	VOLUME (CM³)
0	60
25	65
50	71
75	76
100	82

TEMPERATURE (°C)	PRESSURE (KPa)
0	100
25	109
50	118
75	127
100	137

PRESSURE (UNIT)	VOLUME (CM³)
1	120
2	60
3	40
4	30

In the third investigation you can see that if you double the pressure, the volume is halved.

If you treble the pressure, the volume goes down to one-third of what it was. Volume is **inversely proportional** to pressure.

In the first two investigations you can see that both volume and pressure increase steadily as the temperature rises. These graphs show the results more clearly.

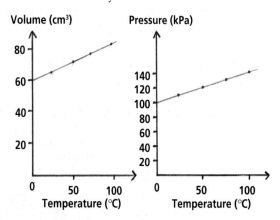

With this Celsius temperature scale, these graphs do *not* go through the origin. The volume of a gas sample increases if you heat it from 50°C to 100°C, but it does *not* double. The same is true of the pressure. It increases but it is not **directly proportional** to the temperature in degrees Celsius.

How low can you go - is there a 'lowest possible' temperature?

The pressure and volume of a gas sample decrease steadily as the temperature drops. So what would happen if you kept cooling the gas down? From the graphs, it looks as if the volume and the pressure would eventually fall to zero!

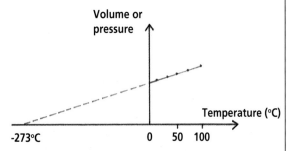

In fact this doesn't happen, because the gas sample becomes a liquid before it reaches this low temperature. The temperature at which the graphs show the volume and pressure becoming zero is called **absolute zero.** It is approximately -273°C.

If you make this point the origin of the temperature axis, the two graphs become straight lines *through the origin*. This is called the **kelvin temperature scale.** Absolute zero is 0 K, and the freezing point of water is 273 K. You just add 273 to every Celsius temperature to change it to kelvin.

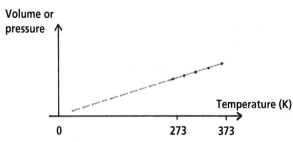

If you double the temperature in kelvin, you double the volume or pressure. Volume and pressure are **directly proportional** to temperature in kelvin. For a fixed sample of gas

- $p \propto T$ (in kelvin) (if the gas is not allowed to expand)
- $V \propto T$ (in kelvin) (if the gas can expand freely).

4. How can you apply these ideas about gases to the atmosphere?

The atmosphere is obviously much bigger than a gas sample. In a flask of gas, the temperature and pressure are the same all the way through. But this is not true for the atmosphere. It contains some air masses which are hot and expanded, and others which are cold and dense – at the same time. These mix – which is what causes the weather!

Why are there air masses at different pressures?
At the equator, the air is warm. So it expands and spreads, like water when you heat it. This means it has a lower density than cooler air. As a result it presses down less on the Earth's surface – the air pressure is *low*.

Over the poles, the air is cooler. It contracts and more air comes in to take its place. The cool air is denser than air at the equator. This means it presses down more on the Earth's surface – the air pressure is *high*.

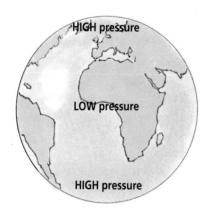

Gases always move from an area of high pressure to an area of low pressure. When you open a lemonade bottle, you hear the rush of gas escaping. The high-pressure gas inside the bottle is moving to the lower-pressure region outside.

What causes the wind?
Wind is the movement of air in the atmosphere from high-pressure areas to lower-pressure areas. You might expect the winds to move in straight lines from the poles towards the equator. Things are complicated, however, by the fact that the Earth is rotating. As the air masses move, the Earth rotates underneath them. As a result, the winds swirl around the high- and low-pressure regions. In the northern hemisphere, winds tend to blow anticlockwise round low-pressure areas and clockwise round high-pressure areas.

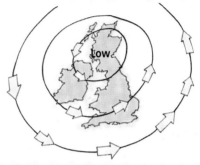

The UK is in the northern hemisphere, so winds tend to blow anticlockwise around low-pressure areas

5. How can we forecast the weather?

Weather forecasts are based on what the weather is like now. So all over the world, on land and at sea, are **weather stations** which record the weather. They continually measure air pressure, temperature, wind direction and humidity (the amount of water vapour in the air).

Land–based weather station – pressure, temperature, rainfall and wind are monitored here

Measuring the sea temperature on board a weather ship

Meteorologists (people who study the weather) use the air pressure measurements to build up a weather map. There are lines on the map called **isobars**. Each isobar links points where the pressure is the same. The heavier lines are **weather fronts** – the boundaries between warmer and cooler air masses. We usually get rain when a weather front passes over us.

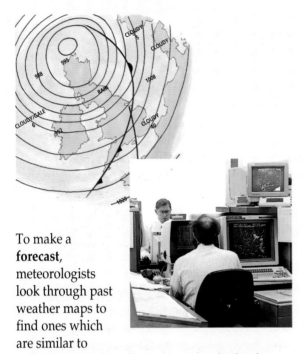

To make a **forecast**, meteorologists look through past weather maps to find ones which are similar to today's map. Nowadays computers do this for them. They know how the weather developed last time the map was like this, so they can predict what is likely to happen this time.

6. What drives the weather?

The energy carried by the Sun's radiation is the 'motor' which drives the weather. It sets up convection currents which cause the winds. The Sun's energy also evaporates water from seas, lakes and rivers into the air, and melts polar ice and snow.

When ice melts or water evaporates, it **changes state**. Energy is needed to cause a change of state.

If you heat a beaker of crushed ice very gently, it gradually warms up to 0°C. The ice stays at 0°C until it has all melted, then the temperature begins to rise again.

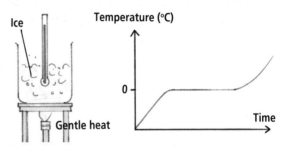

At 0°C, the ice changes into water. Energy is still needed, even though the temperature is not changing. The energy is used to overcome the strong bonds which hold the molecules together in ice, and enable the molecules to move around within the liquid.

Energy needed to overcome strong bonds

In the same way, you need energy to change water into water vapour or steam. If you keep heating a beaker of boiling water, its temperature doesn't rise any further until all the water has turned to steam. The energy is used to overcome all the bonds between the liquid water molecules, allowing them to escape completely and form a gas.

More energy needed to overcome remaining bonds

Evaporation also happens at temperatures below the boiling point. Energy is still needed, as the water is changing state. Because of this, evaporation causes cooling. Wet clothes feel cold because water is evaporating from them. Energy from your warm body causes the evaporation. This cools *you* down.

Taking it further: Explaining the link
The connections between the volume, pressure and temperature of a gas sample are very simple.
So scientists thought that there must be some simple explanation for them. Over 200 years ago the Swiss mathematician Daniel Bernoulli suggested that gases might consist of large numbers of tiny particles, moving around rapidly in all directions. The hotter the gas, the faster the particles move. Pressure is caused by the gas particles colliding with the sides of their container. Nowadays we call these particles **molecules**. Bernoulli's model is called **the kinetic theory of gases**.
It can explain the three gas laws.

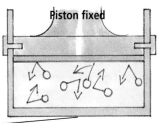
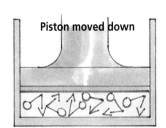
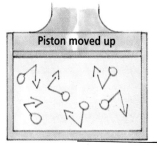

Pressure and temperature: If you heat a gas sample inside a container, the molecules move faster. They collide more often with the walls and the collisions are harder. So the pressure increases.

Pressure and volume: If you squeeze a gas sample into a smaller volume, you pack the molecules closer together. More molecules collide with each square centimetre of the walls every second. So the pressure increases.

Volume and temperature: As you heat a gas, its molecules move faster. They hit the walls harder and more often. The extra force pushes the piston outwards. The gas expands.

Absolute zero
The kinetic theory of gases also explains why there is a lowest possible temperature. At low temperature, the molecules move more slowly. At **absolute zero**, the molecules are stationary. You can't be more stopped than stopped, so you can't get colder than absolute zero! (In fact, scientists now believe that molecules are still moving, even at absolute zero. But they have their minimum possible speed at absolute zero.)

Things to do

The Atmosphere

Things to try out

1 Hold an empty washing-up liquid bottle upside down in a basin of hot water. Don't squeeze it. You should see bubbles coming out of the bottle. Explain why this happens.

Hot water

2 Plan and carry out an investigation to find out how the 'bounciness' of a squash ball changes with temperature. (A squash ball has air trapped inside it.) Use the ideas you have learnt in this unit about the behaviour of gases to explain why the ball is bouncier when it is warm.

3 Keep a diary of the weather in your area for one week. Cut out the weather forecast summary from each day's newspaper, or make a note of what the forecast says on radio or television.
At the end of the week, compare your records of what the weather was *really* like with the forecasts for each day. Give each forecast a rating between 1 and 5 (1 = poor, 5 = excellent). How good do you think the weather forecast is?

Things to find out

4 Thermals are currents of hot air. Glider pilots find them useful, because they will lift a glider. Find out what causes thermals, and then suggest where you would look for them on this map.

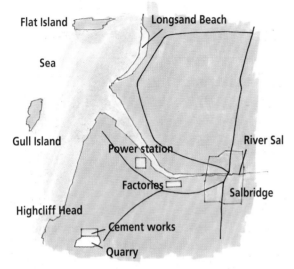

5 Listen to the weather forecast for shipping. It is broadcast several times a day on the radio. If you can, tape-record it. Make a list of all the coastal weather stations named during the forecast, and all the sea areas it gives a forecast for. Use the library to try to find out where these weather stations and sea areas are.

Each weather station makes the same set of observations and measurements. What information does the forecast report for each station?

Points to discuss

6 Explain each of the following using the words **pressure**, **volume** and **temperature**

(a) A dented ping-pong ball can sometimes be fixed by putting it into a saucepan of hot water.

(b) A sponge cake looks like this as it comes out of the oven:

A little later it looks like this:

(c) It is very dangerous to throw an aerosol can on to a fire, even if it is empty.

(d) A bicycle pump holds 100 cm^3 of air and it takes 20 full pumps to get a bicycle tyre hard. But the volume of the inner tube is only 800 cm^3.

7 Discuss the observations in question **6** with others in your group, and then write explanations for each of them *using ideas about how the molecules of the gas are behaving.*

Questions to answer

8 On a cold morning, when the temperature had dropped to -3°C, Carol Evans blew up her bicycle tyres to a pressure of 2.7 atmospheres. Later that week the temperature rose to 7°C. She did the following calculation to find the pressure in the tyres:

> The temperature has gone up from 270 K to 280 K
>
> So new pressure = old pressure $\times \dfrac{280}{270}$
>
> $= 2.7 \times \dfrac{280}{270} = 2.8$ atmospheres

What will the pressure be if the temperature

   (a) goes up to 17°C

   (b) goes up to 27°C ?

9 Jayesh carefully heated an unknown solid substance at a steady rate, and noted its temperature each minute. His results are shown below.

Time (min)	1	2	3	4	5	6	7	8	9
Temperature (°C)	11	13	15	16	16	16	17	17	19

Plot a graph of these results. Explain what you think is happening to the substance.

10 Use the information in *Thinking About 1* to draw a graph showing how temperature changes with height above the Earth's surface.

Introducing

ELECTRICITY IN THE HOME

1 Look at these pictures. Classify them into
- those concerned with producing and delivering mains electricity
- those which use electricity
- those concerned with static electricity.

Make lists of your groups.

2 Look at your list of pictures about static electricity. What other examples of static electricity and its effects can you think of? Add them to your list.

3 You use appliances which run off the mains or off batteries (some can use either). Write down the advantages and disadvantages of each source of electricity.

4 How has electricity changed the way people live? Write an account comparing your lifestyle with that of someone who lived 200 years ago, before electricity was available in the home.

IN THIS CHAPTER YOU WILL FIND OUT

❚ how we can use static electricity

❚ how simple electric circuits work

❚ how to do calculations on simple circuits

❚ how to use electricity safely at home

❚ how to choose the right cable and fuse for an electrical appliance

❚ how cells and batteries work.

Looking at

The Wiring in your Home

How are lights connected to the power supply?
If a bulb goes in a string of fairy lights, they all go off and you have to spend hours finding which bulb blew. But if a bulb goes in the bathroom, the bedroom light stays on. Why is this?

The lights in this house are connected like this...

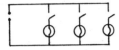

In parallel

...and not like this. (This is how fairy lights are connected, but without the switches.)

In series

(There is more about parallel and series circuits in *In Brief 8 and 9* on pages 124–5.)

You can't see the parallel circuit at home because most of the wires are hidden under the floorboards, above the ceilings or behind the plaster on the walls. Even if you could see the wires, the circuit wouldn't look like the simple parallel circuit in the top diagram.

This picture shows how the wires are connected in a lighting circuit. A **ceiling rose** connects the light fitting to the circuit. 'Bus bars' make it easy for electricians to connect the wires – the wires entering each bus bar are all connected together.

From mains supply via fuse box

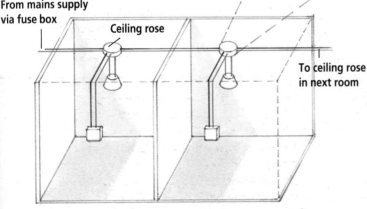

Ceiling rose

To ceiling rose in next room

1 How can you tell your lights at home are connected in parallel? Write down three simple tests (they shouldn't involve a screwdriver!).

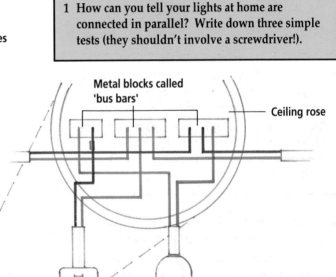

Metal blocks called 'bus bars'

Ceiling rose

Switch

Lamp holder

2 Copy the ceiling rose diagram on a large sheet of paper. The points L (for live) and N (for neutral) are like the terminals of a power supply. Trace out the closed circuit from L, through the switch and lamp, and back to N. Show on your diagram the path the electricity follows when the lamp is switched on.

3 Now draw the ceiling rose in the next room, connected to the right-hand side of your diagram. Show the path the electricity takes.

4 Redraw your diagram, straightening out the wires like a 'proper' circuit diagram, but keeping all the connections the same. Show the switches, the lamps and the wires that are connected. You can shorten and lengthen any wire as much as you want. What do you notice?

How are power sockets connected to the mains supply?

The sockets you plug appliances into at home are also connected in parallel to the mains supply. But this power circuit is slightly different from the lighting circuit.

The power cable has three wires, live, neutral and earth. (Lighting cable also has an earth wire, but it was left it out in the diagram opposite, to make it easier to follow.) Each of the three wires leaves the consumer unit, goes round the house to the sockets, and returns to the consumer unit again. Because of this the circuit is called a **ring main**.

The lighting cable does not return to the consumer unit in this way; it is not a ring.

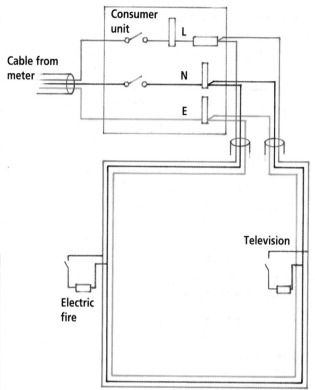

5 Trace the path the electric current takes from the point L opposite, through the electric fire, and back to N. How many possible paths are there?
6 Explain clearly how you can tell from the ring main diagram that the electric fire and the television are connected in parallel and not in series.

When you plug in a one-bar electric fire and switch it on, it draws a current of about 4 A from the circuit. The maximum safe current drawn from any one socket is 13 A. Most appliances draw much less than this. The cable in the ring main has to carry the current for all the sockets. It is designed to carry currents up to 30 A without overheating. The ring circuit has a fuse which blows, breaking the circuit, if the total current in the ring cable gets to 30 A. This prevents the cable from overheating, which would be very dangerous. As most appliances take only a small current, there can be up to ten sockets on a ring main, without too much risk that the total current will get to 30 A.

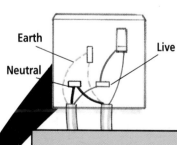

This shows how the ring main cable is connected to the back of a double three-pin mains socket

This house has two ring mains - one for the upstairs sockets and one for the downstairs ones.

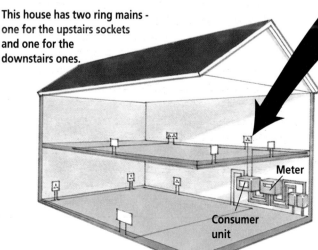

7 Look at *In Brief 13*. Would it be safe to run a 100 W table lamp from all the sockets in the downstairs ring main? Explain.
8 What advantages does a ring main have over a simple parallel circuit?
9 Look at the diagram of a plug on page 34. Draw a colour code for wiring a plug. How is it different from the colour code for the wiring in a socket?

Looking at

Cells and Batteries

Sometimes you need electricity a long way away from the mains, for example for a personal stereo. Batteries provide portable electricity.

4.5 V

9 V

1 **Look at the batteries in the first picture. What are their voltages? Can you see any pattern in their voltages?**

In fact, each battery's voltage is a multiple of 1.5 V. This is because a battery is made up of one or more **cells**. Each cell provides 1.5 V (so strictly speaking a 1.5 V battery should be called a cell!). The second photo shows the cells inside two batteries.

2 **How many cells would you expect to find if you cut open a 6 V battery?**

What's in a cell?
Thinking About 5 on page 130 shows a simple cell. The chemicals in the cell are producing electricity. The cells in the batteries you use do the same thing. The diagram shows a zinc–carbon cell.

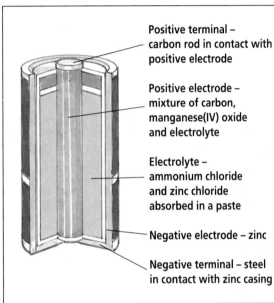

Positive terminal – carbon rod in contact with positive electrode

Positive electrode – mixture of carbon, manganese(IV) oxide and electrolyte

Electrolyte – ammonium chloride and zinc chloride absorbed in a paste

Negative electrode – zinc

Negative terminal – steel in contact with zinc casing

3 **Draw up a table to compare the positive electrode, negative electrode and electrolyte of the simple cell and the zinc–carbon cell.**
4 **Why do you think the electrolyte in the zinc–carbon cell is absorbed in a paste?**

Leaking cells
Because the zinc case of a zinc–carbon cell is also an electrode, it is gradually used up. Eventually holes appear and the electrolyte leaks out.

The more expensive alkaline cells you can buy use the same chemical reaction as the zinc–carbon cell, but the positive electrode is powdered zinc inside a steel case. The electrolyte is potassium hydroxide – a strong alkali, hence the name.

Rechargeable cells
A disadvantage of batteries is that you have to throw them away and buy new ones when they are used up. Some batteries can be recharged, so you can use them over and over again.

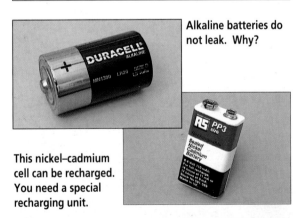

Alkaline batteries do not leak. Why?

This nickel–cadmium cell can be recharged. You need a special recharging unit.

5 **Find out how much rechargeable cells and the recharging unit cost. How many sets of zinc–carbon cells could you buy for this price? What else do you need to consider for a fair comparison?**

Batteries galore!

Nowadays there are lots of different types, shapes and sizes of batteries available. The table shows the results of a survey of different batteries.

Battery type	zinc–carbon	alkaline	mercury	silver oxide	lithium	lead–acid	nickel–cadmium
positive electrode	manganese(IV) oxide + carbon	manganese(IV) oxide + carbon	mercury(II) oxide + carbon	silver oxide	silver chromate	lead(II) oxide	nickel oxyhydride
negative electrode	zinc	powdered zinc	powdered zinc	zinc	lithium	lead	cadmium
electrolyte	ammonium chloride	potassium hydroxide	zinc oxide + potassium hydroxide	potassium hydroxide	lithium chlorate in propene carbonate	dilute sulphuric acid	potassium hydroxide
common sizes (B-button, S-small, M-medium, L-large)	S, M	S, M	B	B, S	B	L	S, M
rechargeable						●	●
can supply a high current		●				●●●	●
suitable only for low current or intermittent use	●		●	●	●		
keep well before use (* OK; ** good; *** v. good)	★	★★	★★	★★	★★★	★	★
energy density (energy stored/weight) (* OK; ** good; *** v. good)	★	★★	★★	★★	★★★	★	★★
price (* cheap; ** medium; *** expensive)	★	★★	★★	★★★	★★★	★★★	★★★

---

6 If you were designing the following appliances, suggest which type of battery you would prefer for each. In each case, explain your choice.

(a) a walkie-talkie for use on an expedition

(b) a heart pacemaker

(c) an automatic camera

(d) a battery powered minibus

(e) a digital alarm clock

(f) a personal stereo

(g) a powerful torch

(h) a satellite (batteries can be recharged from solar panels)

7 Extend the survey by designing an investigation to find out which of two batteries lasts longer. You must make sure that you keep the test 'fair'. Explain how you would go about this, and make a list of all the apparatus you would need.

Looking at

Using Electricity Safely

Plugging it in

Fitting a plug can be a fiddly operation. The point of a plug is to connect an appliance safely to the mains supply. So it is worth making sure the wires are all cut to the right length and fitted neatly to the correct terminals.

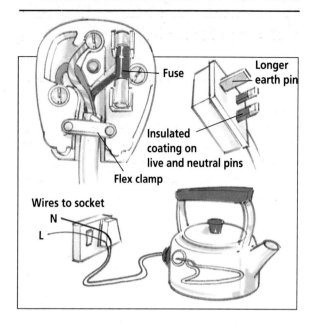

> 1 Make a list of all the safety features which are built into the design of this 13 A plug. Explain what each is for.

When you plug an appliance in, electricity can flow round a closed loop. The loop is formed by the live and neutral wires. The mains supplies **alternating current** (a.c.). This means that the current pulses back and forward round the loop, changing direction 100 times a second!

Earthing it

The live and neutral wires form part of the electrical circuit, but what is the earth wire for? It is another safety feature. Every appliance that has a metal case needs to be earthed.

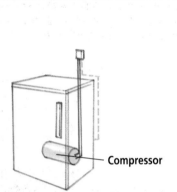

If the wiring inside this fridge is correct and in good condition, the electric circuit involves just the live and neutral wires. The earth wire does nothing.

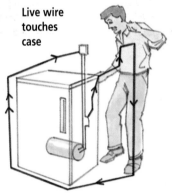

If there was no earth wire and the live wire happened to get worn or damaged so that it touched the metal case, you could be electrocuted. When you touch the case, your body becomes part of the electric circuit.

This fridge has an earth wire. If a damaged live wire touches the case, it forms a closed circuit with the earth lead. A large current flows in this circuit and the fuse in the mains plug melts. This breaks the circuit, so the fridge is safe to touch. You can now have the fault seen to!

> 2 Make a poster for an electricity board showroom explaining what the earth wire is for in an electric fire.
> 3 Some modern appliances have no external metal parts – the whole casing is made of plastic. These are double insulated. They do not need an earth wire because the case does not conduct electricity. Double insulated appliances have a symbol like this:
>
> Make a list of all the appliances you can find in your home which have a double insulated symbol.

Looking at

Static Electricity

Charging up

You will already know about some effects of static electricity. When an insulator rubs against another material, charge is transferred from one to the other. Charge builds up until it suddenly escapes in the form of a spark.

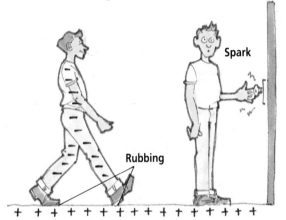

Have you ever walked across a carpeted floor, and then felt a slight shock as you touched a metal door handle? Carpets made from artificial fibres are excellent insulators. As your shoes rub on the carpet, you become charged.

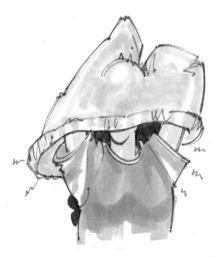

If you pull off an acrylic jumper over a nylon blouse or shirt, you sometimes hear crackles. In the dark you can see that these are really tiny sparks.

Static electricity at work

Small pieces of paper are attracted to a charged object, like a comb. This is why windows sometimes seem impossible to clean completely. The harder you rub, the more the dust particles are attracted to the glass – because it is getting charged! Sometimes this effect can be useful.

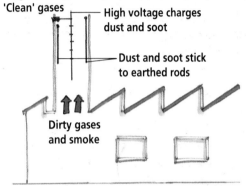

Most of our domestic electricity in Britain is generated in coal-burning power stations. Dust and soot are removed from the chimney gases by an electrostatic precipitator. This greatly reduces atmospheric pollution.

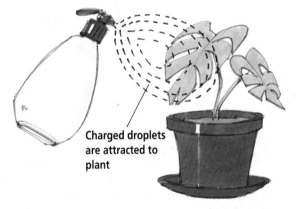

Modern crop sprayers use the effect in reverse – they charge the tiny droplets which are attracted to the plants. The droplets may be charged electrically, or simply by rubbing against the nozzle. A great advantage is that the droplets also stick to the undersides of leaves, where most of the insect pests are.

---

1 Some of the gases doctors use in anaesthetics are inflammable. The floors of operating theatres are covered with a material which is a good conductor. Use the ideas above to explain why.

2 Another everyday device which uses electrostatics is the photocopier. Use a library to find out as much as you can about photocopying and how electrostatics is involved.

Electricity in the Home

1 There are two types of electric charge which we call **positive** and **negative**. Two objects with the same charge repel each other (they move apart). Two objects with opposite charges attract each other (they move together).

2 You can **charge** insulators by rubbing them with a cloth. Electrons are rubbed off one material (leaving it with a positive charge) and stick on to the other (giving it a negative charge).

3 You can also charge conductors by rubbing them, if they are insulated from earth. If they are connected to earth the charge immediately escapes. Sometimes it escapes as a spark – a sudden discharge of static electricity through the air.

4 An electric **current** is a flow of charge. In a wire, the flowing charges are electrons.

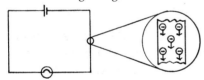

The size of the current depends on how much charge flows past a point each second:

$$\text{current} = \frac{\text{charge}}{\text{time}}$$

We measure current in amperes (or **amps**) and charge in **coulombs**. A current of 1 amp means that 1 coulomb of charge is passing each second.

5 Electric current can only flow round a closed conducting loop called a **circuit**. A source of electrical energy (a cell, battery or mains power supply) makes the current flow. The current is the same at all points round the loop. The circuit transfers energy, for example from a battery to a bulb. But the current which carries the energy is the same before it gets to the bulb (at A) as it is after (at B).

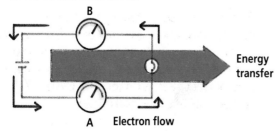

Energy transfer

Electron flow

6 You can vary the size of the current in a simple circuit by changing the battery **voltage** and the **resistance** in the circuit. The voltage (*V*) is the electrical push which drives the current round the circuit. It is measured in **volts**. The bigger the battery voltage, the bigger the current.

A light bulb, resistor or other device in the circuit has **resistance**. With any particular battery, the bigger the resistance, the smaller the current. Resistance (*R*) is measured in **ohms** (Ω).

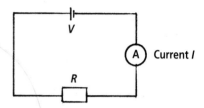

The circuit equation summarizes all this. It can be written as

$$V = IR$$
$$\text{or} \quad R = \frac{V}{I}$$
$$\text{or} \quad I = \frac{V}{R}$$

where V = voltage
R = resistance
and I = current

7 You can use the circuit equation to find the resistance of a component. You measure the current and voltage and from this you can calculate its resistance.

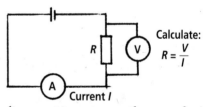

Calculate:
$$R = \frac{V}{I}$$

8 You often want to use more than one device in the same circuit, for example you might want to use two light bulbs or two resistors. You can connect them in different ways.

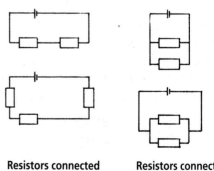

Resistors connected like this are **in series**.

Resistors connected like this are **in parallel**.

9 The devices in most of the circuits you meet in everyday life are connected in parallel. This is because, in parallel circuits

- if one device fails, the others continue to work
- you can switch each device on and off independently
- each device operates off exactly the same voltage, the voltage of the supply.

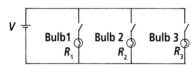

In this simple parallel circuit, you can turn each bulb on and off independently.

10 You can work out the total current drawn from the supply by several devices in parallel. To do this you need to look at each device separately.

Using the circuit equation, the current through bulb 1 above is $\frac{V}{R_1}$. You can work out the currents through bulbs 2 and 3 in the same way.

You can find the total current from the supply by adding the currents drawn by each bulb.

11 If you connect components such as resistors in series, you can find the total resistance by adding the resistances. And the voltages across the resistors add up to the voltage of the battery.

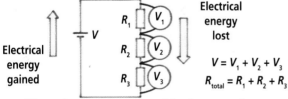

$$V = V_1 + V_2 + V_3$$
$$R_{total} = R_1 + R_2 + R_3$$

The voltage gives you an idea how much energy the electrons gain and lose as they flow round the circuit. Electrons gain electrical energy from the battery and lose it again in the resistors.

The voltage is the number of joules of energy gained or lost by each coulomb of charge.

$$\text{voltage} = \frac{\text{energy}}{\text{charge}}$$

$$V = \frac{E}{Q}$$

12 The energy transferred every second by an electrical circuit is called **power**. It depends on the current and voltage in the circuit.

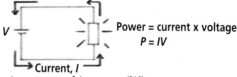

Power = current x voltage
$$P = IV$$

Power is measured in **watts** (W).

13 If you know the power rating of a mains device, such as an electric fire, you can use the power equation above to calculate the current it uses. The mains voltage is 240 V.

$$\text{current (in A)} = \frac{\text{power rating (in W)}}{240}$$

The cable and the fuse used for the fire must be capable of carrying this current. They must have a higher current rating than this.

14 Chemical reactions often give out energy. In **electric cells** chemical energy from reactions is transformed into electrical energy.

15 Electric cells have two electrodes made of metal or carbon. In the chemical reaction, one electrode (the negative electrode) loses electrons. These electrons flow along wires through the external circuit to the positive electrode. The chemical reaction at the positive electrode 'mops up' these electrons. Between the electrodes is the **electrolyte**, which might be an acid, an alkali or a salt solution. In **dry cells** the electrolyte is a paste.

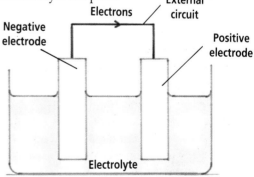

16 Two or more cells joined together make a battery. **Primary** cells cannot be recharged after they run down. You can recharge a **secondary** cell, such as a lead–acid cell, by passing electric current through it. This converts electrical energy back into chemical energy.

Thinking about

Electricity in the Home

1. What happens in a simple electric circuit?

Before you start reading this section, make sure you know the basic ideas about circuits (see *In Brief 4 and 5* on page 124).

A **current** is a flow of charge. A current needs a closed loop (**a circuit**) to flow around. The device in the circuit and the wires **resist** this current. The device could be a resistor, a heating coil, a lamp, or a motor. All of these have resistance.

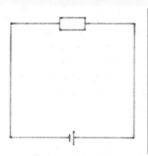 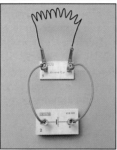

The current flows through the resistor and back to the cell. The resistor limits the current.

The size of the current depends on the **voltage** of the cell (measured in **volts**). The bigger the voltage, the bigger the current. The voltage of a battery (or of a mains power supply) tells you the strength of the electrical push it uses to drive current round the circuit.

The size of the current also depends on the **resistance** of the device. Resistance is measured in units called **ohms**. The bigger the resistance, the smaller the current.

The **circuit equation** summarizes all this. You can write it as

$$V = IR$$ where V = voltage

$$\text{or } R = \frac{V}{I}$$ R = resistance

$$\text{or } I = \frac{V}{R}$$ and I = current

This equation is very useful. If you know two of the three quantities (for example the current and resistance) you can use it to work out the third (the voltage).

Taking it further: Ohm's law

Resistance is defined as $\frac{V}{I}$. This simple definition grew out of an important experimental result first discovered by Georg Ohm, a German schoolmaster, in 1827. In Ohm's day there were no simple electrical meters like the voltmeters and ammeters we have today. It is easier for us to think about a modern form of Ohm's experiment!

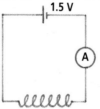 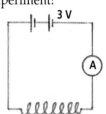

If you make a simple circuit using a 1.5 V cell and a coil of wire, you can measure the current with an ammeter.

If you increase the voltage to 3 V by adding a second cell, you find that the current doubles.

You can go on increasing the voltage by adding more cells. The table shows a typical set of results.

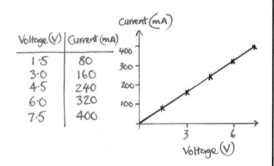

Voltage (V)	Current (mA)
1·5	80
3·0	160
4·5	240
6·0	320
7·5	400

The current increases in proportion to the voltage. If you double the voltage, you double the current. The same thing happens with almost all resistors.

The graph is a straight line. This means that $\frac{V}{I}$ is always the same for this piece of wire. We call $\frac{V}{I}$ the wire's **resistance.**

$$R = \frac{V}{I}$$

The unit of resistance is called the **ohm**, in recognition of Ohm's pioneering work.

2. How can you run several devices from the same supply?

Sometimes you want to use the same electrical supply to run several devices.

The batteries in this cassette player have to run the motor (to move the tape) *and* the amplifier (to produce the sound).

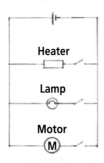

Both the lights in this room come on at the press of a single switch.

There are two basic ways of connecting more than one device to the same supply: in series or in parallel. (See *In Brief 8* on page 124.)

These three devices are connected in parallel.

The parallel arrangement has some important advantages.

Heater

Lamp

Motor

● What would happen if one of the devices broke down? The current can still flow through all the others. So you can easily see which one has stopped working. If the devices were connected in series, a broken one would stop everything working.

● Each device is controlled by its own switch. You can switch each one on and off independently.

● Each device is connected directly to the supply. So all the devices operate at the same voltage – the voltage of the supply.

If you run more than one mains device in your home at the same time, they are connected to the mains supply in parallel. You can switch each one on and off individually, without affecting the others. This parallel arrangement also means that all mains devices can be designed to run off the same voltage supply: 240 V.

Calculating currents

This parallel arrangement is really two simple circuits which share the same battery.

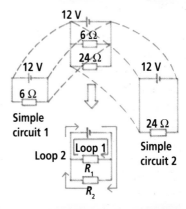

If you think of it as two separate simple loop circuits, it is easy to work out the currents through each resistor and the total current which the battery has to supply.

For loop 1
Current through $R_1 = \dfrac{12\,\text{V}}{6\,\Omega} = 2\,\text{A}$

For loop 2
Current through $R_2 = \dfrac{12\,\text{V}}{24\,\Omega} = 0.5\,\text{A}$

The total current
from the supply is $2\,\text{A} + 0.5\,\text{A} = 2.5\,\text{A}$

Taking it further: voltages in series circuits

If you set up a circuit with several devices in series, you can connect a voltmeter across each device in turn.

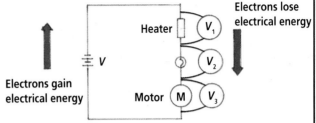

Electrons lose electrical energy

Heater V_1

V

V_2

Electrons gain electrical energy

Motor (M) V_3

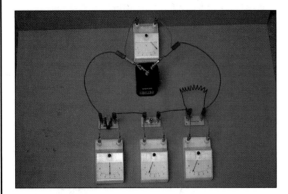

You would find that the voltages across the separate devices add up to the same as the battery voltage.

$$V = V_1 + V_2 + V_3$$

Up to now we have thought of voltage as an electrical push. A better idea of voltage is to think of the circuit as a system for transferring energy. As electrons pass through the battery, they pick up electrical energy. They then flow round the circuit and transfer this electrical energy into heating, or lighting the lamp, or running the motor. The total electrical energy gained from the battery must be equal to the total electrical energy used up by the devices.

The voltage of a battery tells you how much electrical energy it gives to every coulomb of charge which passes through the battery. A 3 V battery, for example, gives 3 J of electrical energy to each coulomb of charge that passes through it.

We define the volt as

1 volt = 1 joule per coulomb

Or, in general,

$$\text{voltage} = \frac{\text{energy}}{\text{charge}}$$

You can think of voltage as rather like height. The battery pumps charges up to a higher level. As they pass through each device they drop to a lower level, giving out some energy. The total energy gain must be the same as the total energy loss.

3. How do we use electrical power at home?

An electric circuit is a way of transferring energy.

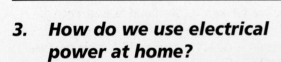

The electric circuit in this cycle lamp transfers chemical energy stored in the batteries into light energy.

The cables from power stations and the wiring in our homes transfer the chemical energy of the coal burnt in power stations into heating, lighting and running various devices.

When people pay their electricity bills, they pay for **electrical energy**. You have seen power ratings on devices. **Power** is the electrical energy the device transfers every second. Current, voltage and power are linked:

$$\text{power} = \text{current} \times \text{voltage}$$
$$P = IV$$

A high power device takes a high current *or* a high voltage, or both. Power is measured in watts (W).

4. How do we choose cables and fuses?

When a wire carries a current, it heats up. The bigger the current, the hotter it gets. Electrical heaters use this heating effect. But all electrical devices, not just heaters, get hot when they are switched on. The device and its cable are designed to cope with this. Cables have different ratings – they can carry different currents without heating up too much. So if you ever have to replace a mains cable, you need to know which rating to choose.

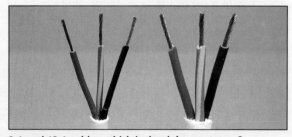

3 A and 13 A cable: which is the right one to use?

Sometimes an electrical device develops a fault, and the current through it becomes bigger than it should be. This makes the device overheat and can cause a fire. All electrical devices are fitted with a **fuse** to protect against this. The fuse is a 'weak link' – a thin piece of tin wire – connected in series with the device. If the current gets too big, the fuse heats up and melts. This cuts off the supply to the device.

3 A and 13 A fuse: which is the right one to fit?

The rating of a cable or a fuse tells you the maximum current it can safely carry. Cables and fuses are now supplied in two main ratings: 3 A and 13 A.

There is a very simple rule-of-thumb for choosing the right cable or fuse.

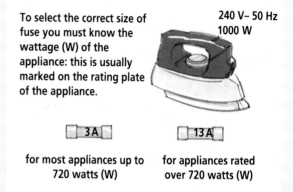

CHOOSING FUSES

To select the correct size of fuse you must know the wattage (W) of the appliance: this is usually marked on the rating plate of the appliance.

240 V– 50 Hz
1000 W

3 A — for most appliances up to 720 watts (W)

13 A — for appliances rated over 720 watts (W)

Wattage is another name for power.

The choice depends on the power rating (in watts) of the device. But why does the changeover come at 720 W?

You can use the power equation to work out the current through a device with a power rating of 720 W. Remember that the mains voltage is 240 V.

$$\text{power} = \text{current} \times \text{voltage}$$
$$720 \text{ W} = \text{current} \times 240 \text{ V}$$

So, $\text{current} = \dfrac{720}{240} \text{ A} = 3 \text{ A}$

If a device is rated at less than 720 W, its current is below 3 A, so a 3 A cable and fuse are enough. A device rated above 720 W draws more than 3 A from the mains and needs a 13 A cable and fuse.

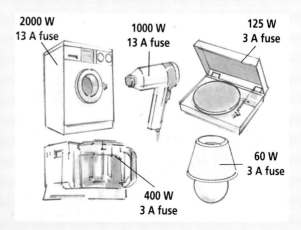

2000 W
13 A fuse

1000 W
13 A fuse

125 W
3 A fuse

400 W
3 A fuse

60 W
3 A fuse

Running several devices from the same supply

Ruth wants to run two lamps and a radio cassette from the same plug in her bedroom, using an extension block. She needs to work out the total current they will use, and decide if the extension block is safe. The devices all work independently, so she knows that they must be connected in parallel. The supply for all the loads is 240 V.

device	rating	current $(= \frac{P}{V})$
bedside lamp	60 W	0.25 A
desk lamp	100 W	0.42 A
radio cassette	24 W	0.10 A

The three devices are connected in parallel. So the total current from the wall socket is the sum of the three separate currents: 0.77 A. A mains extension block is designed to carry currents up to 13 A, so it is quite safe to run these three loads from it.

5. How do we produce portable electricity?

Most of the electricity you use comes from the mains. But sometimes you want a portable supply of electrical energy.

The batteries that run this Walkman are **electric cells**. They use the chemical energy of a reaction to produce electrical energy.

All electric cells have
- a **negative electrode** which releases electrons
- a **positive electrode** which accepts electrons
- a solution (an **electrolyte**) which allows **ions** (charged atoms) to flow through it.

This flow of electrons and ions is the electric current.

What happens inside a simple cell?

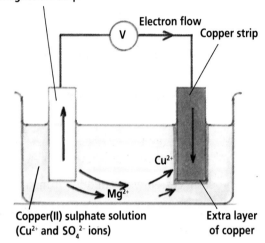

In this simple cell, pieces of magnesium and copper dip into copper(II) sulphate solution. The voltmeter shows that electrical energy is being produced. Magnesium atoms in the strip lose electrons to form Mg^{2+} ions which go into the solution.

$$Mg \rightarrow Mg^{2+} + 2e^-$$

These electrons move round to the copper strip where they attract Cu^{2+} ions from the solution. These ions pick up two electrons each, and become copper atoms which form a layer on the copper strip.

$$Cu^{2+} + 2e^- \rightarrow Cu$$

So as the current flows the magnesium strip gradually dissolves and extra copper is deposited on the copper strip.

This simple cell does not work very efficiently. After a short time its voltage drops, because the magnesium strip gets coated with copper. To make useful cells, we need a better design and choice of materials. *Looking at Cells and Batteries* on pages 120–21 tells you more about the different kinds of electric cells and how they are made.

Things to do

Electricity in the Home

Things to try out

1 The very first working battery was called Volta's pile. You can make a model of Volta's pile using copper coins and milk-bottle tops:

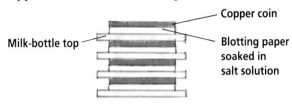

Milk-bottle top — Copper coin

Blotting paper soaked in salt solution

Investigate your model Volta's pile. Try to find out:

(a) what the voltage is between the top and bottom

(b) how the voltage changes as you change the number of coins and bottle tops in the stack

(c) how much current you can draw from the pile

(d) whether the current stays steady or drops off as time goes by.

2 A kite mark is a symbol which shows you that an electrical appliance has passed strict safety tests. You find the kite mark on the rating plate of the appliance.

BRITISH ELECTROTECHNICAL APPROVALS BOARD
PRODUCED TO B.S.3456

See how many appliances you can find at home which have kite marks.

3 With an ammeter and a voltmeter, you can measure the resistance of any electrical component. Draw the circuit you would use for this. Then use it to measure the resistance of a light-dependent resistance (LDR) in the light and in the dark. You should find quite a difference!

Things to find out

4 The three electrical units – the amp, the volt and the ohm – are named after three scientists: André Ampere, Alessandro Volta and Georg Ohm. Another important scientist who studied electricity was Benjamin Franklin. Find out as much as you can about each of these four – when they lived, what they did, and any other interesting facts about their lives and ideas.

5 Car batteries contain lead, which is a valuable metal. The lead can be recovered and recycled once the car battery is no longer usable.

Some small button cells contain mercury. Mercury is very poisonous and so mercury cells should be disposed of carefully when they have run down.

Find out as much as you can about the best way to dispose of old car batteries and mercury cells. Are there any other sorts of cells which should be disposed of carefully, and not just put into the dustbin?

Points to discuss

6 Imagine that one day you plug your radio into a wall socket and switch on, but nothing happens. Something is faulty – but what? Work out a flow diagram to give a safe and logical sequence for finding out what the problem is. A good way to begin is by making a list of all the things which might have gone wrong: from the radio itself, to the electricity supply to your street.

The flow chart has been started for you. Copy and complete it.

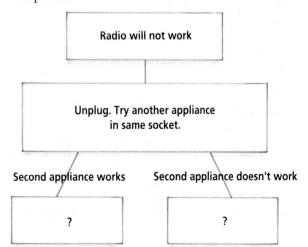

Radio will not work

Unplug. Try another appliance in same socket.

Second appliance works — ?

Second appliance doesn't work — ?

7 Daljit has a Walkman which needs two 1.5 V cells. A set of new alkaline ones cost £1.20 and lasts for about 6 hours of playing time. He is thinking of buying rechargeable cells (which cost £4 each) and a recharger (which costs £6). If he buys rechargeable cells, he cannot make up his mind whether he needs just two, or four, so that he always has two ready charged.

If he buys rechargeable cells, work out how long it will take before he begins to save money. Would you advise him to buy two rechargeable cells, or four, or to stick with disposable cells? Explain your advice.

Questions to answer

8 Find the unknown quantity, *V*, *I* or *R*, in each of these circuits.

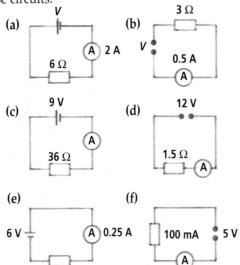

9 These car headlights are both switched on by a single switch. Draw a circuit diagram showing how the two headlights are connected to the switch and battery.

10 Copy the top circuit diagram in the right-hand column on page 127. Use three coloured pencils or pens to mark

(a) the wires where the current is 0.5 A

(b) the wires where the current is 2 A

(c) the wires where the current is 2.5 A.

11 All the meters in these circuits are voltmeters. Work out the readings on all the meters.

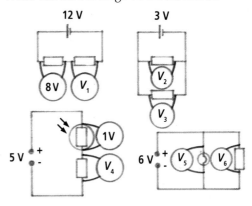

12 Work out the resistance of the filament inside each of these torch bulbs.

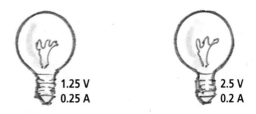

What power does each bulb produce (in W)?

13 Look back at *Thinking About 4* on page 130. Ruth now wants to unplug her radio cassette and plug in a 2000 W hair dryer. Is it safe for her to do this, or will it overload the extension block?

14 A torch contains two 1.5 V cells, costing 90p each. When switched on, the cells have to supply 0.25 A to light the torch bulb. A set of cells gives a total of 6 hours of use. Work out

(a) how many units of electricity the cells supply (1 unit is 1 kilowatt-hour)

(b) how much a unit of electricity from the cells costs.

One unit of mains electricity costs around 6.5 p. Do batteries provide cheap or expensive electricity?

Introducing

MINING AND MINERALS

Have you ever wondered where the materials come from to make the things you use every day? They all come from **natural resources**.
Some materials come from the Earth's crust, some from the sea, some from the air and some from living things. Useful materials in the Earth's crust are called **minerals**.

1 Make a list of all the objects in your school bag. Write down the materials they are made of.
2 Which of the objects on your list do you think are made from minerals?

Before we can extract and use minerals, we need to find them. Mining companies can use satellite photographs to show whether an area is worth mining for a particular mineral. This picture shows an area near Salt Lake City. The yellow area is desert, and the oval area (centre right) contains uranium bearing rocks.

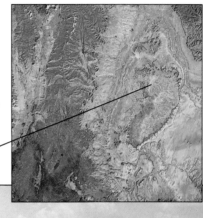

The next step is to mine the mineral. The rock which is dug from this massive copper mine in the USA contains the mineral copper pyrites ($CuFeS_2$).

Chemical processes are used to extract the useful part of the mineral. This is a copper smelter which converts the copper mineral into copper metal.

IN THIS CHAPTER YOU WILL FIND OUT

❚ how minerals differ

❚ how different chemical processes are used to extract the useful parts from different minerals

❚ why industry depends on the materials made from these minerals.

Looking at

How Do Minerals Differ?

Minerals which are used in jewels are called **gemstones**. They are valuable because

● they look attractive
● they are hard-wearing
● they are rare.

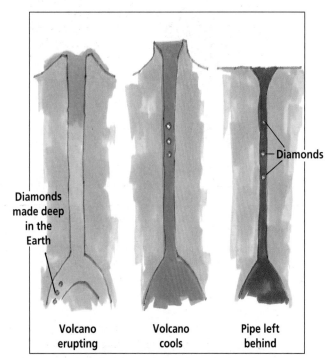

Diamonds made deep in the Earth

Diamonds

| Volcano erupting | Volcano cools | Pipe left behind |

Sometimes diamonds which have been formed deep in the Earth move upwards as part of a rock flow in a volcano. The 'pipe' of rock which is left can then be mined for diamonds. Some of the largest examples of these pipes are found in southern Africa.

The ruby in this ring is a mineral. It is mainly crystalline aluminium oxide. The red colour is caused by small amounts of chromium compounds.

Even colourless gemstones like diamonds look attractive – they reflect light in a way that makes them 'sparkle'.

They are hard because the atoms in the crystal are very strongly bonded together.

They are rare because they crystallize out of molten rock at very high temperatures and pressures. These high temperatures and pressures only occur deep inside the Earth. Over millions of years some of these gemstones have found their way nearer to the surface of the Earth by rock movements and volcanic activity. It is only when this happens that they can be mined – normally they are too deep.

1 Make a list of gemstones that you know.
2 What colour is each gemstone on your list?
3 Use the library to try to find out what the basic mineral is in each gemstone, and what causes the colour.
4 Why do you think gemstones are so expensive? Write a brief explanation.

Mining companies extract other minerals from the ground which go to make the products we use. Some minerals are useful in the form they are dug up in but others need to be chemically processed to obtain particular elements.

Bauxite
- Contains about 75% aluminium oxide (Al_2O_3) and 25% iron oxide (Fe_2O_3)
- Used as a source of aluminium metal
- Aluminium costs about £1200 per tonne

Gold crystals on quartz
- Gold occurs uncombined
- Gold costs about £10 000 000 per tonne

Rock salt
- Contains almost 100% sodium chloride (NaCl)
- Mostly used to make chlorine, sodium hydroxide and sodium carbonate

Limestone
- Contains almost 100% calcium carbonate ($CaCO_3$)
- Used as an ingredient in cement and glass
- Used for building and road making

Copper pyrites
- Contains less than 1% copper iron sulphide ($CuFeS_2$)
- Used as a source of copper metal
- Copper costs about £1500 per tonne

Galena
- Contains about 15% lead sulphide (PbS)
- Used as a source of lead
- Lead costs about £330 per tonne

Haematite
- Often over 85% iron oxide (Fe_2O_3)
- Used as a source of iron
- Iron costs about £80 per tonne

Use the information next to the pictures of minerals to answer the following questions.

5 Which of the minerals is often used in the form it is dug out of the ground?

6 Which mineral is the source of an important non-metal?

7 Aluminium is more abundant in the Earth's crust than iron but it is a more expensive metal. Suggest why this is so.

8 Aluminium is now being used rather than copper for overhead electricity cables. Suggest why this is a sensible policy.

Looking at

A Steelworks

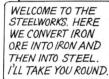

WELCOME TO THE STEELWORKS. HERE WE CONVERT IRON ORE INTO IRON AND THEN INTO STEEL. I'LL TAKE YOU ROUND.

THE BLAST FURNACE CONVERTS IRON ORE TO IRON. IT IS 30M HIGH. ON TOP OF IT IS THE MACHINERY FOR LOADING THE RAW MATERIALS.

THE DIAGRAM OF THE BLAST FURNACE SHOWS THE CHEMICAL REACTIONS GOING ON INSIDE IT. INFORMATION CARD No. 1 EXPLAINS HOW THESE REACTIONS CONVERT THE IRON ORE INTO IRON.

THESE PIPES TAKE AWAY THE WASTE GASES. THE GASES ARE USED FOR HEATING OTHER PARTS OF THE WORKS.

THESE CONVEYOR BELTS TAKE THE RAW MATERIALS UP TO THE TOP OF THE FURNACE.

THIS FURNACE WORKS 24 HOURS A DAY FOR 365 DAYS A YEAR, PRODUCING ABOUT 8000 TONNES OF IRON A DAY. AFTER ABOUT 3 YEARS THE LINING OF THE FURNACE WEARS OUT AND HAS TO BE RENEWED. THAT'S THE ONLY TIME THE FURNACE STOPS WORKING.

WOW!

Iron ore
coke
limestone

IRON and STEEL
INFORMATION CARD No. 1.

The chemical reactions in a blast furnace

Iron ore contains iron(III) oxide (Fe_2O_3). It goes in at the top of the furnace along with limestone ($CaCO_3$) and coke (C). A blast of hot air is forced in at the bottom of the furnace. This burns the coke to form carbon monoxide. This reaction is exothermic and gives out a lot of heat.

$$2C + O_2 \rightarrow 2CO$$

The carbon monoxide reduces the iron oxide to iron. The furnace is so hot the iron is liquid, so it sinks to the bottom of the furnace.

$$Fe_2O_3 + 3CO \rightarrow 2Fe + 3CO_2$$

The limestone is there to react with the impurities in the iron ore. First it is decomposed by the heat.

$$CaCO_3 \rightarrow CaO + CO_2$$

The calcium oxide then reacts with the impurities which are mainly sand (this is silicon dioxide, SiO_2). It forms a liquid called **slag** which floats on top of the liquid iron.

$$CaO + SiO_2 \rightarrow CaSiO_3$$
$$slag$$

$Fe_2O_3 + 3CO \rightarrow 2Fe + 3CO_2$
(iron)

$CaO + SiO_2 \rightarrow CaSiO_3$

$CaCO_3 \rightarrow CaO + CO_2$

$2C + O_2 \rightarrow 2CO$

THE BLA OF HOT A GOING IN HERE GIV IT ITS NA

Slag removed

Molten iron removed

IRON FROM THE BLAST FURNACE IS STILL IMPURE. IT CONTAINS SOME CARBON, SILICON AND PHOSPHORUS. WE REMOVE THESE IN THE BASIC OXYGEN FURNACE BY REACTING THEM WITH OXYGEN. THEY ARE OXIDIZED.

AS THE PURE IRON COOLS DOWN, WE PUT MEASURED AMOUNTS OF CARBON BACK IN TO MAKE DIFFERENT TYPES OF STEEL. STEEL IS MORE USEFUL THAN PURE IRON BECAUSE IT IS LESS BRITTLE. INFORMATION CARD No.2 GIVES SOME EXAMPLES OF DIFFERENT STEELS.

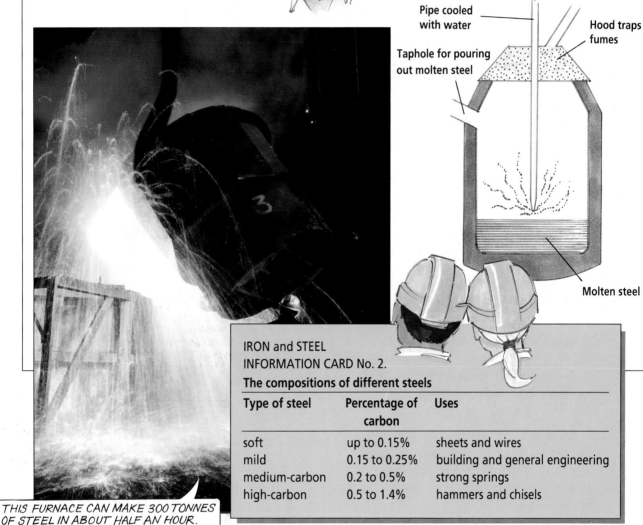

Oxygen

Pipe cooled with water

Hood traps fumes

Taphole for pouring out molten steel

Molten steel

THIS FURNACE CAN MAKE 300 TONNES OF STEEL IN ABOUT HALF AN HOUR.

IRON and STEEL INFORMATION CARD No. 2.

The compositions of different steels

Type of steel	Percentage of carbon	Uses
soft	up to 0.15%	sheets and wires
mild	0.15 to 0.25%	building and general engineering
medium-carbon	0.2 to 0.5%	strong springs
high-carbon	0.5 to 1.4%	hammers and chisels

1 Make a list of all the raw materials needed to convert iron ore into steel.

2 Make a list of all the chemical reactions which happen during the conversion.

3 Make a list of all the products which are formed along with the steel.

4 Draw a flow diagram to summarize how steel is produced from iron ore.

5 Suggest how increasing the percentage of carbon in steel affects its properties. Use Information Card No. 2 to help you.

6 This has been a very rapid tour of the steelworks. What questions would you like to ask? Draw up a list of questions you could ask a guide on a tour of a steelworks.

In brief

Mining and Minerals

1 Rocks are usually mixtures of substances. We call each pure substance in a rock a **mineral**.

2 A rock which contains a useful mineral is sometimes called an **ore**.

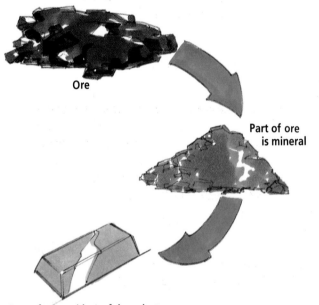

Ore

Part of ore is mineral

Part of mineral is useful product

Limestone is almost pure calcium carbonate. This means the rock which you dig out of the ground is pure mineral.

Copper ores usually contain less than 1% of the useful mineral. The rest of the rock is useless. These are called low grade ores.

3 Mineral resources are very valuable because many products which you use every day come from minerals. But they are a finite resource which means once they have been used they cannot be replaced.

4 A pure mineral is a single chemical compound which can be represented by a formula. For example

galena is PbS

limestone is $CaCO_3$

haematite is Fe_2O_3

These formulas tell you which elements the minerals contain. They also tell you the ratio of the number of atoms of each element.

5 Often a really useful mineral is buried deep underground. Geologists use **remote sensing techniques** to find these minerals rather than go to the expense of drilling holes.

These methods include

- measuring differences in the magnetic or conductivity properties of the layers of rocks under the surface

- doing a chemical analysis of minerals dissolved in rivers and lakes

- examining photographs taken by satellites.

6 The next step after locating a mineral is to decide whether to extract it. Extraction will involve mining or quarrying. A quarry is entirely on the surface. Mines sometimes go underground.
A mining company's decision whether to extract a mineral will be influenced by:

Scientific evidence	What grade is the ore?
Technical evidence	How easy is it to extract the ore?
Market predictions	What is the likely demand for the product?
Environmental and social factors	How will it affect the environment and the local community?

7 Some of the possible benefits and drawbacks of mining are:

Benefits	Drawbacks
More jobs	Spoils appearance of countryside
Produces useful materials	Harms plant and animal life
Creates wealth for company and community	Leaves waste to be disposed of

8 Extracting a metal involves the processes shown here.

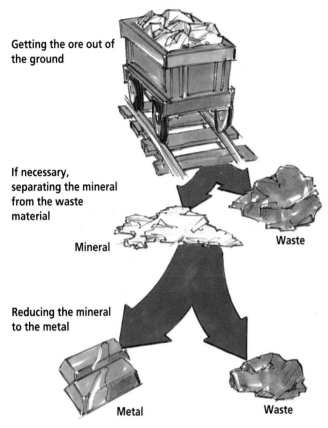

Getting the ore out of the ground

If necessary, separating the mineral from the waste material

Mineral

Waste

Reducing the mineral to the metal

Metal

Waste

Metals occur naturally in different forms.

● Iron and aluminium occur as oxides.

● Lead, zinc and copper occur as sulphides. These are first converted into the oxides, and then to the pure metal.

● Gold occurs uncombined with any other element.

● Sodium and magnesium occur as chlorides.

The method used to extract the metal depends on how reactive it is.

The less reactive metals copper, lead, iron and zinc are extracted by heating the oxide with a reducing agent such as carbon (coke).

The more reactive metals sodium, magnesium and aluminium are extracted by electrolysis.

9 During **electrolysis** an electric current is passed through an **electrolyte.**

Electrolytes are compounds which conduct electricity when they are molten or dissolved in water. They conduct because reactions take place at the **electrodes**.

For example, the electrolysis of molten sodium chloride would form sodium at one electrode

$$Na^+ + e^- \rightarrow Na$$

and chlorine at the other

$$2Cl^- - 2e^- \rightarrow Cl_2$$

10 More limestone is extracted from the ground than any other mineral. It is used direct from the quarry for building roads and for extracting iron. But for some purposes it is first heated. This converts it from calcium carbonate to calcium oxide (quicklime, or lime).

$CaCO_3$	$\rightarrow$	CaO	+	CO_2
calcium carbonate (limestone)	$\rightarrow$	calcium oxide (quicklime)	+	carbon dioxide

11 Halite, sometimes called rock salt, is sodium chloride. Chlorine and sodium hydroxide are made from it. They are used to manufacture various products including:

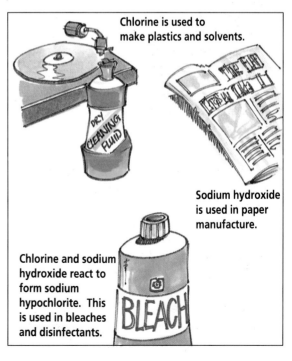

Chlorine is used to make plastics and solvents.

Sodium hydroxide is used in paper manufacture.

Chlorine and sodium hydroxide react to form sodium hypochlorite. This is used in bleaches and disinfectants.

Thinking about

Mining and Minerals

1. What do different methods of extracting metals have in common?

Look at this flow diagram. It asks several important questions. The answers determine what technique to use. Use the diagram to study the methods used for sodium, magnesium, aluminium, iron, lead, zinc and copper.

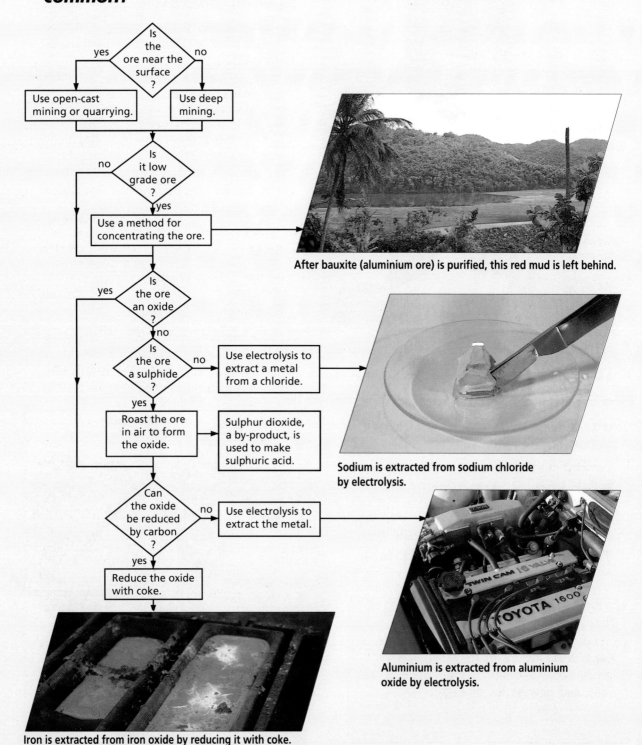

Is the ore near the surface?
- yes → Use open-cast mining or quarrying.
- no → Use deep mining.

Is it low grade ore?
- no →
- yes → Use a method for concentrating the ore.

After bauxite (aluminium ore) is purified, this red mud is left behind.

Is the ore an oxide?
- yes →
- no →

Is the ore a sulphide?
- no → Use electrolysis to extract a metal from a chloride.
- yes → Roast the ore in air to form the oxide. → Sulphur dioxide, a by-product, is used to make sulphuric acid.

Sodium is extracted from sodium chloride by electrolysis.

Can the oxide be reduced by carbon?
- no → Use electrolysis to extract the metal.
- yes → Reduce the oxide with coke.

Aluminium is extracted from aluminium oxide by electrolysis.

Iron is extracted from iron oxide by reducing it with coke.

2. How can low-grade ores be made more concentrated?

Whatever method a company uses to concentrate an ore it will work better if the ore is a powder rather than in big lumps. So the first stage is to crush the ore. The crushing and grinding uses energy and so adds to the cost of the final product.

Concentrating the ore means removing some of the waste material from it. So the method used depends on physical or chemical differences between the ore and the waste material. Here are two methods of concentrating ores.

Concentrating aluminium ore
Bauxite is aluminium ore. It contains up to 70% aluminium oxide. The main impurity is iron(III) oxide. This gives bauxite its red colour.

First sodium hydroxide solution is added to the crushed ore. This dissolves the aluminium oxide part of the ore.

A difference in the chemical properties of these two oxides is used to separate them. Aluminium oxide dissolves in sodium hydroxide solution but iron oxide does not.

Finally purified aluminium oxide is crystallized out of the solution

Then the mixture is filtered to separate the solution from the insoluble iron oxide.

This is called **chemical leaching**. A similar method is used in modern gold mining but a different chemical is used to dissolve the gold.

The problem is what to do with the iron oxide wastes. The photo on the opposite page shows the red mud which is produced.

Concentrating copper ore
Copper ores are very low grade. This means the percentage of mineral present is small. The mineral is separated from the waste material by **froth flotation.** This process uses a difference in their physical properties. →

Most of the mineral sticks to the froth and the waste material sinks. The more concentrated mineral is skimmed off the surface with the froth.

Because copper ores are low grade, large quantities of waste are produced. In the production of one tonne of pure copper about 500 tonnes of waste are produced.

The crushed ore is churned up with water and oils. A froth forms on the top.

3. What chemical reactions do we use to convert minerals to metals?

Useful minerals of metals are often

- chlorides (e.g. halite, NaCl)
- oxides (e.g. bauxite, Al_2O_3) or
- sulphides (e.g. galena, PbS).

If the mineral is a sulphide you first heat it in air to convert it to the oxide.

| lead sulphide | + oxygen | → | lead oxide | + | sulphur dioxide |

$$2PbS + 3O_2 → 2PbO + 2SO_2$$

To convert an oxide to a metal you need to remove oxygen.

metal oxide   -   oxygen   →   metal

**Adding oxygen is oxidation.
Removing oxygen is reduction.**

Zinc oxide, iron oxide, lead oxide and copper oxide can all be reduced by heating them with carbon. In industry coke is used as the source of carbon.

| lead oxide | + carbon | → | lead | + | carbon monoxide |

$$PbO + C → Pb + CO$$

You cannot reduce aluminium oxide with carbon so it is electrolysed to obtain the aluminium.

Taking it further: Extraction and reactivity.
You can link the method used to obtain a metal from its ore to its position in the reactivity series.

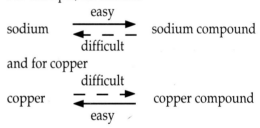

The more reactive a metal is the more it likes to form compounds. This means it is more difficult to reduce its compounds to the metal.

For example, for sodium

sodium $\xrightarrow{\text{easy}}$ sodium compound
    $\xleftarrow{\text{difficult}}$

and for copper

copper $\xrightarrow{\text{difficult}}$ copper compound
    $\xleftarrow{\text{easy}}$

So you can extract copper, lead, iron and zinc by heating the ores with carbon. But you have to use a more powerful method – electrolysis – for sodium, calcium, magnesium and aluminium.

---

4. What happens during electrolysis?

You extract more reactive metals by melting the mineral and passing an electric current through the liquid. This process is **electrolysis**.

Start with this simple example. Use it to build up an explanation.

This diagram shows two carbon rods sticking into some solid sodium chloride. The rods are called **electrodes**.

Solid sodium chloride will not conduct electricity.

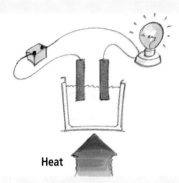

Sodium chloride which has been heated until it becomes a liquid will conduct electricity.

If the sodium chloride is dissolved in water, the solution will conduct electricity.

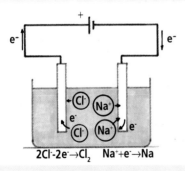

The battery is trying to push electrons around the circuit from the negative terminal to the positive. When the sodium chloride is solid the electrons do not flow through the wire. When it is liquid they do.

Sodium chloride contains particles of sodium and chloride. The particles can move around in the liquid and in the solution, but in the solid they cannot.

So you could suggest that
● the particles in the sodium chloride must be able to move around for it to conduct electricity.

While the liquid sodium chloride is conducting electricity,
● sodium metal is produced at the negative electrode and
● chlorine gas is given off at the positive electrode.
As soon as the current is switched off no more sodium or chlorine is formed.

If you leave the current on but let the sodium chloride cool down, it stops conducting when it solidifies and no more sodium or chlorine is formed.

So you know that
● when liquid sodium chloride conducts electricity, reactions occur at the electrodes.

Sodium chloride consists of
● sodium ions, with a relative charge of +1 (Na^+), and
● chloride ions, with a relative charge of -1 (Cl^-).
One electrode is connected to the negative terminal. Here sodium ions take electrons off the electrode and change to sodium atoms:
$$Na^+ + e^- \rightarrow Na$$
The other electrode is connected to the positive terminal. Here chloride ions give up electrons to the electrode:
$$Cl^- \rightarrow Cl + e^-$$
The neutral chlorine atoms combine to form chlorine gas:
$$2Cl \rightarrow Cl_2$$
So the reactions which take place at the electrodes have the effect of removing electrons from the negative electrode and giving them up to the positive electrode. This means that the battery can keep pushing electrons around the circuit – in other words a current flows.

Whenever electrolysis happens, one reaction occurs at the negative electrode taking electrons from the electrode. Another reaction occurs at the positive electrode, giving up electrons to the electrode.

5. How do we use electrolysis to extract metals?

Extracting aluminium from aluminium oxide

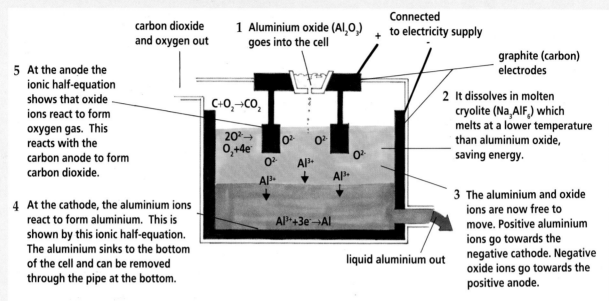

5 At the anode the ionic half-equation shows that oxide ions react to form oxygen gas. This reacts with the carbon anode to form carbon dioxide.

4 At the cathode, the aluminium ions react to form aluminium. This is shown by this ionic half-equation. The aluminium sinks to the bottom of the cell and can be removed through the pipe at the bottom.

carbon dioxide and oxygen out

1 Aluminium oxide (Al_2O_3) goes into the cell

Connected to electricity supply

graphite (carbon) electrodes

2 It dissolves in molten cryolite (Na_3AlF_6) which melts at a lower temperature than aluminium oxide, saving energy.

$C+O_2 \rightarrow CO_2$

$2O^{2-} \rightarrow O_2 + 4e^-$

O^{2-} O^{2-} O^{2-}

Al^{3+} Al^{3+}

Al^{3+} Al^{3+}

$Al^{3+} + 3e^- \rightarrow Al$

liquid aluminium out

3 The aluminium and oxide ions are now free to move. Positive aluminium ions go towards the negative cathode. Negative oxide ions go towards the positive anode.

When aluminium oxide is electrolysed, aluminium is formed at the negative electrode (cathode) and oxygen at the positive electrode (anode).

Extracting chemicals from salt (sodium chloride)
Electrolysing liquid sodium chloride forms sodium metal and chlorine gas. However, the industrial electrolysis of sodium chloride solution produces other important chemicals too. The electrolysis of sodium chloride dissolved in water produces chlorine, hydrogen and sodium hydroxide.

If you try this electrolysis in the laboratory you will find that
● chlorine is given off at the positive electrode, as you would expect, but
● hydrogen is given off at the negative electrode, *not* sodium.

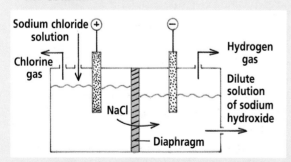

In the industrial process a porous diaphragm keeps the products apart.

Why is hydrogen given off at the negative electrode?
A solution of sodium chloride in water contains sodium ions (Na^+), chloride ions (Cl^-) and water molecules (H_2O).

The negative chloride ions are attracted to the positive electrode and converted to chlorine.

$$2Cl^- \rightarrow Cl_2 + 2e^-$$

At the negative electrode, water molecules take electrons off the electrode.

$$2H_2O + 2e^- \rightarrow H_2 + 2OH^-$$

Hydrogen gas is given off and hydroxide ions (OH^-) are left in the solution. The sodium ions are also left in the solution. This means that the water gradually becomes a solution of sodium hydroxide ($NaOH$) – a mixture of sodium ions (Na^+) and hydroxide ions (OH^-).

Salt and all three products made by electrolysing a solution of it are very important in industry - they are involved in the manufacture of many products.

6. Why do we quarry so much limestone?

We quarry more limestone than any other mineral. This is because it has useful properties, and there is a lot of it near the surface of the Earth. Because it is so readily available, it is cheap.

Limestone is almost pure calcium carbonate. It was formed millions of years ago from the remains of small creatures living in the sea. After being formed like this, some limestone was subjected to heat and pressure. This changed it into a much harder rock – marble. Marble and limestone are both used for buildings.

Magnesian limestone was used to build York Minster. Magnesian limestone contains magnesium carbonate as well as calcium carbonate.

Limestone also provides a cheap alkali. It is used in making iron (pages 136–7) and in making glass. The limestone is added directly to the furnaces and reacts with acidic substances.

It is often useful to convert limestone to **quicklime** (calcium oxide). This is done by heating it in a lime kiln. A lot of the quicklime is then converted to **slaked lime** (calcium hydroxide) by adding water to it.

Farmers use slaked lime to make their soil less acidic.

Eighty per cent of the limestone we extract is crushed and used as 'hard core' under roads. It is ideal for this because, besides being cheap, it is only slightly **porous**. Porous materials absorb water and would crack during frosty weather.

Crushed limestone is used to make a hard base under roads.

Taking it further: How does limestone provide an alkali?

When you heat calcium carbonate it decomposes. Carbon dioxide gas is given off and you are left with a white powder, calcium oxide.

calcium carbonate	$\rightarrow$	calcium oxide	+	carbon dioxide
$CaCO_3$	$\rightarrow$	CaO	+	CO_2

Adding water to calcium oxide causes a vigorous reaction. If you do it in the laboratory you will probably see some steam. The reaction is very **exothermic**. It gives out a lot of heat which converts some of the water to steam. The product of the reaction is calcium hydroxide which is called slaked lime.

water	+	calcium oxide	$\rightarrow$	calcium hydroxide
H_2O	+	CaO	$\rightarrow$	$Ca(OH)_2$

Calcium hydroxide is slightly soluble and forms a solution which turns litmus blue – it is alkaline.

Both calcium oxide and calcium hydroxide can be used as a cheap source of alkali.

7. How can relative atomic masses help people who work in the mining and mineral industry?

How much limestone?

This lorry contains 14 tonnes of quicklime.

George is in charge of a lime kiln. Here he produces quicklime from limestone. How does he know how much limestone to heat to make 14 tonnes of quicklime?

To predict the mass of product the reaction will form he first needs to know the balanced chemical equation for the reaction. The equation for the reaction in a lime kiln is:

$$CaCO_3 \rightarrow CaO + CO_2$$

This equation summarizes the reactants and products of the reaction in a shorthand form. But it also gives George the relative numbers of atoms of the different elements involved in the reaction.

If he knows the relative masses of the atoms of all of the elements in the equation he can use them to make predictions.

The relative mass of an atom of
        calcium is   40
        carbon is   12
        oxygen is   16

Therefore the relative mass of
$CaCO_3$ is $40 + 12 + (3 \times 16)$ = 100
CaO is $40 + 16$ =   56
CO_2 is $12 + (2 \times 16)$ =   44

He can now write the equation for the reaction like this:

$$CaCO_3 \rightarrow CaO + CO_2$$

Relative masses   100   56   44

This means that if George heats 100 tonnes of calcium carbonate, he will get 56 tonnes of calcium oxide (quicklime) and 44 tonnes of carbon dioxide.

Now George can solve the original problem. *Remember*: he is trying to find out how much limestone he needs to give 14 tonnes of quicklime – one lorry load.

He knows that:
56 tonnes of quicklime will be formed when 100 tonnes of limestone are heated

1 tonne of quicklime will be formed from $\frac{100}{56}$ tonnes of limestone.

Therefore, 14 tonnes of quicklime will be formed from $\frac{100}{56} \times 14 = 25$ tonnes of limestone.

George knows that he needs at least 25 tonnes of limestone to produce enough quicklime to fill the lorry.

How much iron?

Mira works for a mining company. She has found that an iron ore like the one in the photo contains about 64% of the mineral haematite (Fe_2O_3). This means that for every 1000 tonnes of ore she would expect 640 tonnes of iron(III) oxide. But how much iron would this contain?

The relative mass of an atom of
        iron is   56
        oxygen is 16

Therefore the relative mass of
    Fe_2O_3 is $(2 \times 56) + (3 \times 16) = 160$

This means that
160 tonnes of haematite will contain
112 tonnes of iron
1 tonne will contain $\frac{112}{160}$ tonnes of iron

640 tonnes will contain $\frac{112}{160} \times 640$

                          = 448 tonnes of iron

Every 1000 tonnes of the ore will contain 448 tonnes of iron.

This is an important step in the calculations the company must do before deciding whether or not to open a new mine, or close an existing mine.

Mining and Minerals

Things to try out

1 Look round your school for minerals. Have different minerals been used in the building? What minerals are there in the grounds?
  Find examples of
(a) minerals used in their natural, unchanged form
(b) minerals that have been processed in some way before being used.
  Use your list to make a mineral trail around the school that could be used by parents or other visitors.

Things to find out

2 Go to a local DIY warehouse. Find the price of different types of building materials, include any different types of sand, gravel and ballast. Which is the cheapest? Which is the most expensive?
  What reasons can you suggest for the differences in price?

Points to discuss

3 Suppose that there was a sudden world shortage of copper, so that the price of copper suddenly doubled. What effects might this have on people in Britain?

Questions to answer

4 Which of the substances below are
(a) made from a mineral which needs virtually no processing
(b) made from a mineral which has to be purified and processed before it can be used
(c) not made from a mineral?

| Zinc | Gravel | Bread | Brick |
| Glass | Iron | Polythene | Wood |

5 Look at *Thinking About 5* on page 144.
  What products would you expect if you passed electricity through potassium bromide solution? Write ionic half-equations to explain your answer.

6 This question is about extracting zinc from zinc oxide. The object is to work out the mass of zinc that can be extracted from 1 tonne of zinc oxide.

Zinc is extracted by heating zinc oxide with coke (carbon).

zinc oxide + carbon → zinc + carbon monoxide

$$ZnO + C \rightarrow Zn + CO$$

(a) What are the relative masses of (i) zinc oxide, (ii) carbon, (iii) zinc, (iv) carbon monoxide involved in this reaction?
(Relative atomic masses: Zn = 65, O = 16, C = 12)

(b) Copy and complete:

____tonne of zinc oxide produce ____tonne of zinc

(c) From (b) work out the mass of zinc that could be obtained from 1 tonne of zinc oxide.

7 Chromium can be prepared by reducing chromium oxide with aluminium. The chromium oxide and aluminium are heated together. The object of this question is to find out the mass of aluminium needed to react with 1 tonne of chromium oxide.

chromium + aluminium → chromium + aluminium
  oxide   oxide
$$Cr_2O_3 + 2Al \rightarrow 2Cr + Al_2O_3$$

(a) What are the relative masses of
(i) chromium oxide, (ii) aluminium,
(iii) chromium, (iv) aluminium oxide involved in this reaction?
(Relative atomic masses: Cr = 52, O = 16, Al = 27)
(b) Copy and complete:

____tonne of chromium oxide react with
____tonne of aluminium

(c) From (b), work out the mass of aluminium that reacts with 1 tonne of chromium oxide.

8 Look at a periodic table.
(a) In which part of the table do you find
  (i)   the most reactive metals
  (ii) the most reactive non-metals
  (iii) the metals that are most commonly used for construction
  (iv) metals that are often used as catalysts?
(b) Give the symbols of six elements that occur commonly in the Earth's crust.

9 Use the information on this data card for copper, and the *Thinking About* section of this chapter to help you.

COPPER

Main mineral : copper pyrites

Formula : CuFeS$_2$

Grade of ore : copper ores contain typically less than 1% of copper.

Method of mining : usually open cast – a single pit can be enlarged at the rate of 2 million tonnes per week.

Method of extraction : the ore is concentrated by froth flotation, then smelted to form impure copper by mixing with sand and 'blasting' with air, and then the impure copper is purified electrolytically.

Production: world production is about 8 million tonnes of which about 7 million is primary copper extracted from the ore and 1 million is secondary copper made by refining scrap copper.

The production and demand in thousands of tonnes for several countries is given in the table.

Country	Supply		Demand
	Metal mined as ore	Metal produced	
USA	1150	1560	2000
UK	–	180	400
Zaire	500	–	–

Uses :		
	electrical equipment	58%
	plumbing and roofing	19%
	machinery	17%
	other including coins	6%

(a) Draw a pie chart for the uses of copper. Choose one of the uses and discuss the advantages and disadvantages of its being a source of scrap copper.

(b) Suggest which of the countries in the table

(i) does not mine any ore

(ii) exports most of its copper

(iii) mines ore but still needs to import some copper.

(c) Suggest what environmental problems are likely to occur during the mining and extraction of copper.

(d) During the smelting process the ore is reacted with oxygen. Which gas would you expect to be produced during this process and what other important chemical could be made from the gas? What environmental problems would occur if the gas was allowed to escape into the atmosphere?

(e) The electrolytic method for purifying copper can be copied in a laboratory using the apparatus in the diagram.

At the positive electrode copper atoms dissolve by forming copper ions, Cu^{2+}. At the negative electrode copper ions are converted to copper atoms which are deposited on the electrode.

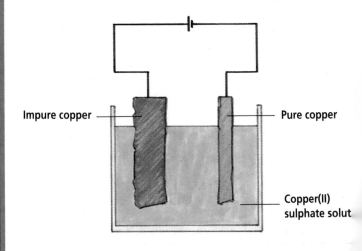

Impure copper — Pure copper — Copper(II) sulphate solut

(i) Write ionic half-equations for the changes which occur at the electrodes.

(ii) Explain how these two changes result in the conversion of impure copper into pure copper.

Introducing

BALANCING ACTS

Your **environment** is your surroundings. Any environment is made up of living and non-living things. Each part of an environment can affect any other part. All the parts of an environment are delicately balanced with one another.

Hillside meadow with wild flowers

Rainforest in Rwanda, central Africa

Rainforest in Brazil being cleared to build a road

Cultivated meadow growing wheat

1 How have people affected the environmental balance in these photographs?

2 Give two more examples where people have changed the balance of an environment. Try to choose one example where you think the effect is good, and one where it is bad.

IN THIS CHAPTER YOU WILL FIND OUT

▌ how organisms are balanced in an environment

▌ how people change the environment

▌ how changes in the environment can upset the balance of organisms

▌ how scientists can monitor the environment, so that they can detect changes early

▌ how we can protect the environment.

Looking at

A Blue Pearl in Space

The first astronauts were launched into space in the 1960s. They were the first people to see the planet Earth as a whole. They were astonished by the beauty of the planet and described it as looking like 'a blue pearl in space.'

The astronauts sent back descriptions of our planet that started people thinking differently. Up until then the Earth had seemed very large. Suddenly, it seemed very small with resources which were limited – they would run out sooner or later, and could not be renewed.

Looking at the world from space made people realise how special the planet was. All its different parts were not separate, but together made up the whole planet. All the parts of the planet affected one another. People suddenly realised how important the environment was. The Earth has its own finely balanced cycles, and if we upset them the results could be catastrophic.

> 1 'A world of limitless potential'
> 'A world of limited resources'
> Write a poem that shows the difference
> between these two views of the world.

Recycling oxygen

Plants use sunlight to make sugars and oxygen from carbon dioxide and water. So without plants we would soon run out of oxygen. Plants recycle our waste carbon dioxide back to the oxygen we need to breathe. Microscopic plants in the ocean supply nearly three-quarters of the oxygen in the atmosphere. Some of the oxygen in the upper atmosphere is turned into ozone, which forms a layer around the Earth. This layer protects us from harmful ultraviolet radiation.

Recycling water

The temperature of the Earth is high enough to evaporate water continually from the seas. Convection currents in the atmosphere move water vapour around the Earth, and as it cools it falls as rain. Water is essential for life, and the water cycle constantly distributes it over most of the planet.

Recycling carbon dioxide

Plants use up the waste carbon dioxide we pump into the atmosphere. Carbon dioxide is produced when things burn, and also when living things respire. Microscopic plants living in the seas allow the oceans to act as 'sinks' for much of the carbon dioxide produced. Even so, recent human activity has caused a build-up of carbon dioxide in the atmosphere. There is more about the effects of this on pages 104–5.

Recycling minerals

All living things need certain minerals, such as nitrates, phosphates and calcium, to grow and function healthily. Plants absorb these from the Earth. There is only a limited supply of these on the Earth, but they do not run out because they are continuously recycled. This recycling is done by decomposers, which are often microbes, living in the soil or in shallow lakes and seas. They feed on the bodies of dead organisms, causing decay and allowing the useful minerals to be absorbed by plants.

What do you think would happen if

2 the temperature of the planet went up and killed all the microscopic plants in the oceans

3 soil and water became so polluted by industrial waste that decomposers could no longer survive

4 the protective ozone layer in the atmosphere was destroyed

5 the temperature of the planet went down so that very little water evaporated?

---

6 Use the information on this page and any other ideas to produce a poster showing people that the Earth is one large environment, and why they should try to protect it.

Looking at

Fishing

Finding fish

Most of the fish we eat come from the sea.

> 1 Make a list of the different types of fish you have eaten.
> 2 Think of some ways of dividing them into groups.

Fish are not evenly distributed in the sea. Some parts of the sea contain very few fish, while others have huge amounts. It all depends on the balance of the ocean environment. Fish are part of a food chain, just like other organisms. One typical food chain is shown in the diagram.

In a particular region of the sea, if the food chain is left undisturbed, a balance would be reached. Each consumer would reach maximum numbers depending on how much food was available.

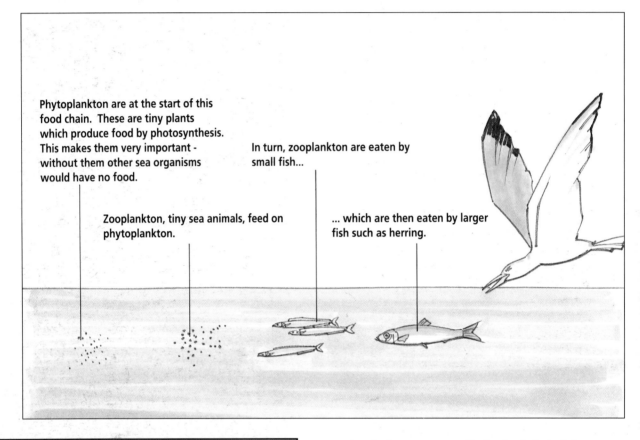

Phytoplankton are at the start of this food chain. These are tiny plants which produce food by photosynthesis. This makes them very important - without them other sea organisms would have no food.

Zooplankton, tiny sea animals, feed on phytoplankton.

In turn, zooplankton are eaten by small fish...

... which are then eaten by larger fish such as herring.

> 3 Why are phytoplankton important? What can they do that other organisms in the chain cannot?
> 4 What would happen to the herring if the phytoplankton population fell?

If people affect any part of this chain then a new balance will have to be found which takes this effect into account.

If the sea becomes polluted and this affects the growth of phytoplankton then this would affect the numbers of all the organisms higher in the chain.

An obvious way we affect a food chain is by becoming part of it ourselves. We catch fish to eat but we do not depend entirely on fish to survive.

If we are careful about how many fish we catch then the food chain will reach a new balance and all will be well. But if we catch too many fish and the population of the fish begins to decline then that will have a serious effect on the food chain as well as on our food supply.

> 5 Suggest what the effects could be of reducing the herring population in a particular area.

Catching fish

The technology of fishing has improved over the years. People have realised that fish can be a cheap source of food, so they have designed more efficient ways of finding fish and catching them.

However, this does not mean they always catch more fish.

These figures show what happened to herring fishing in the Norwegian Sea in the 1960s.

Year	Number of fishing boats	Total catch (tons)
1963	16	32 419
1964	195	189 668
1965	284	604 754
1966	334	454 900
1967	326	335 071

(Source:Burd, Sea Fisheries Research)

6 Calculate the number of herring caught per fishing boat and display the results as a graph to show what happened to the catches in the period 1963–67. Describe the changes during this period.

7 Why do you think the number of fishing boats increased up until 1966? Why do you think they decreased in 1967?

The herring population had been **overfished.** Too many fish were caught, so the remaining fish could not produce enough young to replace them. The total population went down.

The balance for a fish population can be summed up as follows:

$$\text{Stock of fish} = \text{Stock of fish} - \text{fish} + \text{fish} - \text{fish}$$
(at end of year)   (at beginning   dying   born   caught
of year)

If the fish stock is the same at the beginning and the end of the year, the population is balanced. If the number of fish caught and dying goes above the number of fish born, the balance is destroyed.

If overfishing is not checked, whole populations can be wiped out.

Seventy years ago there was a huge herring fishing fleet based at Yarmouth. The herring population in the North Sea was overfished and the population declined. There were no longer enough herring for the boats to catch, and the enterprise was abandoned.

8 When catching fish in a natural environment we have to be careful about the effect this has on the fish population and the food webs that they are involved in. An alternative is to create an artificial environment and farm the fish. Write an article for a magazine which discusses whether or not fish farming is a good idea.

In brief

Balancing Acts

1 The environment contains many different types of plants and animals. Human activity can change the environment. This affects the other living things on the Earth – what kinds there are, where they live and how many there are.

2 Human activity can kill organisms, or even whole species. We *can* manage the environment to encourage and protect living things, instead of killing them.

Food and other goods have to be transported from place to place.

Houses are needed for people to live in.

Fertilizers improve crop yields so provide more food.

3 We need to collect information about the environment so that we can judge whether it is changing. Sensors connected to computers are an important tool in this task.

4 The environment is very complex. Improving one part of the environment can have a harmful effect on another part. Modern farming has become very efficient thanks to agrochemicals, such as fertilizers and pesticides, but these need to be handled carefully. For example, fertilizers may improve crop growth, but they can also pollute rivers and lakes if not used properly.

5 Changes in the environment can affect how quickly populations of organisms grow. The total population that an environment can support is limited by factors such as space, food and light.

6 There is a limited amount of material available on the Earth. Important materials are used again and again, as part of a **cycle**.
Energy cannot be recycled. It is transferred between organisms as part of a **chain**.

7 Organisms can be classified as **producers** or **consumers**. Green plants **produce** food by photosynthesis. Animals then **consume** this food, either by eating plants or by eating animals that have eaten plants.

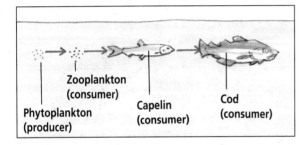

Zooplankton (consumer)
Phytoplankton (producer)
Capelin (consumer)
Cod (consumer)

8 Animals that eat other animals are called **predators**. The animals that they eat are called **prey**. You can draw a **food chain** to show the relationship between predators and prey. **Food webs** are more complicated and show the relationships between different food chains.

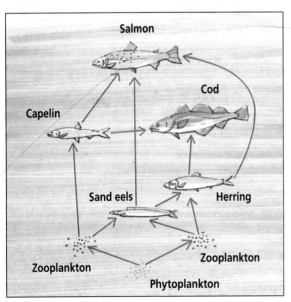

Salmon
Cod
Capelin
Sand eels
Herring
Zooplankton
Zooplankton
Phytoplankton

9 All the animals in a food web get their energy from the Sun, via a food chain. Not all the energy which enters a food chain is transferred to the final predator. Energy is used in the chain by the other organisms, for example, for moving, excreting or reproducing (see *Thinking About 6*). You can draw pyramids **of numbers** and **pyramids of biomass** to represent feeding relationships which take account of this energy use.

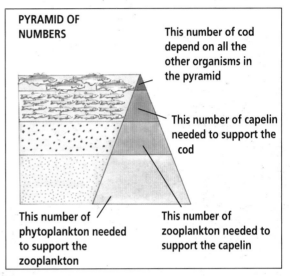

PYRAMID OF NUMBERS
This number of cod depend on all the other organisms in the pyramid
This number of capelin needed to support the cod
This number of phytoplankton needed to support the zooplankton
This number of zooplankton needed to support the capelin

10 The oceans are a rich resource of food, but we need to manage fishing carefully. If we upset the balance, stocks of fish may be wiped out.

11 The planet Earth is a finite resource. It is made up of different environments that all affect one another. We need to manage all these environments carefully to avoid destroying them. We may have to pass laws to protect the environment.

Thinking about

Balancing acts

1. What is an environment?

Our environment is what surrounds us. It is made up of living and non-living parts. The organisms in any environment depend on both the non-living parts and the other living organisms. There is a balance between them.

The word 'environment' is often used in a general sense. A more precise term for the organisms and non-living factors in an area is an **ecosystem**.

The organisms in an **ecosystem** can be grouped into four types:

Producers

These are **green plants**. They transfer some of the energy in sunlight into food – they store it as chemical energy. They **produce** the food that the rest of the ecosystem uses.

Primary consumers

These are **herbivores** – animals which feed on plants and so consume the food the plants have produced.

Secondary consumers

These are **carnivores** – animals which feed on other animals. They also consume food produced by plants, but at a second stage. Secondary consumers are **predators**. The animals that they eat are their **prey**.

Decomposers

These organisms obtain their energy by breaking down the remains of dead animals and plants. They are a very important part of the ecosystem, as they help to recycle essential chemicals.

This diagram shows how all these types of organisms interact.

Trees are producers – they produce food using sunlight.

This caterpillar is a primary consumer – it eats green plants.

This nightingale is a secondary consumer – it eats the caterpillar which eats green plants.

This fungus is a decomposer – it lives off dead organisms.

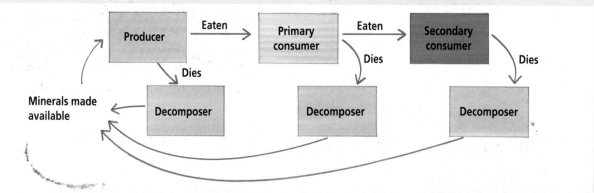

2. How can we protect the environment?

We need to protect the environment because our lives and the lives of all other organisms depend on it. But actually doing this is not easy, because everything we do affects the environment in some way.

We need to know more about the environment in order to protect it. The more we know about the environment, the sooner we can spot changes and do something about them. This monitoring is discussed in *Thinking About 3*.

Some changes in the environment may not be obvious at first. To avoid damaging the environment over a long period of time it may be necessary to have rules and regulations. It is important to explain to people why the regulations are necessary, otherwise they will ignore them.

As all environments have an effect on one another, different countries have to cooperate in protecting the global environment. Scientists and governments often disagree about which factors to monitor and what levels are acceptable. They need to find a common view if laws about the environment are to be effective.

3. How can we monitor the environment?

We need to **monitor** (watch) the environment to detect any changes that might be taking place. In particular, we need to detect pollution early to prevent destructive changes.

There are many factors that are delicately balanced in the environment. Dissolved chemicals such as nitrates and phosphates, pH, temperature and oxygen levels all need to be monitored. And one measurement is not sufficient – they need to be measured regularly and accurately.

The Greenpeace ship *Rainbow Warrior* monitors dolphin deaths

Samples of river water are tested for pollution

The air is monitored on this London rooftop

Computers are useful tools for monitoring the environment. By connecting sensors to a computer, scientists can record accurate measurements at regular intervals. Some sensors are **remote** – they are not attached to a computer by wires, but they transmit the data to a central laboratory. Here a computer stores the data and prints it off when required.

This small computer prints the results of roadside pollution monitoring on site

4. *How do populations grow?*

Most populations in an environment are **stable**. They are not getting bigger or smaller, but are balanced. The number of new individuals born is balanced by the number dying of old age or being eaten by predators.

If you set up a fresh ecosystem, such as an empty pond, and introduced a few individuals of one species such as duckweed, the population would not change very much at first. The individuals need to grow before they are old enough to reproduce so only a few will reproduce at a time. Section A on the graph shows this stage.

After a while more individuals start to reproduce, and the number of individuals begins to increase dramatically. This stage is shown by section B on the graph.

Eventually, the population stabilizes. The number of new individuals is the same as the number of individuals dying, so there is no overall change in the population number. This stage is shown by section C on the graph. The population has reached its limit for that environment. The limiting factor may be lack of space, lack of food, too much waste, or other factors.

Plants take some time to establish in a new pond like this one in Telford.

Eventually an equilibrium is reached and the pond supports the maximum number of individuals, as in this pond in Sussex.

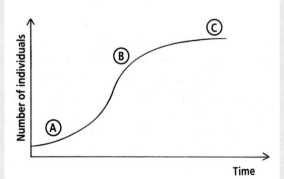

The duckweed population gets bigger until it reaches a limit.

5. How does energy flow through an ecosystem?

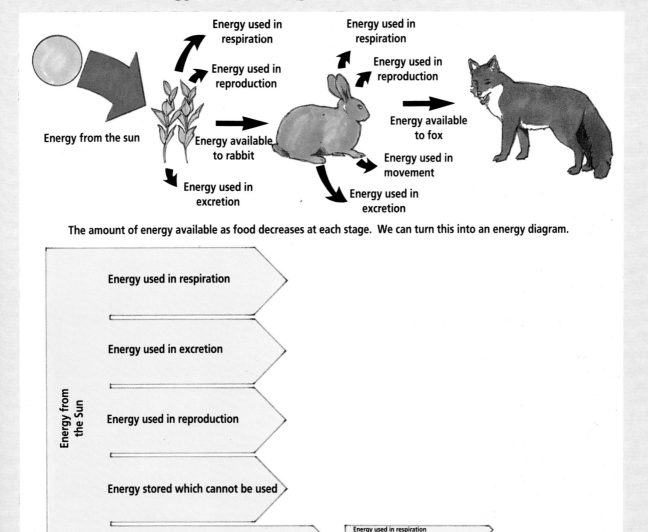

The amount of energy available as food decreases at each stage. We can turn this into an energy diagram.

Producers are the only organisms that can use energy to make their own food. Most producers are green plants which transfer the energy in sunlight into chemical compounds. (There are also some bacteria which can use chemical energy to produce food.)

The chemical compounds produced in photosynthesis are passed along a food chain. The compounds pass from one organism to another by the process of feeding. Each different feeding stage is known as a **trophic level**. Between 80% and 90% of the energy gained from feeding is used at each stage – it is not passed on to the next stage. This is because the organism has to feed, respire, excrete, reproduce and move. Animals do a great deal of moving, so they consume a great deal of energy.

Taking it further: What are trophic levels?

Trophic levels are the stages in a food web. The first trophic level consists of all the producers in an environment. The second trophic level contains all the different primary consumers, and the third trophic level is all the animals that feed on the primary consumers. At each trophic level the amount of energy available for transfer gets smaller.

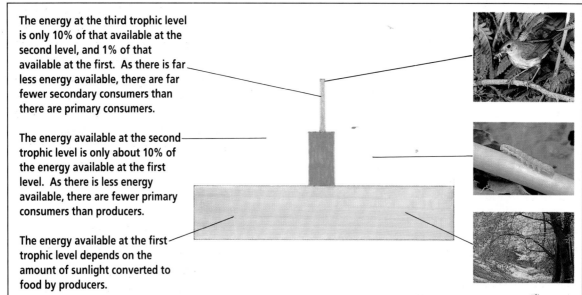

The energy at the third trophic level is only 10% of that available at the second level, and 1% of that available at the first. As there is far less energy available, there are far fewer secondary consumers than there are primary consumers.

The energy available at the second trophic level is only about 10% of the energy available at the first level. As there is less energy available, there are fewer primary consumers than producers.

The energy available at the first trophic level depends on the amount of sunlight converted to food by producers.

You can show these decreasing numbers in a **pyramid of numbers**. The number of organisms at each trophic level of a food chain is represented as a layer. The layers form the shape of a pyramid.

However, a pyramid of numbers does not take into account the size of the organisms. One oak tree may support thousands of insects and many birds that eat them. One cow may support many thousands of insects such as ticks.

A **pyramid of biomass** solves this problem. Each layer represents the dry weight of the organisms in the food chain. This gives a more accurate picture of the flow of energy through the food chain, but it is much more difficult to work out. Instead of just counting organisms, you have to collect them, dry them (which means killing them) and weigh them.

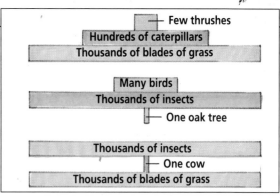

Few thrushes
Hundreds of caterpillars
Thousands of blades of grass

Many birds
Thousands of insects
One oak tree

Thousands of insects
One cow
Thousands of blades of grass

Some pyramids of numbers do not look like pyramids!

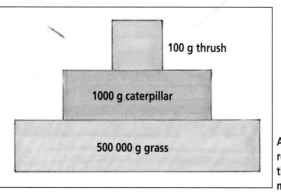

100 g thrush

1000 g caterpillar

500 000 g grass

A pyramid of biomass represents energy flow through a food chain more accurately.

Things to do

Balancing Acts

Things to try out

1 Find a tree growing near a busy road, and a tree of the same species growing in a park or garden.

Make a list of the differences you can observe between the two trees.

Are there any differences that could be due to pollution?

What other factors could explain the differences?

Things to find out

2 Look at collections of local newspapers in your local library to find out about environmental issues in your area in the last few years.

Some examples to look out for include

(a)   new road schemes

(b)   housing developments

(c)   landscaping of derelict sites.

What issues were at stake? What were the views of different groups of people? What was the outcome?

Points to discuss

3 A theme park wants to add some new fairground rides to its attractions. The owners think the theme park will lose popularity and business will suffer if they don't keep developing the park.

They plan to add the rides at the edge of the park, near some houses. They could put them in the centre, but this would spoil their 'wild garden' which provides a habitat for many plants and animals, as well as being popular with the visitors.

The local people are against the idea because they think the rides will be too near their houses. They think they will be noisy and spoil the view.

Any environment is a delicate balance. Where do you think the balance lies in this issue?

Questions to answer

4 (a)   Use the food web to predict the effect of clearing the ferns from the area.

(b)   Owls regurgitate the parts of animals they eat which cannot be digested. These are called owl pellets. A girl collected some owl pellets and found that they mostly contained the bones of mice. Use the food web to put forward possible explanations for this observation.

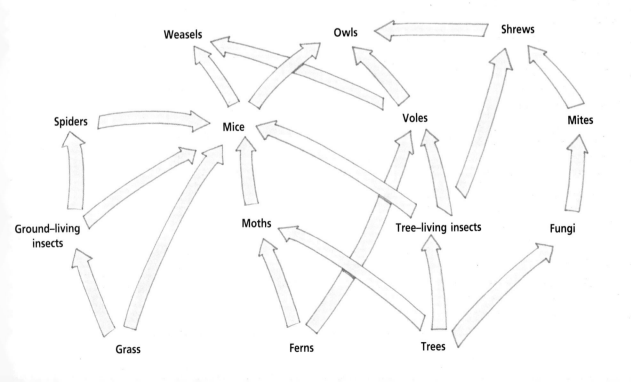

5 This graph shows how the human population has grown over the last 10 000 years.

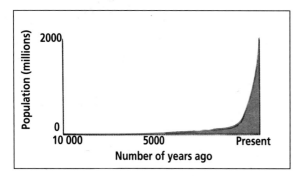

(a) Compare this with the duckweed population growth graph on page 158. What differences can you see? What similarities are there?

(b) How do you think the human population will change over the next 100 years? (Use the graph on page 158 to help your prediction.)

6 The chart below shows what happens to a stream when it is polluted with sewage. It shows how the levels of chemicals and the numbers of living things change as the sewage flows down the stream. There is a lot of oxygen dissolved in the water before the sewage enters, but the level of oxygen drops immediately the sewage is added. The oxygen level builds up again in stages further downstream.

(a) Describe what happens to the levels of nitrate and phosphate.

(b) What happens to the numbers of bacteria and midge larvae?

(c) How do the types of animals change as the oxygen level changes?

(d) If you were sampling a river, what animals would indicate that the water was badly polluted?

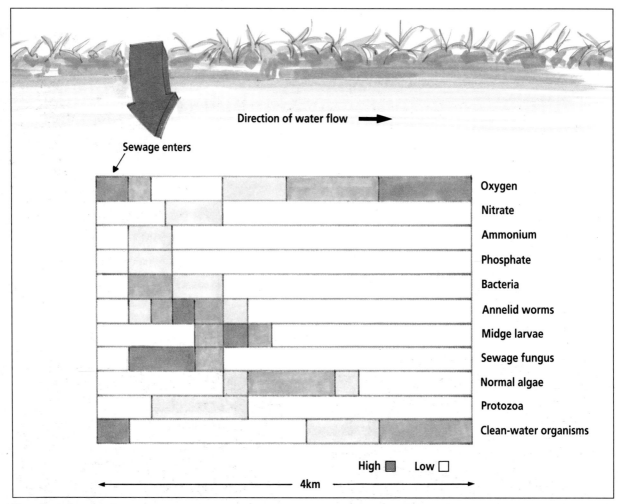

The effect of sewage on a stream.

Introducing
COMMUNICATING INFORMATION

What makes humans different from other organisms? For one thing, we can communicate with each other in a very sophisticated way. This means we can share knowledge.

We use **codes** to communicate, such as words which we hear and signs which we see. Sometimes we convert information into an electrical code or a code in patterns of light to transmit it over long distances.

DIM MYNEDIA
NO ENTRY

1 The picture shows some ways of communicating. Which of your senses does each method use? Make a list.
2 Add to your list the type of code which each method uses. Choose from
   - shape patterns
   - sound patterns
   - light patterns
   - electrical codes.

IN THIS CHAPTER YOU WILL FIND OUT
▌ how you speak and hear
▌ how you see
▌ about lenses and light
▌ about light and colour
▌ about the electromagnetic spectrum.

Looking at

From There to Ear

If you want to speak to someone a long distance away, there are two things you can do.
- You can send your message along a wire.
- You can use waves from the invisible electromagnetic spectrum to carry your message.

1 Make a list of communication devices you can think of that use wires.
2 Make a list of devices that use waves to carry messages.

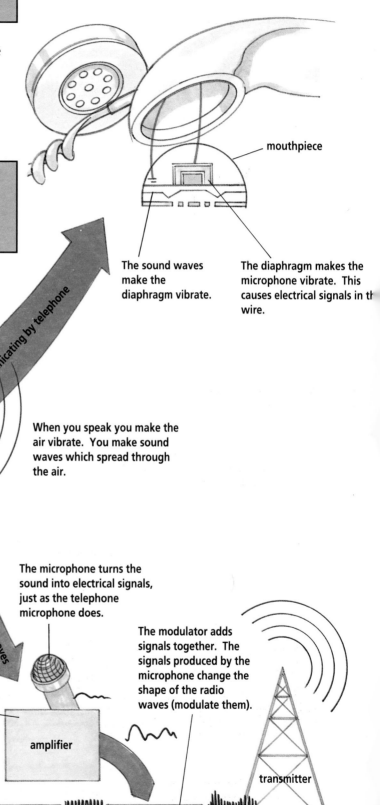

mouthpiece

The sound waves make the diaphragm vibrate.

The diaphragm makes the microphone vibrate. This causes electrical signals in the wire.

Communicating by telephone

When you speak you make the air vibrate. You make sound waves which spread through the air.

Communicating by radio waves

The microphone turns the sound into electrical signals, just as the telephone microphone does.

The modulator adds signals together. The signals produced by the microphone change the shape of the radio waves (modulate them).

The amplifier makes these signals bigger.

amplifier

The amplifier makes the radio waves bigger.

transmitter

The oscillator produces radio waves. Radio waves can travel over long distances.

oscillator

amplifier

modulator

modulated radio wave

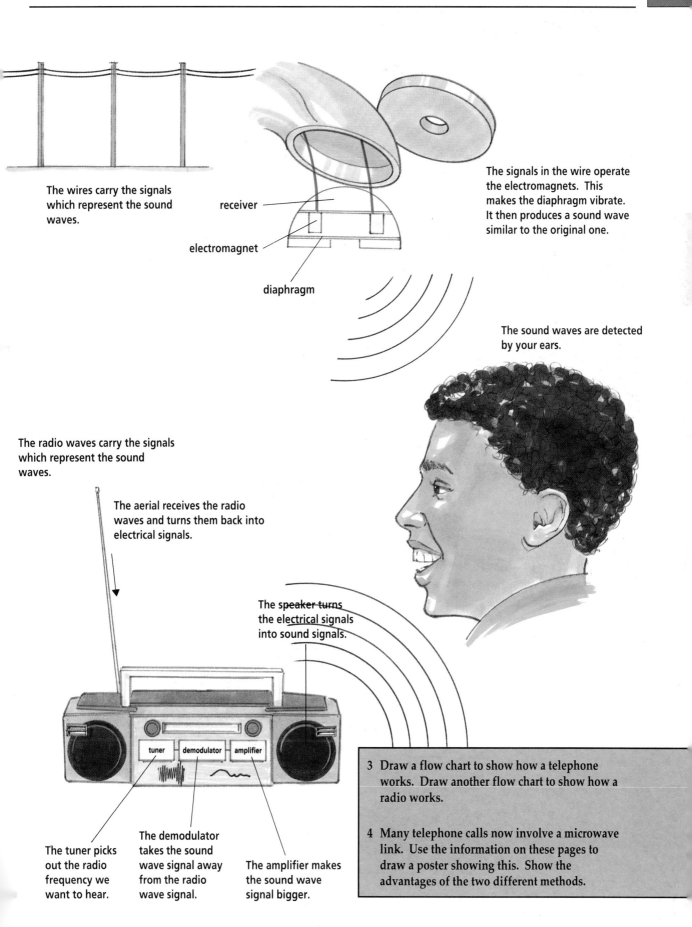

The wires carry the signals which represent the sound waves.

receiver

electromagnet

diaphragm

The signals in the wire operate the electromagnets. This makes the diaphragm vibrate. It then produces a sound wave similar to the original one.

The sound waves are detected by your ears.

The radio waves carry the signals which represent the sound waves.

The aerial receives the radio waves and turns them back into electrical signals.

The speaker turns the electrical signals into sound signals.

tuner   demodulator   amplifier

The tuner picks out the radio frequency we want to hear.

The demodulator takes the sound wave signal away from the radio wave signal.

The amplifier makes the sound wave signal bigger.

3 Draw a flow chart to show how a telephone works. Draw another flow chart to show how a radio works.

4 Many telephone calls now involve a microwave link. Use the information on these pages to draw a poster showing this. Show the advantages of the two different methods.

Looking at

Prisms and Spectra

If you shine a beam of white light at a triangular prism at an angle, the beam which emerges is coloured.

Where do these colours come from? This question was asked by many scientists in the seventeenth century, and earlier.

I THINK THE PRISM IS DYEING THE WHITE LIGHT.

SOMETHING IN THE PRISM IS MAKING THE COLOURS.

MAYBE THE COLOURS ARE ALREADY IN THE WHITE LIGHT BEFORE IT ENTERS THE PRISM.

> **1 What do you think of these arguments? Suggest an investigation which might help you find an answer.**

The problem was finally solved by Isaac Newton. He carried out a series of detailed investigations during the year 1666.

This engraving shows one of Newton's important observations. Sunlight enters a darkened room through a circular hole in the window shutter and strikes a prism. A rainbow coloured spectrum appears on the screen.

Newton was particularly puzzled by the fact that the spectrum was oblong in shape, even though the hole in the blind was a perfect circle.

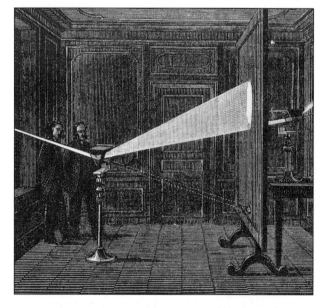

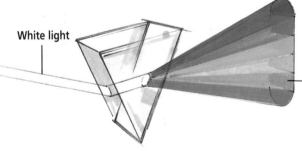

White light

Spectrum of colours

> **2 Try to think of reasons to explain the shape of the spectrum Newton saw on the screen.**

Newton thought his observation could be explained if white light is a mixture of rays, which are bent by different amounts as they pass through the prism. Blue rays are bent more than red rays so blue appears higher up the screen. Each colour arrives at a slightly different point on the screen. The overlapping circles of colour make up the oblong shape.

To test his ideas, he made a small circular hole in the screen. By moving this hole, he could allow through one spectrum colour at a time. Then he used a second prism to bend this coloured beam.

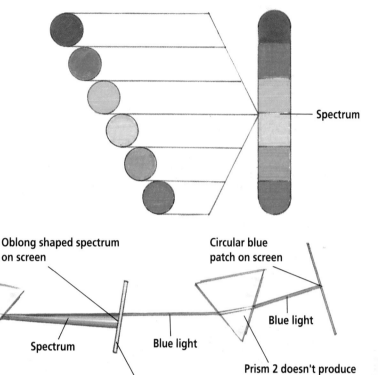

Spectrum

White light

Oblong shaped spectrum on screen

Circular blue patch on screen

Prism 1 produces a spectrum

Spectrum

Blue light

Blue light

Screen with hole only allows blue light through

Prism 2 doesn't produce a spectrum

He discovered two important things
● the light was not broken into any more colours by the second prism
● the light beam from the second prism cast a circular patch of light on the second screen, not an oblong.

Newton concluded that the coloured beams are not split up any further by the second prism.

> **3** Newton's work on spectra began with a *question*, which led to an *observation*. He then developed a *hypothesis* from which he made a *prediction* that he could *test*. Set out the story above in the form of a flow diagram of five boxes, each labelled with one of these words.

Newton did a final experiment to round off his investigations. He used a second prism to recombine the spectrum back into white light.

This confirmed that the colours were present in the white light and were not produced in the prism. This old diagram from 1721 edition of Newton's book **Opticks** showed how he did it.

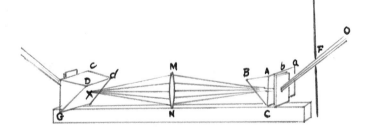

> **4** Why do you think Newton carried out this final investigation? Did it lead to any new theory or discovery?

Looking at

Optical Fibres

This picture was taken using fibre optics. An optical fibre is a very thin strand of glass. Optical fibres can be very long. Bundles of optical fibres are put together to make a flexible tube which can be inserted into the body to take pictures. This tube is called an **endoscope**.

Endoscope picture of a human foetus at 10 weeks. Mouth and nostrils are just developing.

1 When do you think doctors might want to see inside the body?
2 Where else might people use an endoscope to take pictures of the inside of things?

How do optical fibres work?

Optical fibres are made of very clear glass, so light can travel a long way down them. Light cannot escape from an optical fibre because it is reflected at the sides.

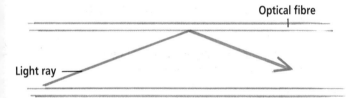

Optical fibre

Light ray

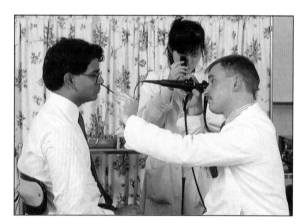

Doctor examining patient's throat using an endoscope. A separate eyepiece allows another doctor to watch too.

A ray of light bounces from side to side of an optical fibre, being reflected each time it gets to the edge. It doesn't matter if the fibre is bent – the light ray still passes all the way along it.

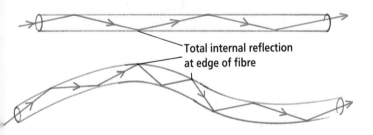

Total internal reflection at edge of fibre

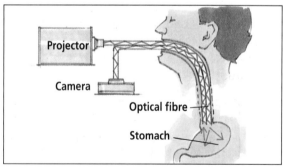

Projector

Camera

Optical fibre

Stomach

Light comes from the projector, is reflected off the stomach walls and goes back up to the camera.

There is no light inside the body for an endoscope to carry back up, so endoscopes have two bundles of optical fibres. One takes light from a projector into the body. The other takes light from a focusing lens back to the observer or a camera.

3 People going into hospital may be worried about having an endoscope inside them. Design a leaflet to show people how an endoscope works and to reassure them that the technique is painless and does not involve anything harmful. Explain when the technique is used and any advantages it has over X-rays.

In brief

Communicating Information

1 We have five senses to receive messages. Other animals use their senses in different ways.

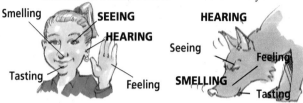

2 We use language for communicating. When we write a message, we use letters – a sort of code – to represent the spoken sounds.

3 If we want to communicate quickly with people who are far away, we convert speech into coded electrical signals. These can be transmitted over long distances along telephone wires or carried by radio waves.

4 You make spoken sounds in the voice box in your throat. You receive sounds with your ears. Hearing defects happen when people damage some part of their ears.

5 You use your eyes to receive information in the form of writing or pictures. Your eye acts as a lens and produces a focused image of the thing you are looking at on your retina.

6 We can use additional lenses – glasses or contact lenses – to correct sight defects. Other optical instruments, like microscopes, telescopes, cameras and projectors, also use lenses to produce images.

7 Lenses produce focused images of objects. They do this by bending the light as it passes through them. The thicker the lens, the more strongly it bends the light.

8 We can use **ray diagrams** like the one here to explain how a lens forms an image, and to predict the size and position of the image.

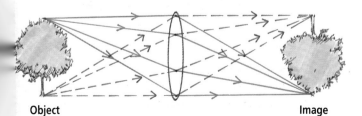

Object   Image

9 By experimenting with convex lenses, you can discover two general rules about images
- as an object comes closer to the lens, the image moves further away from the lens, and also gets bigger
- the stronger the lens, the closer the image is to the lens.

These rules are true as long as the object is not too close to the lens. They are useful in understanding how cameras and projectors work.

10 If you pass white light through a prism, you can see different colours. White light is made up of these colours. The prism separates the colours in white light.

11 Light from two sources can produce an **interference pattern,** just like water waves do. This suggests that light is a sort of wave. Light consists of vibrating electric and magnetic fields – it is an **electromagnetic wave.** Electromagnetic waves can travel through empty space.

12 Different coloured lights have different **wavelengths.** Red light has a longer wavelength than blue light.

Wavelength   Wavelength

13 There are other electromagnetic waves with wavelengths shorter than blue light and longer than red light. You cannot see these waves. We use them in various ways, for example, radio communication and taking X-rays. Electromagnetic waves all travel at the same speed, the speed of light (300 000 000 m/s).

14 Light rays change direction when they pass from air into a clear medium like glass, or from glass to air. This is called **refraction.** Lenses and prisms work by refraction.

15 Light rays which strike the surface inside a clear medium may be reflected back into the medium. This is called **total internal reflection.** It is used in optical fibres. Even if the fibre is bent, light inside cannot escape and passes all the way along. Optical fibres can be used to carry coded information in light beams, instead of using electrical signals in wires.

Thinking about

Communicating Information

1. How do humans communicate?

If you want to communicate with a friend who is nearby, you speak – you use sound to carry the information. If your friend is further away, you might use one of the methods shown on pages 164–5. Telephones and radio links are more complicated than speaking, but the basic result is the same: you send information in the form of **sound**, and this is picked up by your friend's ears, using the sense of **hearing**.

Another way to communicate with your friend is to write your message down and send it. Your friend uses the sense of **sight** to read it.

For humans, the two most important senses for communicating are hearing and sight. Most of the information we receive is picked up by either our ears or our eyes. So how do these work?

How do your ears work?
The diagram below shows a cross-section through an ear.

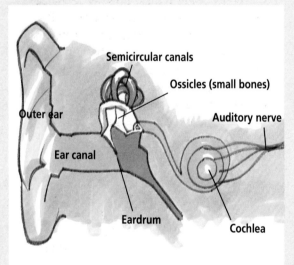

Semicircular canals

Ossicles (small bones)

Outer ear

Auditory nerve

Ear canal

Eardrum

Cochlea

The **outer ear** is the part you can see. It helps you to collect sound and to judge where it is coming from. Sound waves are tiny vibrations in the air. When a sound wave enters the **ear canal**, the vibrating air makes the **eardrum** vibrate. The eardrum is a membrane stretched across the end of the ear canal.

In the **middle ear** are three tiny bones, the **ossicles** – the smallest bones in your body. These magnify (amplify) the vibrations of the eardrum and pass them on to the **inner ear** or **cochlea**. Here the vibrations produce an electrical signal which the **auditory nerve** carries to your brain. The brain interprets these signals and makes sense of the sounds you have heard.

The middle ear also contains three **semicircular canals**. These have nothing to do with hearing, but help you keep your balance.

How do your eyes work?
The diagram below shows a cross-section through an eye.

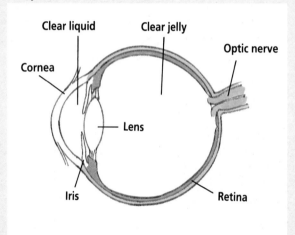

Clear liquid

Clear jelly

Optic nerve

Cornea

Lens

Iris

Retina

Your eye is almost exactly spherical in shape, apart from a bulge at the front – the **cornea** where light enters. There is a space between the cornea and the **lens** which is filled with clear fluid. Another space between the lens and the **retina** is filled with a clear jelly. The **iris** can expand and contract, controlling the amount of light which enters your eye. (It is your iris which gives your eye its distinctive colour.)

· The retina is made up of a very large number of special cells which are sensitive to light. When light strikes a cell in the retina, it produces an electrical signal, which passes along the **optic nerve** to the **brain.** The brain interprets all these signals and makes sense of what you see.

Because of its shape, the whole eyeball behaves like a convex lens, focusing light from the objects we are looking at on to the retina. The lens makes small adjustments so that you can focus sharply on either close or distant objects.

2. What do lenses do?

People have used lenses for over 600 years. This picture, painted in 1392, is the earliest to show someone wearing spectacles. They were probably first worn by monks who used to copy manuscripts, before the invention of printing.

Lenses are useful because they can produce an image. The photograph below shows a convex lens casting an image of two crossed wires on to a screen.

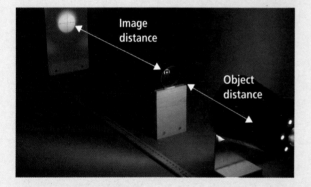

Getting a small image

You can use this apparatus to investigate lenses and images. If you move the object further from the lens, you have to move the screen closer to the lens to get a sharp image. The image distance gets smaller, and so does the image itself.

This idea is used in a camera. The image needs to be very small as it is focused on the film. The object distance is much bigger than the image distance.

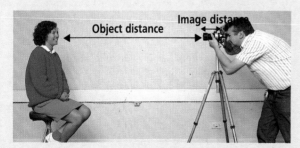

Getting a big image

On the other hand, if you move the object towards the lens, you have to move the screen back to get a sharp image. As the image distance gets bigger, so does the image size.

This happens in a slide projector, where we want to produce a large image of a small object.

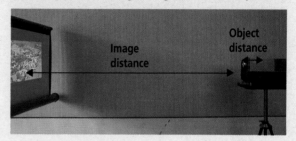

Taking it further: How lenses form images

A lens looks quite simple – it is just a shaped piece of glass. But lenses do something quite complicated! Think about what happens when an image is formed.

Take any one point on the object, such as the midpoint where the two wires cross. Light rays spread out from this point in all directions. Some of these rays happen to be travelling in the right direction to strike the lens. The lens bends *all* these rays by just the right amount to bring them all back to a single point on the screen – the image of the midpoint. But the lens is not just doing this to the bundle of rays from the midpoint of the object – it brings together all the bundles of rays from *every* point on the object to the equivalent point on the image.

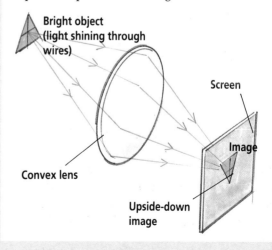

3. What is light?

You can see the straight rays of light through this window

Laser display at Glastonbury festival

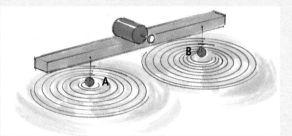

A and B both hit the water at the same time so they produce waves at the same time. At some places a peak from A meets a peak from B – both waves combine to form a bigger wave. At other places a peak from A meets a trough from B – they cancel each other out.

When you see light coming through a window, or if you have seen a laser beam, you can reach the conclusion that light consists of **rays** which travel in straight lines from their source.

The idea of light rays is not new – you have already used it to explain how lenses form images. But what is light and how does it travel?

One important clue comes from the double-slit experiment, originally carried out by Thomas Young in 1801. He made two narrow slits on a sheet of blackened glass. When he shone light through them they formed two identical light sources, side by side. In a darkened room, he saw that the light from these two sources produced a pattern of bright and dark lines on a screen.

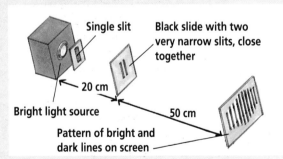

Single slit

Black slide with two very narrow slits, close together

20 cm

Bright light source

50 cm

Pattern of bright and dark lines on screen

We can explain this by comparing it with the behaviour of water waves. Waves from two dippers in a ripple tank produce an **interference pattern.** In some places the two waves are in step – both peaks add to produce a stronger wave. In other places they are out of step – peaks and troughs cancel each other out to produce a very weak wave.

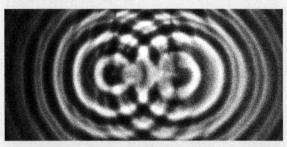

The interference pattern shows where waves add together and where they cancel each other out.

The light from the two slits seems to be doing the same – adding in some places to produce brighter light and cancelling out in others. So Young concluded that light was some form of wave.

All waves need a medium of some sort to travel through. For water waves, the medium is water. For sound waves, any solid, liquid or gas can be the medium. But light can travel through a vacuum. It has to cross 150 million kilometres of empty space to reach Earth from the Sun. What sort of wave can use a vacuum as its medium?

The answer came from James Clerk Maxwell in the 1860s. He did calculations which showed that a wave made of vibrating electric and magnetic fields could exist in a vacuum and would travel at the speed of light. A wave like this is called an **electromagnetic wave.**

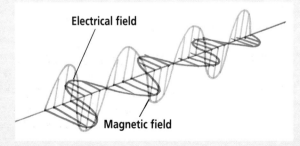

Electrical field

Magnetic field

4. How do we use the electromagnetic spectrum?

The idea that light is a wave helps us explain what the difference really is between different colours of light. They have different **wavelengths** (or different **frequencies** – it amounts to the same thing). Red light has a longer wavelength than blue, with the other spectrum colours in between.

But are there other electromagnetic waves, in addition to light, with longer and shorter wavelengths still? The answer is yes. Light is just one member of a much larger family of waves. The full electromagnetic spectrum (or e.m. spectrum for short) looks like this:
All electromagnetic waves travel at the speed of light and can travel through a vacuum. Many of them have important applications.

Radio waves Long-wave (LW) and medium-wave (MW) radio waves are used to carry radio broadcasts. The waves can spread round obstacles, so your radio can pick them up even if you can't see the transmitter. Short-wave (SW) radio waves are used for shorter distance radio links, like police radio and CB. VHF means very high frequency and UHF means ultra high frequency (compared with other radio waves). These are used for high-quality stereo radio transmissions and for television. For good VHF and UHF reception, you need a clear route from your aerial to the transmitter.

X-rays These are produced by specially designed X-ray machines. They can pass through skin and muscle but not so easily through bone. So X-rays can be used to take a shadow picture of the inside of your body. However, X-rays damage living cells and so a large X-ray dose can be harmful.

Gamma rays These come from some radioactive substances. They pass easily through most materials and can damage living cells. Gamma ray sources must be handled with great care.

Microwaves These are very short wavelength radio waves. They are now used instead of cables for many telephone links. There has to be a direct line without any obstacles from the transmitter to the receiving dish. You may notice microwave receiving dishes on high masts near your home. Some microwaves are absorbed strongly by water and they heat it up. This is how microwave ovens heat food.

Infra-red waves These are given out by every hot object. Your body emits long wavelength infra-red waves. The hotter the object, the shorter the infra-red wavelength it emits. A red-hot electric fire element is hot enough to emit short wavelength infra-red waves along with some visible red light.

Visible light Sunlight is a mixture of infra-red waves, visible light and ultraviolet light. Most light sources emit infra-red waves along with visible light.

Ultraviolet waves The special tubes used in sunbeds produce ultraviolet waves. They cause a chemical reaction which tans the skin. It is dangerous to expose your skin to too many ultraviolet waves as they increase the risk of skin cancer.

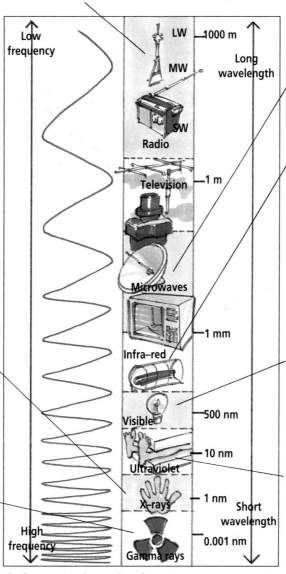

Low frequency — High frequency

Radio
LW — 1000 m
MW
Long wavelength
SW

Television — 1 m

Microwaves — 1 mm

Infra–red

Visible — 500 nm

— 10 nm

Ultraviolet — 1 nm   Short wavelength

X-rays

Gamma rays — 0.001 nm

The frequency in the number of complete waves per second. The shorter the wavelength, the higher the frequency.

5. What happens when light crosses a boundary?

When light passes through a lens, it changes direction. The light ray is bent. The same happens in a prism: here the different colours (wavelengths) are bent by different amounts.

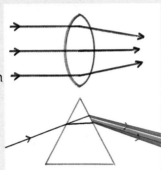

The light bends at the boundary between the glass and the air. This is called **refraction**. We can study refraction in more detail by looking at what happens when a single light ray enters or leaves a glass block.

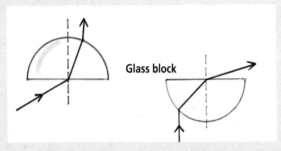

Glass block

The light ray bends *towards* the centre line as it enters the glass and *away from* it as it leaves. Refraction happens because light travels more slowly in glass than in air. This difference in speed causes the ray to change direction if it enters or leaves the glass at an angle.

If a ray which is inside the glass hits the boundary at a shallow angle, it does not come out into the air. Instead the light ray is completely reflected, as if the edge of the glass block was a mirror. This is called **total internal reflection**.

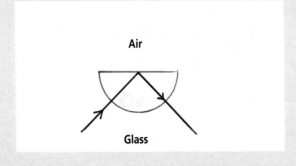

Air

Glass

Optical fibres make use of total internal reflection. An optical fibre is a very fine glass thread. Once light has entered the end of the fibre, it cannot escape through the sides because it is reflected each time it hits the boundary. If the fibre is very fine, it can be bent without changing the angles enough to make the light ray come out. The light travels all the way along the fibre to the other end.

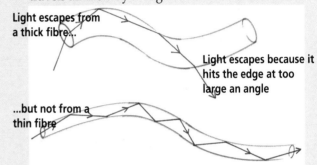

Light escapes from a thick fibre...

Light escapes because it hits the edge at too large an angle

...but not from a thin fibre

Optical fibres are now replacing copper electrical wires for telephone and computer links. They can be made smaller and lighter than wires, and glass is made from materials which are cheap and readily available – unlike copper, which is in shorter supply. Information is sent along the fibre by switching a light beam on and off very rapidly, rather like a very fast Morse code. The light pulses travel down the fibre at the speed of light and are decoded at the receiving end.

Optical fibres can also be used to look in inaccessible places. This is explained on page 168.

Things to do

Communicating Information

Things to try out

1 You can make a simple light detecting circuit using a light-dependent resistor (LDR).

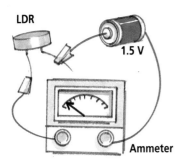

Design an investigation to find out whether this circuit can detect all wavelengths of visible light, and whether it can detect any electromagnetic radiations beyond the visible range.

2 Make a disc from white card and divide it into six sections. Colour these with the six colours of the spectrum: red, orange, yellow, green, blue and violet.

Then make the card into a spinner. What do you notice about its colour as it spins? How would you explain this?

Things to find out

3 Animals communicate without using language. Use the school or local library to find out as much as you can about the following examples of animal communication:
(a) the dance of bees
(b) a robin sitting on a branch and singing loudly
(c) a dog sniffing a tree trunk.

4 This diagram shows part of the tuning dial of a radio. Make a list of all the scientific terms and abbreviations used in the diagram. Try to find out what each of them means.

Points to discuss

5 In a group make a list of all the signs you can see around your school. Discuss how the information they communicate might be presented without words. Discuss and decide which of these you think would be an improvement.

6 Copy the object, lens and screen in the diagram on page 171. Now draw four rays coming from the top of the object, and show where these go to after they pass through the lens.

7 Use the information about the electromagnetic spectrum on page 173 to draw and complete a table with these headings:

Type of radiation	Source(s)	Detector(s)	Uses

Questions to answer

8 Part of each of these diagrams has been hidden under a card.

Copy and complete the diagrams showing what you would expect to find under the card.

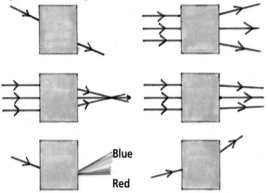

9 Jane carried out an investigation using a convex lens to find where the image was for various object positions.

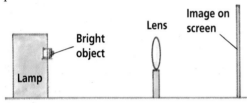

Unfortunately she wrote some of her measurements of the image distance in the wrong place in her results table.

Reading	Distance from filament to lens (cm)	Distance from image to lens (cm)
1	25	60
2	30	33
3	40	100
4	50	30
5	60	40

(a) Make a correct version of the table.
(b) Which reading would give the largest image?
(c) Which reading would give the smallest image?

10 What kinds of electromagnetic radiation might you be able to detect at points **a** and **b** in the diagram below?

11 Look at *Thinking About 4* on page 173. Name one kind of electromagnetic radiation which

(a) can pass through your body
(b) makes some chemicals fluoresce
(c) carries radio signals over long distances
(d) carries high-quality radio signals but only over short distances
(e) can cook food quickly and efficiently
(f) is emitted by every hot object.

12 (a) Look at *Thinking About 2* on page 171. A photographic enlarger can produce a focused image on paper in either position A or position B. Which setting will make the larger photograph? Explain your answer.

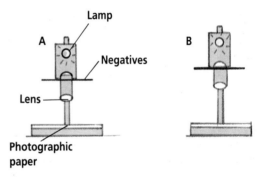

(b) The slide projector can give a focused picture on the screen in either position C or position D. Which will give the larger picture?

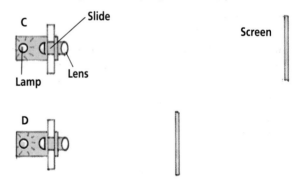

(c) The slide projector in diagram D gives a sharp image. To make the picture bigger, the projector is moved back, away from the screen. This makes the picture go out of focus. Which of the following would you do to focus the picture again

(i) move the lens outwards, away from the slide
(ii) move the lens inwards, closer to the slide?

Explain your answer.

Index

Scientists mentioned in the text

The authors and publishers are grateful to the following for permission to reproduce photographs:

Contents:
p1 TL Trevor Hill; BL Shell UK; R Sporting Pictures UK Ltd; p2 TL Robert Harding Picture Library; BL Trevor Hill; R J.C. Allen/Frank Lane Picture Agency; p3 TL GeoScience Features; BL Robin Millar; TR GeoScience Features; p4 TL Barnaby's Picture Library; B Chemistry Photographics, University of York; R GeoScience Features.

Energy Matters:
p4 Trevor Hill; T Michael Prior; p5 T Robert Harding; M Michael Prior; p8 TR Sporting Pictures UK Ltd.; BR Michael Prior; BL Robert Harding; ML Vauxhall Motors; MR Trevor Hill; p9 ALL Trevor Hill; p10 TR Valor Gas; BL Michael Prior; ML British Gas; MR Trevor Hill; p11 TL Trevor Hill; BL Michael Prior; BR Robert Harding; p13 Philips Lighting; p14 Michael Prior.

Keeping Healthy:
p15 L Sporting Pictures UK Ltd.; TR Grapes/Michand/Science Photo Library; MR CNRI/Science Photo Library; BR St Bartholomews Hospital; p17 Biophoto Associates/Science Photo Library; p18 T St Bartholomews Hospital; B Hulton Picture Company; p19 Wellcome Institute Library, London; p20 TL Science Photo Library; TR Robert Harding; BR Science Photo Library; p21 St Bartholomew's Hospital; p22 Trevor Hill; p24 John Olive/Chemistry Dept, University of York; p25 John Olive/Chemistry Dept, University of York.

Transporting Chemicals:
p31 TL Shell UK; BL Hugh Ballantyne/Millbrook House; TR Shell UK; BR Whitbread Brewery; p32 ICL; p33 ICI; p34 TR Vivien Fifield; TR The British Library; B Vivien Fifield; p35 Vivien Fifield; p39 London Fire & Civil Defence Authority; p41 TL Trevor Hill; TR Barnaby's Picture Library.

Construction Materials:
p46-7 Pilkingtons; p48 TL J Allan Cash; TR Elizabeth Ann Kitchens; MR J Allan Cash; ML Armitage Shanks; BR Robert Harding Picture Library; p49 Barnaby's Picture Library; p50 TL Robert Harding Picture Library; M&R John Lazonby; BL Glasheen/Barnaby's Picture Library; M&R John Lazonby; p52 Barnaby's Picture Library; p54 Barnaby's Picture Library; p56 Barnaby's Picture Library; p57 Barnaby's Picture Library.

Moving On:
p59 T&ML Trevor Hill; BL John Lazonby; R Barnaby's Picture Library; p60 TL Barnaby's Picture Library; TR MIRA; BL & p61 Reproduced from *Verkeer and Veiligheid*, PLON, Pub. NIB of Zeist, Netherlands; p64 B&C Trevor Hill; L John Olive; TL The Guardian; p66 Sporting Pictures (UK) Ltd; BR Aviemore Photographic; p70 Trevor Hill; p71 Trevor Hill & B Allan Cash; p73 Reproduced from *Verkeer*, PLON, Pub. NIB of Zeist, Netherlands; p74 T Barnaby's Picture Library; Ford Motor Company; BMW; Sealink; Barnaby's Picture Library.

Food for Thought:
p75 TL L West/Frank Lane Picture Agency; BL ICI; TR Derek Robinson/Frank Lane Picture Agency; BR Hutchison Library; p76-7 S McCutcheon/Frank Lane Picture Agency; p79 L National Dairy Council; TR & BR AFRC Institute of Food Research; M Hellman's; p81 T Gamma Press/Frank Spooner; M John Wright/Hutchison Library, B Trevor Hill; p82 L ICI; TR J Burgess/Science Photo Library; BR H Binz/Frank Lane Picture Agency; p83 L Vivien Fifield; R ICI; p84 Trevor Hill; p86 L Mazola; TR JC Allen/Frank Lane Picture Agency; BR Trevor Hill; p87 Trevor Hill.

Restless Earth:
p89 GeoScience Features; p90 GeoScience Features; p91 GeoScience Features; p93 Steve Smyth; p94 Photri/Barnaby's Picture Library; p96 TL GeoScience Features; BL Barnaby's Picture Library; TR GeoScience Features; BR Ronald Sheridan Picture Library; p102 GeoScience Features.

The Atmosphere:
p103 L GeoScience Features × 2; TR NASA/Science Photo Library; BR John Sanford/Science Photo Library; p108 BL Tony Morrison/South American Pictures; TR John Cleare/Mountain Camera; p113 BR (above) P.J.B. Nye/Meteorological Office; BR (below) Crown Copyright/Meteorological Office; p114 TL Crown Copyright/Meteorological Office; BL Christiana Carvalho/Frank Lane Picture Agency.

Electricity in the Home:
p117 National Power × 1; Chemistry Photographics, University of York × 11; Robin Millar × 2; Trevor Hill × 1; Lightning - H. Binz/Frank Lane Picture Agency; p118 TR Robin Millar; p120 Chemistry Photographics, University of York; p121 Robin Millar × 1; Chemistry Photographics, University of York × 6; p126 Chemistry Photographics, University of York; p127 TL (above) Chemistry Photographics, University of York; TL (below) Robin Millar; TR Trevor Hill; p128 TL Chemistry Photographics, University of York; BL Robin Millar; BR (above) National Power; BR (below) Trevor Hill; p129 Chemistry Photographics, University of York; p130 TL Robin Millar, BL Trevor Hill; p132 Robin Millar.

Mining and Minerals:
p133 Main Picture Photri/Barnaby's Picture Library; BL Hutchison Library; TR Earth Satellite Corporation/Science Photo Library; p134 Zales Jewellers Ltd; p135 GeoScience Features; p136 British Steel; p137 British Steel; p140 T J. Wright/ Hutchison Library, GeoScience Features × 3; p141 T GeoScience Features; B Colin Johnson; p145 TL John Olive; BL Holt Studios; TR ICI Chemicals & Polymers; p146 GeoScience Features.

Balancing Acts:
p149 TL Roger Tidman/NHPA; BL Marion Morrison/South American Pictures; TR GeoScience Features; BR David Woodfall/NHPA; pp150–51 NASA/Science Photo Library; p153 Topham Picture Source; p156 GeoScience Features × 2; ML Ron Fotheringham/NHPA; MR A.P. Barnes/NHPA; p157 Greenpeace Picture Library × 2; BL Environmental Picture Library; p158 Environmental Picture Library × 2; MR Telford Development Corporation; p160 TR A.P. Barnes/NHPA; M Ron Fotheringham/NHPA; B GeoScience Features.

Communicating Information:
p166 TR David Parker/Science Photo Library; BR Vivien Fifield; p168 TR St Bartholomew's/Science Photo Library; MR Petit Formatt/Science Photo Library; p171 TL Reproduced by permission of Trustees of Science Museum, Chemistry Photographics, University of York × 3; p172 TL (left) Sonia Halliday; TL (right) Tim Malyon/Science Photo Library; MR Paul Brierly; p174 Telefocus, a British Telecom photograph.

(T = Top; B = Bottom; R = Right; L = Left; M = Middle)

Picture research by Jennifer Johnson.

Heinemann Educational Publishers,
a division of Reed Educational and Professional Publishing Limited,
Halley Court, Jordan Hill, Oxford OX2 8EJ

OXFORD FLORENCE PRAGUE MADRID ATHENS
MELBOURNE AUCKLAND KUALA LUMPUR SINGAPORE TOKYO
IBADAN NAIROBI KAMPALA JOHANNESBURG GABARONE
PORTSMOUTH NH (USA) CHICAGO MEXICO CITY SÃO PAULO

First published 1991
This edition 1996

ISBN 0 435 629 980

Designed and typeset by KAG Design Ltd, Basingstoke
Cover designed by Leigh Harrison
Cover illustrated by Eikon Ltd, Leicester
Printed in Spain by Mateu Cromo

The authors are indebted to many companies and institutions for their
encouragement and financial assistance; in particular to
BP
Heinemann Educational Publishers
ICI
The Salters' Institute of Industrial Chemistry
The Training, Enterprise and Education Directorate
The University of York